The View From Here

The View From Here

A Collection of Dr. Bob's Sunday Columns and Other Musings

Robert Hallstrom

*The Vet's Corner
Publishing Company*

Copyright © 2015 by Robert Hallstrom

All rights reserved.
Published in the United States by
The Vet's Corner Publishing Company.

Edited versions of columns dated from October, 1999, through July, 2011, appeared in the *Contra Costa Times*. An edited version of "The Spark That Ignited The Flame" appeared in *The Bugle*, March/April 2012.

ISBN 978-0-9967280-0-3

Printed in the United States of America

Jacket Design by Ryan G. Gates, DVM
Photo by Joanne Hallstrom

First Edition

*for Bob & his family,
both relatives & friends*

Contents

Foreword	1
Introduction	2

Part One: Observations of Life and Family   5

Hitting The Road Cures That Closed-In Feeling	7
Have Fun Before You Die	10
Character Revealed In The Parking Lot	13
Money Grab	16
Bon Voyage	22
Remembering Frankie	26
Holiday Time Calls For Reaching Out To Family	31
Old Studebakers	34
Preserving Memories In Mundane Locations	37
Kijana	41
Discovering the Real America	44
Meeting Nova	47
We Must Needs Die	52
Wandering In The Desert	55
Man, The Toolmaker	60
Deep Roots And Respect On The South Dakota Plains	63
Ghost Towns Reveal Our Humanity	67
When It's Time To Carry Your Dad	70
Witnessing An Awe-Inspiring Homecoming	72
The Touch Of Evil	75
You Gotta Be Grown Up To Understand	80
Glorifying Copycats Becomes Self-Fulfilling	83
Dude, You're Pissing On My Wall!	87

A Requiem For A Rogue 92
Some Animal Lovers Are Becoming
    People Haters 94
I Must Get Old, But I Do Not Have To Like It 97
Takes A While To Get In Christmas Spirit 100
Birds' Familiar Tune Brings To Mind Our Own Chaos 103

Part Two: The Commies and The Fascists 105

For Last Resort Only 107
First Column After Termination 109
Some Things Never Change 114
Bison Diaper Wisdom 119
That Piece Of Fan Mail 123
Demonstration And A Hammer 128
What To Expect From Uncle Sam 132
Looking Back With the Luxury of Time 135
Programmed Stupidity 138
Considering Integrity 141
The Great American Novel 149
Calling for Reason 160
Letter To An Assemblywoman 164
Make That Cheese Easy To Find 168
Film Comes A Long Way From
    Cowboy Stereotypes 171
Saying Proper Thanks To A Very Brave Man 174

Part Three: X Number of Mornings 177

Key To The City 179
If Wishes Could Make It So 182
Entering Wyoming 185
Lessons From The Truck 189
The Window Seat 197

Winter Rains Scare Tourists, Bring Special Beauty To The Coast	200
California Winter	202
Appreciating The Pioneers Of Mountaineering	205
The Wedding Back East	209
Sierra Experience Lives On	216
Inspiration Comes In Many Forms	218
The Morality Of The "Hunt"	221
The Spark That Ignited The Flame	225
Kehoe, Revisited	234
Discovering Betty Jane	237
Riding Betty Jane	242
A Bird On The Head Is Worth Two In The Bush	252
Getting Away From It All	255
Grizzly Bears' Place In California Society	260
Franklin Wrong On Eagle Vs. Turkey	262
A Picture Worth A Thousand Words	264
Seeking A Photograph, Redux	267
Backyard Offers An Escape, Even As An Adult	269

Intermission   273
Cooperisms	275

Part Four: My Invisible Friend   279
Just Why Must We Debate Death?	281
Don't Take Rights Away From Wrong People	284
Havana & Berkeley Sister Cities?	287
Don't Take Care Of Stray Cats	289

Part Five: Veterinarian Behaving Badly   293
Homemade Baby Food	295

This Shouldn't Be Necessary, But Here...	299
I'm Tired	304
Judge Not Lest Ye Be Judged	308
Murder, By Internet	311
A Soft Spot	320
Bums And Bullies	324
Penny and Ed	328
Petting Puppies	332
Pot Calling Kettle, Uh... Names	336
Wasting Time	340
Bourbon And Bandages	344
Real Doctor	347
Peddling Your Ass About Town	351
Did I Do OK?	355
Why Bother?	362
Almost Perfect	367
Acknowledgments	*372*

The View From Here

Foreword

In January of 2015, Ryan and I found out our veterinary colleague and mentor Bob Hallstrom was retiring at the end of this year. Bob practiced veterinary medicine in Pittsburg, CA, for 43 years, building his small animal practice and building his life around it. He found himself at the end of his professional life doing unaccustomed work of valuing his practice for sale- and wondering what the career it represented was worth.

Now, in addition to being a veterinarian, Bob is a writer. Ryan and I had read a number of his columns, as well as pieces in various veterinary forums. He wrote to get what he saw out of his head as much as he did to produce the weekly column his local paper published for ten years. Bob observed the world around him closely and with appreciation for what he saw- both the people and the landscape, the beautiful and the ugly. His wife, Joie, became his constant companion, co-creator of many of his experiences and editor of his columns.

Bob has been a friend and mentor to Ryan and me and a large number of other veterinarians including his daughter, Jody. When he shared with us how his impending retirement had him questioning what he'd spent his life on, we immediately thought of this book. Bob's writing is a gift he gave us, a gift bought with the clarity, practicality, humor and humility of forty years of thoughtful practice. Helping Ryan guide its assembly has been my privilege, and this resulting book of select columns is our gift to ourselves, and to Bob.

Eden Myers, DVM, MS
justvetdata.com

Introduction

> *Most everybody knows we're trying to get out of this, and they collectively couldn't be nicer. Although if one more tells me I can't retire I might scream. They mean well, but I've been chewing the leg in the trap for some time now.*
>
> Bob Hallstrom
> *The Vet's Corner, August 11, 2015*

My father retired from veterinary medicine at the end of 2014. He was loved and adored by his support staff and many, many clients. I had the pleasure and privilege of working with him professionally for almost nine years, and before that as a college and veterinary student gaining valuable experience. He showed me tremendous work ethic and character, the type that characterized his generation of veterinarians.

Bob Hallstrom is of my father's generation, and I have had the pleasure and privilege to get to know him over the past number of years in a very special online community of forty-some-odd veterinarians. Through a variety of interactions with Bob, I have seen much of my father in him.

Having recently celebrated the career of one retiring veterinarian, I felt called to celebrate the career of another upon his retirement. Not out of a sense of duty, but of gratitude.

For those who cared or were even able to notice, Bob uniquely illustrated the practice of veterinary medicine over the course of his career: employing a sense of humor, tempering the depressing times with time spent deep in our national parks, meeting his clients' needs in ways that were accessible to them, venting through writing and finishing the race with his head held high.

Bob gave us a *bunch* of material to sort through over the years in general, and for this project in particular. Joie supplied us with the workable material for the project. Bob had no knowledge of this, which is exactly how we wanted it. And as Bob has been quite the prolific writer, we couldn't wedge 500-plus columns into a book that you'd want to carry around, so Eden Myers and I whittled this collection into a representative sample for your reading pleasure.

This book is a tribute to Bob, a gift to him on the event of his retirement. It is also a tribute to the veterinarians of his and my father's generation, the gold standards of the golden age of veterinary medicine. The columns included here have their original publication dates specified (if known), and while they've been mildly edited for formatting purposes, the spirit, the language, and the vernacular are untouched so that you hear Bob's voice. He, and you, deserve nothing less.

Ryan G. Gates, DVM
Cuyahoga Falls Veterinary Clinic, Inc.
fallsvetclinic.com

Part One: Observations of Life and Family

Hitting The Road Cures That Closed-In Feeling

One of Bob's first Sunday Columns. (RG)

Dogs are smart. They see through the clutter of life, right to the important stuff, things like dinnertime, walks, and pats on the head from the people they adore. And they know the value of rides.

My dog was sleeping on the floor in front of the fireplace, a perfectly reasonable thing to do on a chilly autumn day. He was snoring, oblivious to his surroundings, until I pulled my keys from their hook on the wall. The tiny clinking sound resurrected him and he shot past me to stand expectantly at the door. Go for a ride? You bet!

We piled into the cab of my truck and were off. My dog's nose stuck out of the window, taking in the smell of strange country. After only a short ride he bounded out of the truck and ran into the house, as eager to come home as he was to leave.

Recently I endured a period of quiet desperation; the world seemed off its axis. Trapped in that proverbial box with the walls slowly closing in, I didn't know what was wrong. My dinner dish was full, I didn't need a walk, and my wife gave me all the pats I needed, but I couldn't see the important stuff through the clutter… I needed to get the smell of strange country. Go for a ride? You bet!

No two rides are the same, but I know a few simple rules, which anyone may follow. The first day, go as far as practical to put that box behind. Drive across a place like Nevada if you can. The vast open spaces and distant blue mountains stretching to the horizon are so intimidating they force you to view your problems from a new perspective. Listen to country music, the poetry of the common folk, on weak radio stations that fade in and out as miles blur beneath your tires. Use the solitude to wander around inside your head and reacquaint yourself with the person living in there. In such desolate country you will discover time to clean out the closet a little. It is OK to cry.

If you know where you are going, and there are two roads, take the smaller. If you don't know where you are going, take the smaller road anyway.

Explore a short detour, perhaps a spur road into the Ruby Mountains just before dusk, when shadows are long and colors warm. Spend time in aspen groves watching the sun sparkle through the golden leaves. Then drive on through all the phases of the sunset and into the darkness.

Breakfast on the second day should be in the coffee shop of a second-rate casino. Get up very early, the call of the road will prevent sleep anyway, and be sure to flirt with the old waitress with the gravelly voice. Talk with people who have lived their lives differently than you; do not judge, instead try to learn. Listen to the old folks. We may be in the information age, but we should acquire knowledge the old fashion way.

Seek out settings so awe inspiring that you lack words to describe them to your friends. Stand shivering alone on a sage flat in Jackson Hole for instance, just as dawn breaks and elk begin to materialize from wisps of ground fog all around you. Bugles from unseen bulls echo on four sides and you can see the small clouds of steam billowing from an antlered bull as he poses in front of you, silhouetted by the dawn. Remember to look behind and watch the summits of the Tetons turn to glowing embers with the first brush of the morning sun.

Later, note the wonder reflected in the eyes of a small boy as he watches half a ton of bison saunter past his dad's car, four feet away, as the great beast leisurely strolls down the yellow stripe in the center of a road in Yellowstone. Acknowledge the twinge of envy you feel when you realize the boy, unlike yourself, is just beginning to experience all the wonders he will see. Then go out and find some new wonders for yourself.

Find places so beautiful you don't know where to look first. It is OK to cry here, too. Then photograph or draw or write so you can prolong the lessons when you get home.

As you pass by, contemplate the lives of people memorialized by little white crosses on the side of the road. They also went for a ride, but they can never go home again. Hope that they were at peace with their lives when they were asked to leave. Then count your blessings.

When it is time, and the ride is over, you will bound out of the truck and run into the house, as eager to come home as you were to leave. And you will find the important stuff will be clear again.

So, the next time you feel the walls closing in and you cannot see through the clutter, take a lesson from a dog. Go for a ride? You bet!

October 28, 1999

Have Fun Before You Die

I thought I was going blind. They say you start losing your night vision as you become ancient, and since I am fast approaching that definition, I figured that must be what was happening. When ya can't see where you are going, it can be a bit disconcerting.

Where we were going was east on the New York State Thruway. We managed to catch the tail end of the evening commute, and the locals who knew where they were going were going there rapidly. Apparently, those speed limit signs on the shoulder are just for decoration, kinda like they are around here, and to stay in line I disregarded the traffic law and adopted the law of the jungle. So we motored on, in the dark, in the rain and the spray, in the traffic, at extra-legal speed, and I couldn't see squat. I couldn't see the lane markers. I couldn't see the shoulders. I set my sights on a pair of taillights and kept my foot on the throttle. It was an act of faith that I did not enjoy.

My blindness under these circumstances confused and annoyed me. Other folks seemed to see well enough to power through the darkness without care. Couldn't understand what was wrong with me. Finally panic took over from where common sense had left off, and I pulled off the road for the night. And I concluded that I was simply too old for this nonsense anymore.

Then two nights later I turned on the headlights while parked behind another car. And only half of that car lit up. Duh! The Jetta was a perdiddle. In case you don't remember, a perdiddle is a car with one headlight burned out. And we was one. No wonder I couldn't see in the dark. The Jetta needed a new headlight.

So I was sitting in the Volkswagen dealer in Springfield, Massachusetts making a cup of coffee in that little sitting area where they park the waiting folks, and thinking to myself that I needed to buy one of those coffee makers like they had, onnacounta how well it worked, and I looked to my left and there sat the new cars. I think they do that on purpose. Because right then and there a seed was planted. So while they changed out my old Jetta's oil and put in a new headlight, I checked out the new models.

Once we arrived home, I wore out the internet looking at cars, and comparing features, and memorizing things like 140 horsepower and 236 foot pounds of torque, with EPA rating of 30/42. Then I put it all on the shelf, 'cause we really didn't *need* a new car, and despite rumors to the contrary, I am a practical kinda guy.

During the drive to Boston (p.209), by the time we were cruising across North Dakota, we had realized that the nimble little Jetta had some advantages over the big diesel pickup truck on road trips, so long as said trips didn't involve pulling the trailer. It was quieter, rode out the bumps better, and burned far less fuel. And we had amazed ourselves with how much stuff we had crammed into the back of that thing with the backseat folded down. So we added the possibility of touring with a small car after we retired (p.374), figuring on picking up something like the diesel Jetta sportwagen when the old Jetta died, so we'd even have room for the kayak and some camping gear for those times when we didn't want to haul the trailer. It fit in well with the other dreams we hold for retirement time.

Anyway, after taking our first two-week vacation in over 14 years, and enjoying just how good that felt, we showed up back at the clinic to face the crush of catching up, the whining from those who couldn't let us off the hook for slacking off when they needed us, the quiet resignation that we had years of six day, 55 hour weeks to weather before we could even consider trying to retire, and the realization of all that settled around our shoulders with the subtlety of a 50 pound pigeon turd dropped from above. So rather than dutifully waiting patiently to grow old and die, we began discussing the possibility of having some fun before that happened.

Last Sunday we took the new Jetta for a nice long scenic drive to see a site that had been on the list of places to visit for decades. And it was wonderful! The weather cooperated with intermittent showers, cloud shows, cool weather, rainbows, and sunbeams highlighting the hills and valleys. Pinnacles National Monument lived up to its billing as a sparsely visited, well preserved, teaming with wildlife, and populated by rock spires and chaparral lit by fall color kind of place.

Did I mention that we bought a new car? Well, we did. We went for the sedan rather than the sportwagon, to enjoy a more nimble feel. We sprang for the turbo diesel for longevity and way better fuel economy. With the six speed manual transmission, satellite radio and GPS. And it rocks!

The way we figure it, the new Jetta will be nearly paid off by the time we might retire. So my practical side can sorta explain away this indulgence. The little diesel purred along at over 40 miles per gallon on this tour, which should improve after we get her broken in. And we are laying plans to actually take off a weekend every month and go do fun stuff, rather than just talking about doing this. And sometimes we will take the trailer, and sometimes we will fly low and fast in the new Jetta. We'll see ya when we get back.

November 13, 2011

Character Revealed In The Parking Lot

"I know sage, wormwood, and hyssop, but I can't smell character unless it stinks."

Edward Dahlberg
"On Human Nature"
<u>Reasons Of The Heart</u>

A long day at work finally wound down, and the thought of lemonade brought us to the local supermarket. I sat in the truck, two disappointed little dogs standing in my lap, watching through the window as my wife disappeared past the automatic doors. The radio murmured quietly as a gentle breeze filtered into the cab, and I watched a slice of the local population filter into and out of the store. People watching. My favorite pastime.

One of those imported sport/luxury sedans was parked two slots over. Nice chrome custom wheels graced four corners. Low profile performance tires were wrapped around those rims. He paid extra for those. The front tires were worn nearly to the chord. The rears looked almost new. Somebody appeared to have been smokin' those tires around the neighborhood more than absolutely necessary. And he had not mastered the art of rotating them. I put a mental check in the bad column over that one.

When the driver returned to this car, and unloaded his shopping cart through his passenger door, I watched. I won the bet with myself when he left the cart sitting in the adjacent parking slot, rather than returning it to the store or pushing it into one of those cart parking areas that the store provides. And no, I was not surprised when, after he had consumed the contents of those take-out food containers, they just slipped out his window to splat on the pavement. Two more checks in the bad column.

OK, so the guy is a slob. That is not exactly equivalent to mass murder, but I do believe his acts add up to what you might call bad character. And if you add up enough bad character, pretty soon you end up with a society like ours, which often seems sorely lacking in the good version.

Swinging your fists around in the air is not bad character. Swinging them into some innocent person's jaw in a crowded room is. Bad character has a signature. Trying to park your car in that slot in the parking lot in which the shopping cart sits reminds you of bad character. Finding the litter next to it confirms the suspicion. Watching the hillside go up in flames because someone thinks that smoking cigarettes is a license to litter, well that smells of bad character, too.

Lying, cheating, and stealing demonstrate bad character. Those merchants in China slipped melamine into the wheat and rice gluten that recently showed up in your pets' food. They just wanted their protein to assay higher, so they could sell it at a better price, and they didn't care a wit if somebody died. Bad character.

"As I know more of mankind, I expect less of them, and am ready now to call a man a good man upon easier terms than I was formerly," said Samuel Johnson.

Perhaps this is where we end up. Spend enough time in a world rife with bad character, and our standards drop. A certain quiet resignation settles down upon our shoulders as we face the hopelessness of it all.

And then there is that mirror on the wall, where our own examples of bad character come home to roost. We live in glass houses. Perhaps we shouldn't be too quick with that stone. And we are not without sin, so we shouldn't cast the first one. So what should we do when we realize, as the radio guy pointed out the other day, "The world changes, but human nature does not."

Perhaps we could listen to Marcus Aurelius, from the 2nd century:

> *"Waste no more time arguing what a good man should be. Be one."*

May 6, 2007

Money Grab

Bob's column from Thursday, November 18, 2011, (not included in this volume) which he references here was one long rant against the Occupy Wall Street crowd and their misguided ideas. What follows is the column he intended for that Thursday, which instead emerged two days later. Bob proved his wit and wisdom can shine through no matter the day. (RG)

All the times I've talked of how a column of mine starts out in one direction, putters around a bit, and then takes off only to end up way over there somewhere... well that was never more apparent than the one I sent around on Thursday. Ya see, I never intended to do much more than mention the Occupy people in Oakland, with their core of old worn out communists still rankling over the '60s and '70s, when they blew their chances to take over the world, and the latest delusional young generation living the obligatory we-can-save-the-world-and-Marx-is-the-way mantra which has been drummed into them by *all* those overpaid university and college professors. No, I was simply reacting to their harsh noise in support of Obamagenda, and of course, in the process, their need to reject the American way of life and that embarrassing successful capitalism thing. I know they simply want to save the world, which is a good thing, if impossible, and I cannot trifle much with that, for I was once that naïve myself. And besides that, they are probably going to win in the end, to all of our detriment.

No, I didn't intend to spend the day riled about that. But I get carried away. You all know this.

What I wanted to eventually talk about was the simple logistics of saving the world. And that would mostly be the reality of paying for it. I didn't have to invest all that energy in rehashing that same old stuff, 'cause y'all already know it, and either nod your heads yes, or get all aghast when you disagree. No middle ground there, whatsoever.

My reference to leaping off a bridge had far less to do with the revulsion I feel for the rock-throwing, shower-needing, disrespectful mob than it did with one phone call with one dimwitted but very persistent monotone speaking robotic clog person in the bureaucracy. And in that column I never got around to telling you about it. Sorry about that.

So, here's what got me all stirred up...

Our mail comes, when it does, to one of those aluminum 8-boxes-on-a-stick just down the street from our house. I drive right past it every day coming home from work, but I'm usually too tired to stop. When I finally get round to it, the box is generally crammed so full of junk mail that ya gotta tear that all to heck just getting it out. Which you have to do to find those three bills and the bank statement you've been waiting for to see if you can afford to hit the Safeway tomorrow. So I finally got around to it on Wednesday night. And I carried two armfuls of shredded junk and my three bills and, "Yea!" my bank statement into the house. And I carefully picked through the junk before tossing it unread into the recycling bin, because every once in a while there is a fourth bill hidden in there, and you know how embarrassing that can be when you don't pay that one. Very carefully I searched.

And I found something. It was a nondescript but official looking letter addressed to the two of us living in our home. And for some reason, I opened it. Two words on page one caught my eye.

FINAL NOTICE.

They were in large print and highlighted in a *black box*, so I guess somebody wanted to catch my eye. Maybe they should have done something similar on the envelope, but that is another argument.

I don't get many
FINAL NOTICE
letters, except from those out there who wish to refinance my home or in some other way put my money into some other pocket. And this was no different. Only this was to be a government pocket, so
FINAL NOTICE
takes on another meaning. Credit card companies can't hurt me if I don't want their card. Governments can.

The letter was a not-so-social, nor polite, request for a response from us, mostly me, since I had ignored all those other letters the city had sent to me in the past, and boy were they going to go serious on me now. Besides the, *"Huh?"* part, as I have not received any such letters, I felt that little sense of outrage I tend to get when the government wishes to communicate with me. It's that boot on my neck feeling.

The letter suggested that I should finally send in the money for the business license that the CITY OF CONCORD politely requested. Onnacounta that home business that I run out of my home. You remember, the one I don't run. 'Cause you see, I don't run a business from my home. Oh, and don't forget the 50% penalty because I'm so late. And while I'm at it, don't forget to pay for the years 2008, '09, and '10. So with '11 tossed in there, that adds up to… let's see… That will be $366.00. Before December 12, or we will start fining you up to $500.00 a day thereafter. ACK!!!

I'm still kinda naïve, so I dialed up the CITY OF CONCORD FINANCE OFFICE at the supplied number, for, ah, clarification. I was her first caller of the day. I was very polite in the beginning. Marisol filled me in, and the call ended, abruptly. I applied for an exemption for 2011, per their rules. Maybe they will argue with that, 'cause I didn't turn 62 until the year was part gone. I guess we will see. I'm doing my part to fund my government, and getting used to the fact that I'm gonna need to grow real comfortable with a lot more of this as we descend toward the future utopian world.

Meanwhile, here is the letter I sent in, as the CITY OF CONCORD needs my version of an excuse to shirk my responsibility in this matter. I'll have someone let ya know if I end up in jail over this.

11/16/2011
Robert G. Hallstrom, DVM
Delta Animal Clinic

Dear City of Concord, California,
My name is Robert Hallstrom. I own and work full time at the Delta Animal Clinic in Pittsburg, CA. I spend nearly 60 hours a week in that building. I sleep at YYY XXX Place, Concord, CA.

I am requesting an exemption from the Concord Business License Tax for the year 2011. I marked the exemption box for "I am 62 years of age, operating my business from home, and I make under $3,600 per year," under protest for I do not operate a business from my home.

I most certainly do not earn more than $3,600 from any business in my home. And I am 62 years old. Ask my mother if you need verification.

I do attempt to write and once wrote a weekly column for the East County edition of the Contra Costa Times, *for which I received the princely sum of $40 a week. I no longer write for this esteemed rag. And on one (1) occasion I sold a magazine article, but that was last year, and my income from writing this year (2011) will be zero.*

I write in my office in Pittsburg, in my trailer while camping on the coast near Mendocino and in the Mojave, and only occasionally while staring at the ceiling of my bedroom in Concord in the dark of night when sleep will not come.

I have never conducted the "business" of my "business" from my home in Concord. I have never emailed my newspaper column to my former editor at the newspaper from my home. I have never received payment at my home. None of my correspondence or phone calls with my editor were received at my home, and none of the tax related forms descending from my writing came addressed to me in my home. And the throngs of well-wishers clamoring for more of my writing rarely clog the street in front of my home.

If you wish to call my writing efforts a business, feel free. You flatter me. But I do not run a business from my home.

I do file state and federal income tax annually. And I dutifully included the small fortune I garnered from my writing when I submitted said tax forms. And I included my home address when I filed, figuring those folks expect that. If this means to you all that I run a business from this humble home, you have a much looser definition of business than anyone I can imagine, and frankly I think you should be ashamed of yourself.

But since you clearly hold the proverbial gun to my head, I shall pay your Business License Tax for the requested years: 2008, 2009, and 2010. I cannot afford to argue with you, and certainly do not wish to increase your booty to the tune of $500 a day simply because you get to write the rules. I would however, like to take advantage of your rule exempting us old folks from your victim pool, hence my request for this exemption.

I won't be standing in Todos Santos Plaza with a sign, after skipping my showers for a week, in protest of this situation. But I do thank you for the inspiration as I write my next submission for my blog. In case you are wondering... you folks won't come off well.

The View From Here

  I apologize for contacting you folks so late in this process, but I have never received any previous notification from you regarding this little matter of a business license tax. And since I do not run a business in Concord, it never crossed my mind to ask.

  The young lady in the Finance office, Marisol, who answered my phone call this morning, was very patient and polite and you should laud her. She sounded a bit tired when I finally let her go. I hope I didn't ruin her entire day. None of this nonsense is her fault, and I trust I wasn't too hard on her. In fact, I kinda feel sorry for her, having to bite her lip as she implements her superiors' mandates.

  I retain my sense of humor. My editor at the paper fired me because my final column submitted was a defense of two of your fine Concord police officers. My editor was never in favor of complimenting any police officers, but since I have made the acquaintance of so many of your officers, I like to give them praise when I can. And I shall continue to do this. But I do find it ironic that the city these dedicated officers work to protect has so poorly managed its affairs that it feels it must stoop to this level of chicanery to extort money from its residents.

  Thank you ever so much for your time

  Bye the bye, this is written in Pittsburg, CA... not my home.

  Robert G Hallstrom, DVM

Nov 20, 2011

Bon Voyage

They do things differently on ships. They call stuff by different names. For instance, you can't just go to the john. You have to go to the head. And ships don't just move… they make way. And they do other stuff along the way, like when they launch a ship, once it is built to the point where it will actually float. Because if you haven't noticed, you cannot build a steel ship in the water.

So ya see, they build those big steel ships on land on top of a wooden framework. Then later, when they figure it'll hold water (out), they build a big slide, called a ways, and then shift the weight of the ship onto wooden sliding thingys, called sliding ways, and with great swings of heavy hammers, they remove the various things holding things together until the crash of a champagne bottle provides the straw for this camel, and the ship goes, "WHEE!!!!!" all the way down the ways and into the water. With a nice splash. And hopefully, the thing stays right side up, 'cause when it doesn't, it is *so* embarrassing.

They always leave at least one rope tied to the ship, lest it wander off and get into even more trouble. With this rope, you can pull the ship back to shore and hold it there until all construction is finally finished, and then eventually you let other people drive the ship away and it heads for places all around the world.

So one of the things we got done when we went to Germany for the wedding was the first re-gathering in about five years of our brood in its entirety. We've seen the kids in ones and twos a few times, but not since the famous diarrhea summit in Wyoming have we snuck as many as three into one room for our enjoyment, and longer than that for all four. I had borrowed a trick taught me by my own parents. They found the best way to get the kids together when we didn't want to be called kids anymore, was to set the meeting in Wyoming. Worked every time for them. Well, apparently watching one of them get married works, too. We sat in a jet lag fog in Frankfurt, watching them interact, admiring them, and marveling at the simple reality that they all were still afloat.

I don't know if you've seen the film, but I remember it well. It was shot in black and white, like all the newsreels. The workers stood about in hard hats and leather gloves, large heavy hammers in hand. And the dignitaries in their dark suits and the designated champagne bottle smasher, a large women slightly overdressed, were perched on the stand by the bow. Intricate scaffolding surrounded the hull of the ship. The bottle swung from its ribbon, and burst in splendor against the bow, men swung hammers against the last shims, and then the ship slowly started down the ways, building speed, and finally splashing into the water. Where it promptly turned turtle, and sank below the dirty water. Bummer.

I once described a high school graduation by recalling the opening scene from "Top Gun," where amid the chaos and noise on the deck of a nuclear aircraft carrier, stern but excited looking pilots were launched, along with 14 million dollar aircraft, from steam catapults on the bow of the ship. Well, this week's cheap trick will try to compare the assembly and final release into the world of children with the construction and launch of a steel ship. Neat, huh?

I know... it ain't the same. But bear with me.

You can't build a kid in the water, either. Sure, sometimes you wonder if you shouldn't just kick them in and let them sink or swim, but most of us prefer the traditional way. So we assemble a complex of scaffolding and supports in a safe place. We start with a blueprint, which we follow up to a point. Sometimes when the parts we ordered don't fit just right, we will *ad lib* the thing for a while until you can't see light through the cracks any more. For it doesn't pay to blindly follow the rules if you can see they are leading you to a serious leak.

There is a schedule, but leave some room for overtime that you didn't plan for. 'Cause there is always overtime. Don't hesitate to call in an outside consultant if needed. And never hesitate to buy that retired foreman a beer so you can pick his brain when ya just can't figure where that one piece of the puzzle goes.

It's always more difficult than you thought, and even when you work from the same blueprints, no two ships ever turn out the same. And when you are standing there watching, when the work seems finished, and you see the men hammering away the shims so the ship can begin to launch, and the fat lady swings the bottle, that knot still forms in your throat, each and every time, no matter how many ships you have successfully launched, 'cause ya just never know what can go wrong.

So you get the big splash, and then you wait while the ship sways back and forth in the water for a moment, and then it settles down perfectly straight, and the cheer reverberates through the crowd, and you know ya did good. And then you tug on the rope and pull the ship back in, and you finish the rest of the assembly. Then there are sea trials, where you test the ship on short journeys and there is no rope to tug it back, and then finally you watch as the ship heads across great oceans, to far distant ports, and you hope the folks that take over for you and sail with that ship are capable and wise.

And you know that there are storms. And you wonder just a bit if you see your ship sailing in loose circles while it seeks its best course, and you wonder even when you cannot see the ship if it has yet found its course. But you cannot change a thing once it has sailed.

The View From Here

What we saw when our fleet came together last month made our hearts soar. Four ships, each looking shipshape. We no longer follow every inch of every journey of these ships, because we don't have to. They are doing just fine on their own.

August 4, 2011

Remembering Frankie

Unless you were across the international dateline in Japan, the attack on Pearl Harbor that thrust the U.S. into World War II happened on December 7, 1941. Tokyo had it as December 8. John Lennon was murdered on December 8, 1980. Lennon would have turned 70 this year. My father-in-law's baby brother would have turned 85 this year. Frankie was serving on the battleship *USS Oklahoma* in Pearl Harbor when the Japanese attacked. He never had a 17th birthday.

Not too many people remember Frankie. There is a plaque in a small town park in Massachusetts with his name on it. Maybe a sailor or airman said a little, "Here's one for you, Frankie!" when he pressed the trigger or released the bomb later in that war. Mostly, Frankie has been forgotten.

Used to be, on the anniversary of the Pearl Harbor attack everybody took notice of the date. There were speeches in Congress and in small parks around the country. The History Channel talked about it, and some TV network would run one of the movies. Old men remembered. Every one of 'em. Sometimes they went silent for the day, 'cause they remembered lots.

This year, December 7 came and passed with little notice. I don't recall seeing anything about it on The History Channel. If they said anything in Congress, I missed any reference to it on the six o'clock news. The old men remembered, but there aren't near as many of them anymore. It was almost as if it had never happened.

As I saw it, December 7 this year was all about John Lennon, 'cause that was what filled the radio and TV. Rather a large fuss was made about him this year on the anniversary of his death. Maybe that's because the Baby Boomers are getting to the nostalgia stage of life. And most of my contemporaries would

The View From Here

rather remember the Beetles than some long ago war. I turned to The History Channel to see what they had on special for the anniversary of Pearl Harbor, and got Ice Road Truckers or some such drivel.

I grew up reading about WWII, watching documentaries and movies about WWII, and listening to the stories about WWII. My bookshelves are peppered with books about WWII. So I don't mind at all when my wife comes home from one of her forays into the second hand stores with a history book or picture book pertaining to that war. You should see the one she brought back last week.

This one has over a hundred full-page photographs, most in black and white, taken by Navy and Marine Corps cameramen, most captured during the heat of action. Page one has the shot everyone has seen of the *USS Shaw* exploding during the Pearl Harbor attack. And the last few show solemn looking men signing the peace document in Tokyo harbor.

About halfway through the book, on a right hand page, they show a low altitude aerial photograph of a Japanese aircraft carrier. It was a clear South Pacific day, with excellent visibility, and the photo jumps off the page. The flight deck sports a distinctive camouflage, painted to resemble a battleship or cruiser from the air. In the South Pacific, no one wanted to look like an aircraft carrier, because these ships were the threat, and thus became the targets. Battleships stopped being the prime target that Sunday morning in Pearl Harbor.

Looking carefully at the photo, I can see a five inch anti-aircraft battery on the starboard bow, twin barrels pointed at the camera, essentially useless when the aircraft was that low. Early in the war, no one took low altitude photographs of Japanese aircraft carriers. No one who survived, anyway. But this airplane was pretty safe.

The ship is turning sharply to starboard, black smoke pouring out of the stack, showing full power from the engines, and white smoke billowed from the stern, from those holes blasted through metal. No aircraft sat on the flight deck, which was buckled from an interior explosion. If an aircraft carrier could look scared, it would look like this ship. The book's index confirms the inevitable, stating that she was sunk later that afternoon. The date was October 24, 1944.

You can see a few men standing on the flight deck. Their shadows stretch across the deck. They were just standing, powerless to stop the attack. I decided that I needed to find out all I could about this ship. I wanted to learn her name, and hear her story.

So I wandered into the vast internet, and hiding in there, waiting for me, was a list of the Japanese fleet carriers, with their life stories and the details of their destruction, including dates. One, the *Zuikaku* was listed as sunk on October 25, 1944. Japan time. Right date. Bombs and torpedoes found her off the coast of Luzon, while the Japanese were being blasted out of the Philippine Islands.

She was the last of the carriers that had decimated Pearl Harbor in 1941. The other five were long since gone to the bottom. The pictures of her on my computer were not good, but this clearly was not the carrier in my book. She had a different camouflage pattern, and she sported a raised island on the starboard side and three aircraft elevators. My carrier only had two, and no superstructure.

But in her history it was mentioned that she was accompanied to this battle by three light carriers, the *Zuihō*, *Chiyoda*, and *Chitose*. The paltry remaining aircraft assigned to these four ships totaled perhaps 102. The U.S. Navy fleet that attacked them had ten carriers, with somewhere between 600 and 1,000 aircraft. None of the U.S. ships sustained damage in this battle. All of the Japanese carriers were sunk. Once their few planes were shot down, these ships were nearly defenseless.

The first photo I found of *Zuihō* told me I had found the carrier in the book. The flight deck had the proper camouflage, and two elevators. The date of her sinking matched. Heck, it was the exact same photo. So I had the name of my ship.

In the 1930s, treaties limited the size and number of Japan's warships. So she built other ships, like luxury passenger liners, and then converted them to aircraft carriers right before the war began. *Zuihō* began her life as a submarine tender, but during that construction they switched her over to be a light carrier. She was ready in 1941 to play a support role in the Pearl Harbor attack that started the war. She also was in support during the battle of Midway, the carrier battle that finally turned the tide of war against Japan.

I found much on the net. I could have read about the surprise attack on Pearl Harbor where the large and very effective Japanese carrier force killed over 3,000 Americans. I could have read about the war Japan's military leaders brought to China earlier, and the city of Nanjing where for fun, Japanese soldiers massacred many thousands of unarmed civilians. I could have read about the prisoners of war they herded onto the beach and machine-gunned near Singapore or about the Bataan Death March.

The Japanese military had it pretty much their own way early in that war because they had a war machine no one could resist. It took a while before the combined resolve of the American people built the weapons and filled the ranks in the army, navy, and marines and put an end to that nightmare. By the time they carried the fight to the Philippines, the tables had turned. By then, it was the Japanese army and navy that could no longer resist.

Zuihō was sent all over the South Pacific during the war, but as Japan's stolen empire was slowly ripped from her bleeding fingers, her few remaining carriers became almost an afterthought. They could no longer defend even themselves, and the remnants of the once invincible air fleet were pressed into duty in the kamikaze attacks. The admirals had sent *Zuihō* and the other three carriers to the Philippines as bait, rather than as an attacking force, and the 800 defenseless men aboard when that photo was taken, like those guys on the flight deck in the photo, were just hoping not to die. Kinda like Frankie, three years earlier.

August 6, 2011

Holiday Time Calls For Reaching Out To Family

When reaching out to Joie about putting this project together, I asked if there were any columns in particular that she wanted to see included. She requested only one specific column: this one. Bob wrote this shortly after his mother-in-law's passing. (RG)

Rex answered the bell, swinging open the front door, peering out through the glass of the storm door. No one there.

"Hi Rex!"

Looking down, Rex spotted his little friend Davey standing on the stoop. Davey is five years old. He was cradling in his tiny hands a plate of cookies and other goodies snuggly wrapped in clear plastic.

"Rex, I'm sorry about your wife. Why didn't you call me? I would have been here. I'm your best friend."

Davey and Rex are indeed best friends. Somehow they have discovered a common bond despite the 85 year difference in their ages. Davey comes down the block whenever he sees Rex working out in the yard. They hang out together, talking, telling stories, laughing. You know… like friends.

Even though he is only five, Davey knows what a friend does when his buddy is hurting. He shows up.

Rex and Edna were married for 64 years. Those who knew and loved her called her Saint Edna. She earned that title. My father in law, Rex, is one of my favorite people, but I concede that he is a challenge to live with. Brilliant, innovative, creative, he is also a bit impulsive, and once started he changes direction as easily as one of those super tankers.

Edna was up to the challenge. She loved him, took care of him, and accepted him through all those many years. And she loved to skunk him at cribbage.

Edna reared three children, chips off the block of Rex, three disparate, impulsive, brilliant and creative children, also a challenge. Saint Edna. She truly earned the title.

Eighty-five years of wear and tear, rheumatic heart disease, emphysema, and the vicissitudes of time finally caught up with her, and Edna left us two weeks ago. Saint Edna's job here on earth is finished, and now heaven has a new angel. From the look of things around here, God can use the help.

I put off writing this column for a long time. I really wanted to write something good about this holiday season, since today is Christmas, but all I had was a head full of desperate clutter. 'Twas the night before deadline before I even got any decent ideas. I don't have many secrets from those of you who have been reading this column for any length of time. So I hope you will excuse me if this is too personal. Our family is only a small piece of humanity, but we are as representative as any other piece. We have learned some valuable lessons in the last two weeks. Some very valuable lessons.

Losing a wife, mother, mother-in-law, grandmother and great grandmother has devastated our whole family. But it has brought us all together, closer than we had been, as close as we should have been all along. And our friends have converged upon us, offering compassion, a shoulder to cry upon, a good listen, and a plate of cookies and goodies snuggly wrapped in plastic.

This holiday season has been sullied in this country by much squabble over what we are celebrating, and whose celebration is better than the next. Some have suggested we shouldn't celebrate anything, since one celebration might bother somebody else. Take down this decoration, change that song, tone down everything except the sales down at the mall. This distresses me.

I don't care if you celebrate Christmas or Chanukah, gather for Kwanza, worship a tree, or simply decorate one so you can stack the fruits of consumerism beneath it. I don't care if you only mark the winter solstice. Whatever you do, this is the time to call the family home and bring together your friends. Wrap all these wonderful people around you. This is important. This is special. This is what grounds us, comforts us, enervates us, saves us. It's what, in the end, keeps us all going. Bring 'em together. Bring 'em home. Or give 'em a call if you can't. Don't wait until you lose them. Then it is too late.

Merry Whatever. I wish you a good one.

December 25, 2005

Old Studebakers

The clinic exit door is glass, so I can see out to a slice of the parking lot from the hallway in front of the exam rooms. A variety of cars and trucks, and the occasional motorcycle take their turns in the two slots closest to the door. I check them out, like I always do. Some are more interesting than others, just like the folks who arrive and depart in them. Such is life. Much of life is routine, and perhaps will become a blur in memory, and then there are those unforgettable moments, and the people with whom you share those moments.

I don't know if cars remember much from their past. Like us, they probably pass through their time in a colorless rush to the next place, and they pass by without seeing the bulk of things. But I'm sure they remember some. And when you see an old car parked in a driveway or garage, and you realize that it doesn't get out on the road as much as it used to, or perhaps it doesn't get out at all, don't ya wonder if it doesn't reminisce about the special times and places it has seen while it quietly sits there? Surely it now has the time to do this. And like us, as we mature, old cars spend more time with, and savor, the memories.

A while ago I looked out the glass door, and sitting there was a 1963 Chevy. I did the math quickly in my head. Forty-eight years old. That is older than Norm's Studebaker.

Norm was my best friend through high school. I've lost touch with him over the years. He wanted to be a concert pianist playing for the assembled masses, and he tried really hard for that. He ended up running his dad's lumberyard in our little town instead, and he did well enough at that to buy a concert piano, a twenty-foot long or so Bosendorfer I think it was, and it sat in his living room and he played it every day, for himself. Alone.

Anyway, back in the late '60s Norm bought a '27 Studebaker. In the '60s you could go to the Sears catalog and find any part for an old Model T Ford you wanted, and if you were trying to rebuild an old one you just wrote a check and the parts came and you rebuilt the car. Studebakers were just a bit less ubiquitous than Model T's, and in the '60s, if you wanted to fix one old Studebaker you needed another old Studebaker from which to cannibalize parts. So even with a few friends helping, that old Studebaker never regained its former glory. I think Norm finally ended up giving up and selling the car to someone else. Poof... gone.

I recall that driving that old car around was really neat for us. Cars had changed a lot from '27 to our time. I loved the old pinstripes we found when we took off the old paint covering the older paint, 'cause that told of the proud past of this car. And I remember how forlorn the car felt. That old Studebaker had an aura of sadness about it. I didn't realize it at the time, but that is what I now remember most of it. And I got a completely different feeling from that '63 Chevy in the parking lot.

Now, this Chevy was not one of those absolutely perfectly frame off restorations you see at the custom and classic car auctions on TV, the ones that sell for a king's ransom. Far from it. In fact, it died in the parking lot, and if the car parts store wasn't walking distance away, and a new battery was thus forthcoming, it wouldn't have made it home that night. And the folks who owned this old car were as far removed as you can imagine from those people who write six figure checks to buy restored vehicles with the same ease as the rest of us buy a sandwich down at Togo's. Heck, this guy could have spent his few discretionary dollars on teeth, and no one would have minded.

But with the new battery, the engine fired right up, and settled into a contented idle. I told the guy that it sounded happy. He agreed. Turns out this car had been in his family since day one. Through forty-eight years of the evolution of the nation, and the progression of a family, this car had stuck around, and the folks in this family have kept it alive and part of things. And the car felt happy.

Somewhere in this there may lay a lesson. I started writing about something way different than this, when I began this thing rather late last night. And I ended up here. Don't know why. The fun columns always seem to end up way different from where they start. Maybe next week I'll write the column I started this week. Meanwhile, I'll just think some more about where this one went.

August 11, 2011

Preserving Memories In Mundane Locations

My best photographs have long or interesting stories behind them. The big photo that hangs in my exam room is one of these. I took it in September 1979 while visiting the Tetons on my motorcycle. The photo shows the length of the Teton Range from the viewpoint you can drive to on the top of Signal Mountain, a view you can't photograph anymore because the trees grew up too much, and now you can't even see the forest for them. Sure, you can walk over there and look around the trees and get some of that view, but it's not the same. In the photo, lots of fresh snow color the peaks, for it was well into September and the first snowstorm had already come through.

The storm that brought this snow had also visited the Uinta Mountains in Utah, where I camped high in an aspen grove off a gravel road, and awoke to a winter wonderland that was something less than conducive to motorcycle travel. Later I crossed into Wyoming on I-80 along the only lane that was plowed, and spent the night in Kemmerer, the home of the original JC Penney store, and then rode on the next morning with the thermometer hovering around the 14 degree mark in order to get to the Tetons that day. The things I did for fun...

The motorcycle was a divorce present to myself, one of those self-indulgent things you do to help rebuild your self-esteem in the wake of certain unpleasantries. I camped alone beside Jenny Lake, in the campground that was closed and nearly deserted for the season, and I squatted to take clear cold water from the lake for meals and drinking, with the mountains looming overhead. I didn't think about climbing the Grand on this trip, because the last journey to this place had kinda soured me on that plan. And I knew the climbing school and guide service was closed for the season. Did I mention that this was a long story?

Dad and I had talked of climbing the Grand from the very beginning, when we first saw it in the mid '60s. Mom gave us the look; you know the look, the one that silently suggested we take up some other nonsense and forget this one. So the notion sat on the shelf, to be talked about only in the abstract. And when his doctor told him that no way was Dad getting his permission to climb a mountain at his age, his dream seemed dead.

I still thought about doing the climb. Two years before the motorcycle trip I had driven to the Tetons in September, alone. That marriage was terminally ill already, but the truth hadn't been revealed to me yet, although she would have known. I drove the new car, the one that I took off the dealer's lot on 7/7/77, which I had figured was a sign of good luck, and it wasn't. Approaching from the Idaho side, I had a brief look at the Grand from near Victor, and it felt just a bit weird. And after transiting Teton Pass, where you can turn left just past Wilson and take the back road to Moose, and the Grand fills the sky in front of you, I got this terrible feeling in my gut looking up at the peak, and since I harbored the notion that I would seek out the climbing school and actually try to climb the Grand on this trip, I asked the mountain if it was going to kill me. And the mountain laughed. At me.

That was an annoyance. I was trying to create something positive in my life, 'cause things were clearly spiraling out of control about then. The Grand Tetons had always grounded me and given me meaning in my life, and here they were taunting me, and I didn't get it.

That trip was cut short, just like the one before we got married, when she called me, and I drove home at her request. She only did it to see if she could tug the string and I would snap back, and then of course when I got home, I got the who-are-you-and-what-do-you-want look upon arrival and that was a disappointment. Both times. And I knew why the mountain laughed at me. I wasn't ready for the mountain.

The motorcycle trip felt better 'cause I felt better, and I think the mountain knew it. I was still looking up at the Grand and thinking about climbing it. So I mentioned it to Dad and he still wanted to climb it, too. He found another doctor, the one who told him he should go, and he somehow got the idea past Mom, and then at age 59 he began beating himself into shape. And that's how the other photograph came to be.

Our climbing guide used my camera to take the other photo (p.219), because Dad's had kinda got ruined during that little dunking we took when we paddled our kayak into deep trouble in the spring runoff on the Snake River. But that's another story. In this photo, the coil of rope lay in the foreground, and the line led to its tie off on Dad's waist. He wore one glove cause the other had floated away, and I stood at his shoulder. Behind us stretched snow covered mountains and then the haze over the distance of Idaho. Everything else was rock, the top rock on that big piece of rock, the Grand Teton (elevation 13,770 feet). We were on the summit. And we be smilin'.

So I was talking with some clients in the exam room, and we looked up at the photo on the wall, and I showed them the Grand, and then I mentioned that we had climbed it on June 25, 1980, and it just happened to be June 25 as we talked. Thirty one years later. And they asked, "Why?"

"Because it was there."

Been there, done that, got the T-shirt. My sister had a shirt made up with that photo on the front and gave it to Dad when he turned 90. I'm thinking he just might have been wearing that shirt while I talked to that client last Saturday. And that would be OK.

June, 2011

Kijana

> *We do not see nature with our eyes, but with our understandings and our hearts.*
>
> William Hazlitt
> *"Thoughts on Taste"*
> *Edinburgh Magazine, October 1818*

In Swahili, Kijana means "little boy." I guess in relative terms he was, but when I first stood beside him, little was not the word I considered. He weighed about 150 lbs when he was born, and his adoptive mother said he was pushing 400 lbs on the day we visited. She had to keep reminding him not to lean against us, because he had no idea yet how to be bigger than everybody else. Kijana was about waist high to me, but I could sense his mass whenever he came close, and I didn't want to get between him and anything hard. Kijana wasn't interested in hurting anyone, but he could get frisky, like any toddler.

Most all of us have been sniffed by a dog. This can be a bit intrusive, but it pales in comparison to being checked out by an elephant. Kijana was already skilled in the use of his trunk, and within moments he knew each of us quite well. He passed the end of his trunk all over us, very quickly and adroitly. It never bumped into us, but would brush ever so gently across our skin as he sniffed. And he made eye contact, and held it, and I came away convinced he was every bit as intelligent as he needed to be, and that he welcomed our attention.

His favorite trick was to grab a few strands of our hair with the end of his trunk and tug a bit. Not too hard. Just for fun, I guess. My nine year old stepdaughter had long straight blonde hair. Kijana had a ball with her. She stood barely taller than this baby elephant, and I have photos of the two side by side.

I was sitting on a hay bale a few feet away when I took the photos. An adult elephant stood on the other side of the massive bars of her enclosure, just behind me. Sitting on my hay bale, I looked up at her knee. This lady weighed about 10,000 lbs. From my angle below her, that was mighty big! Pictures cannot do an elephant justice. To truly know one takes up close and personal.

I watched from a surf side bluff as a 40 ton gray whale and her calf swam by, just outside the breakers. Alamere Falls dove off the cliff to my left, headed for the ocean. The sun was setting into the western horizon, making that sizzling sound as it slid into the sea. But all I could see were those two huge beings slowly slipping through the clear water in front of me.

I've known friends who have traveled to San Ignacio lagoon to float in rubber rafts an arm's length from these massive creatures, to touch them and look deeply into their eyes as they looked back. And I would give much to have that chance.

The whales are doing well these days, recently recovered from the hunting of the past, but that could change. The elephants' fate is a bit more tenuous. I remember well the day I heard the sad news of 11 month old Kijana's sudden death. I cried like a baby. I cannot imagine a world without elephants or whales.

I've tried here to condense an elephant and a whale into mere words, and believe me, I don't come close. And a little photo you hold in your hand is just not the same. So I hope the time never comes when I must try to explain an elephant or a whale to a child of some future generation, if none are left to actually know.

May 20, 2007

Discovering the Real America

So I looked at the scenery, she read her magazine
And the moon rose over an open field
"Kathy, I'm lost." I said though I knew she was sleeping
I'm empty and aching and I don't know why.
Counting the cars on the New Jersey Turnpike
They've all gone to look for America

          Simon and Garfunkel
             America, 1968

  Way back in '79 I straddled my brand new motorcycle, fired up the engine, and headed off to look for America. I didn't call the trip that name at the time, but I ended up singing this song over and over again as I motored across the waist of Nevada on Route 50, according to Life Magazine the "Loneliest Road In America." My bike had no radio, and such novelties as MP3 players wouldn't come along for another several years, so if I wanted tunes to go with my scenery, I had to supply them myself. And so it became the Look For America trip.

  At first I didn't realize I was looking for America. I'd always thought I had long ago found America. I figured I had spent my entire life in America. But I was wrong.

  No, I had spent my time in the greater Chicagoland area, and then in California. These places call themselves America, but in many important characteristics, they are not. It was only later that I discovered the real America. And of course I realized that I like the real thing much better than the impostor.

  I recommend Route 50 across Nevada to you. It traverses a land of stark lonely beauty. Very lonely, and very stark. Whilst driving it you will pass only the occasional car. You will pass through only the rare tiny town. You will lack much of anything you could call "services." And you might see a raven or perhaps if lucky a pronghorn, but you had best be comfortable inside your own head for you likely will be your own company for most of this trip.

I had passed on the opportunity to top off the fuel tank in the quaint burg of Austin. Eureka didn't look that far off on the map. I could make that easily…

Route 50 is even lonelier when you are parked on the shoulder for a bit, lamenting the local shortage of fossil fuel. Eureka was down the road somewhere, out of sight. No idea how far. Might be a long walk. But hark! A vehicle cometh! A motorhome, with California plates. Drove right on by in a cloud of dust and indifference. Apparently, these folks from California could not be bothered to help a stranger stranded out in the middle of less than nothing.

California corrupts human behavior, because we have compressed together far too many people, mashed into inhuman conditions, and to keep them happy in that unhappy and unhealthy environment, we tell them that all the wrong stuff, the unimportant stuff, is really the important stuff. So folks obsess on the bad and let the good in them dissipate.

The old pickup truck that did stop, piloted by a local man, not only carried me into Eureka, but back to my bike with a can of gas. Not insincerely friendly, the man driving was however helpful when needed, and polite, and decent. You know, like an American.

He didn't act like a Californian. I've found many other Americans in the less traveled, rural places that fill that bit of the continent the coastal urban denizens call "fly over country." Such folk lead perhaps simpler lives that we have here in California. Might even call them boring. But you can spot 'em right away because they are lacking in the scowls that daily fill your rearview mirrors, and they don't wave to you with only that one finger as you interact in traffic. And they are not always in such a danged hurry.

Such people are so unaccustomed to fearing for their very lives if they so much as make eye contact with the wrong stranger that they will actually help you if ya need it. You know, like an American.

When I wander out into America, I can feel the oppression of living in pseudo-America peel off in layers. The relief is palpable. It feels so good that I look forward to repeating the pleasure whenever possible. So when the time came to deliver ourselves to New England for a wedding (p.209), and we contemplated the airline flight from one crowded oppressive coast to yet another, we decided to drive through America instead. We plan on enjoying the trip.

Some have questioned this project. The last thing they would wish to do would be to drive across what they feel is interminably boring landscape. They see things a mite differently than we do. Such folks really should stay on the coasts, and just fly over the middle when needed. They'd hate our trip. For me, I expect to find much less "empty and aching and I don't know why" out in the middle of nowhere important than I find here in California.

September 25, 2011

Meeting Nova

"Don't worry, be happy!"

It'sa kinda silly song. This time it was sung by a fake rubber fish mounted on a wooden plaque. You've seen these novelties... Ya press the red button and the fake rubber fish moves its head and tail as if swimming, and the fish's mouth opens and closes with the lyrics. Oh, and it plays songs, like the Bobby McFerrin song, "Don't worry; be happy." This giz is best appreciated when tipsy or two years old. We weren't imbibing. But Nova is two years old, and she loved it.

So OK... who is Nova?

Well, let's see if I'm up to this.

Some people you can sum up with a few short sentences. And frankly, most two year olds fall into this category. Many two year olds will eventually grow and expand and their sentences will become longer and more enjoyable to read. But some people will never warrant much more than a short story, and you gotta keep the descriptions uncomplicated with these.

Not Nova.

She is one in a million.

After meeting Nova, I wanted to tell you all something about her, and I've plenty of time and energy to do this, what with being on vacation and all. I have all those gigabytes on my 'puter to play with, and those dozens of words in my vocabulary to arrange and rearrange, and yet it will take me a bit to do this, and I will rewrite it a few times, and still I fear I shall only scratch the surface of whom Nova is and what she does and how impressed I am with this tiny child. I know this already, and I have only spent maybe three hours with her.

The wedding was Sunday, and on Monday I had the headlight fixed and the oil changed early (p.10), and got the Jetta packed for the long journey home before noon, but we hung around because the offspring were gonna show up and we wanted to be there for this. We were at my father-in-law's, Rex's house, and his grandkids wanted to spend more time with him and they showed up, since they were in town and home was far away for most of them. And Rex has some health issues and he is 96 and so you stop by when you are in town. Ya know.

Anyway, we found out that Nova's parents could bring her by for a visit after she woke up from her nap, and we figured that was worth waiting just a little, since meeting her was on the short list. And we were so right.

I was washing the dishes after the pizza, onnacounta I'm a nice guy and such (and I always need the points), when Jason, Elizabeth, and Nova arrived. So Nova was well into enjoying herself when I came into the room. She stood next to the little coffee table with all the magazines in front of the couch, and she was looking at fish. Pictures of fish. In the Orvis catalog.

Nova likes fish. She has been to the aquarium, and it's full of fish and she saw every one of them. And she has books at home and she goes through them looking for fish. And she finds every one. So Nova found every fish in the Orvis catalog, and she was delighted. She was so delighted that she wanted to share, and so if somebody was sitting there watching her, and everybody was, she would pick someone, walk over and take that grownup's finger, and haul them back over to see her fish. And she did this to several grownups. And when I walked into the room, she was doing this and I thought it was pretty cool.

Nova eventually had seen all the fish in the Orvis catalog, and so she found a rocking chair to climb upon, and she rocked herself for a while. And then great grandfather Rex brought in the rubber fish on a plaque that plays songs when you push the red button, and presented it to Nova. And *wow*, was that OK with Nova. She had the red button figured out right away, and with each push she enjoyed a new song from her fish, and she danced with each, and the smile would melt steel.

Ya see, Nova has a hearing aide that puts the sound into the bones of her head so she hears the music just fine. The bones in her ear are just a bit mixed up, so the usual way to hear won't work for her. But with the help of the hearing aid the dancing comes naturally along with the smile. And she sees anything she wants by just cocking her head a little to get things into focus. And without question, this works fine for her, too.

Once in a while Elizabeth or Jason need to suction out Nova's tracheotomy tube, but she is accustomed to this. And she wears the backpack that holds her food that feeds through the plastic tube to that other tube into her stomach, and that's just normal for her. No problem, ya know. She squeals with joy over life's little discoveries and she is starting to eat tiny bits from a spoon finally, and some day that will be fine too.

Nova has about 200 words now, which ain't bad for a two year old. She does this with ASL, which is American Sign Language, if you haven't been paying attention. If you get the chance, you should learn some ASL, 'cause it comes in real handy with some folks who don't talk with their mouths yet. Nova holds up the "I Love You" thing with her fingers, and it will melt your heart. Trust me.

Something about Nova that I just have to share. When she is pushing the red button and the fish is singing, and she wishes to show this wonder to you, she will walk over to you. And she *will* take your finger, and lead you over to experience this with her, and you will know you have been selected by someone very special for something very special, and if you don't tear up just a little with how happy it makes you feel to be selected by Nova, you are beyond redemption. And yes, every single person in the room was so honored.

Nova doesn't miss a thing, and she enjoys most things, and every eye in the room follows her everywhere and she enjoys the world, for she is just that wonderful.

And you are probably wondering about the hearing aid and the trach tube and the way Nova must be fed. Nova was born with a thing called Pfeiffer Syndrome. You can look it up, but what we have here is an incredibly uncommon, one in one hundred thousand babies-deal that happened to land on Nova. Craniosynostosis. Big word.

When things work as they should, a baby has these gaps between the bones in their skull, and this lets them grow into "normal" and then the bones knit together later and you have a "normal" head. With Pfeiffer Syndrome the bones fuse together prematurely and unless the surgeons move things around fairly often while the child grows, this messes up everything. So Nova has had a few surgeries, and she will have several more, and when she is finally grown she will have a nearly "normal" head. And if the early returns bear fruit, Nova will be one heck of a neat human when it is all done.

Nova has several little friends with whom she plays, and they have a ball together. And you can tell that she is going to have many more. Because of the roll of the dice, Nova doesn't look like every other child. She looks like Nova, a happy, bright, gifted child, but that isn't enough for a few fools.

Apparently some moms have 'rescued' their little children from time spent with Nova, which proves that the human race is gonna go on like it always has, with prejudice and ignorance and irrational fears and dislikes propagated for eternity. And I feel so sorry for those little children, for they will not learn the joys of friendship with Nova, and they will advance through life incomplete and deprived because of their parents' ignorance.

Some folks would tell you that Nova is handicapped. But I would suggest that if you ask Nova, the operative word here would be inconvenienced. Not handicapped. And this is Nova's choice. She seems totally cool with things as they are, which of course would be a lesson for all of us.

October 9, 2011

We Must Needs Die

For we must needs die, and are as water spilt on the ground, which cannot be gathered up again.
                                                    2 Samuel 14:14, *KJV*

Sharla lost her grandfather last week. Don Ford was only 60 years old, but the asthma and diabetes conspired to take him long before anyone expected. Don died very quickly. He didn't even have time to be surprised, for he left before he knew anything was happening. Death doesn't care if he was planning to move to Tucson with his lovely wife to enjoy a quiet retirement.

An old proverb holds that death always comes too soon or too late. Our loved ones are either snatched so quickly and unexpectedly that we have no chance to prepare for the loss, or we must endure their protracted pain and suffering before they finally earn their release. It seems there never really is a good day to die.

Don's death caught all of us by surprise. It was hard on everyone who knew him of course, but I thought it was particularly difficult for Sharla, because she hasn't had to endure the loss of someone close. At sixteen, her life is filled with excitement and disappointment, often both in the same hour, as she copes with the perpetual trials of adolescence and high school. As massive as these upheavals must seem to her, grandfather's death suddenly landed on her with an impact that makes a canceled date to the junior prom seem pretty insignificant.

Sharla has two families dedicated to keeping as much of life's pain away from her as possible. Nobody gets divorced because they are getting along too well. Sharla's mother and father split years ago for some pretty good reasons. Greg found love again and married. Joie stumbled across and married me.

When Greg and I first met, we sized each other up and then decided that Sharla's well-being was far more important than any need we might have to knock heads with each other. So we formed a loose liaison dedicated to rearing and protecting one little girl. But how do you protect someone from this?

Greg caught a double whammy, for Don was his father. Not only did he have to guide Sharla through all this, but he also had to find a way to cope with his own grief.

As much as I have tried to participate in her life, I suddenly found myself on the outside looking in. I had met Don. He read my column every week and claimed he liked it. And Sharla's wonderful grandmother, Ann, helped us refinance our home twice. But this wasn't my family. I wanted to hold the safety net in case it was needed to catch Shar, but I also tried to stay out of the way.

So from the other side of the room I watched helplessly as innocence melted away and reality slowly took its place. Sharla was never going to see Don again, and she would never be quite the same person because of this.

But, I also watched as she accepted her grief and settled in to comfort Ann. Sharla flowed into the difficult gap between our two families, smoothing out, for a while at least, any differences we might have, so this terrible time could pass without conflict. And then she thanked each of us for being there for her... as if we had done anything at all. Kids are tough, and so wise.

During one of the uncomfortable lulls that occur during such times, I walked outside with Greg while he loaded some things into his car. He felt like talking, and expressed his gratitude that he was able to spend an entire day with Don right before his death. Like most of us, Greg works many long hours, and he could easily have missed this opportunity while he was busy just trying to do his job. So of course, I agreed that this was a good thing. He must have caught my wry smile, for he asked me what was up. Well, I said, I guessed I had learned something from him, as well. For it was high time I called my parents, too.

I hope you all still have your parents and grandparents, for once they are gone there is no going back. Perhaps you could find some time to call or visit soon. Someday, you might be glad you did.

April 2003

Wandering In The Desert

I am a rock; I am an island... and a rock feels no pain; and an island never cries.

Simon and Garfunkel
I Am A Rock, 1965

We turned on to the road at a perfect time. Headed almost straight east, the sunrise unfolded for us through our windshield as we fled toward Needles. Just enough smog overflowed into the desert from the L.A. Basin to the west to allow the sun, from its hiding place just below the horizon, to color the sky a gory red. It backlit the sawtooth mountain ridge which was our horizon, and cast just enough light to purple the lesser ridges lined up in front of the first, each veiled slightly by the haze. The vast foreground for this show was flat empty desert, blessedly devoid of manmade light, and thus still black as night.

I have this special set of nerve endings for such moments. Groupings of said nerves are aligned along my shoulders, scattered about the back of my neck, loosely attached to the hair on my head, embedded deep in my chest, and buried in that special vault somewhere in the center of my belly. When stimulated, they go all gonzo, and they let me feel quite tingly and warm. They lie in these places, patiently waiting for the excuse, slowly building up the charge until ya gotta wonder how they can hold it. And then a such moment comes along, the trip wire gets tripped, the poles depolarize, the synapses hook up, and it's, "Oh, Goodie!" time. Often the levees are broached (the ones inside, built up over the years, whose job it is to make sure I don't let myself get too happy), for they are designed only for the usual floods and not the once in a long while weather event. The overflow triggers the seventh cranial nerve, which, as we all know, cannot help itself. The seventh cranial nerve operates the "muscles of expression" in my face, so this becomes the secondary trigger, and from its stimulation we get a smile.

So with the cruise control locked on an expedient 73 MPH, the Jetta purring contentedly in 6th gear at 2,000 RPM, and while the satellite radio provided our old music, I watched the free show through the window. I exulted in the presence of the desert, experienced my pleasure, and sported my smile. Oh, and I got to thinking.

An artist might wonder at such a time how she might find the perfect clay to mix with some salts and minerals and a little oil to exactly match that luscious red color when she applies it to canvas or fine pottery. And the scientist might marvel at the refraction angles of light intermixing with smog, or the rod to cone ratio of our retinas, or even the cholinesterase levels flying around our nerve connections that allow us to see this scene. Meanwhile, the tortoise over there might only wonder how long before the sun would warm up a fellow enough for him to wiggle his toes.

But me… I chose to wander about inside my head, and therein I found a can of worms. And why not open a can of worms? I utilized this spectacular moment to wonder if all this exhilaration running around inside me meant that there really is a God or not. 'Cause that's what a gory red sunrise in the desert can do to a man.

I have no problem with the notion that so many religions got their start with folks who wandered about in deserts. I have tried to capture the beauty of the desert with mere words, and I don't know enough words. So I guess I could say that the desert is something so wonderful that it defies description. The desert is also a bit harsh. It can and will kill you. And it doesn't need a reason. Since much of what a god is supposed to do revolves around trying to explain the unexplained wonder of the world, and also the horror of it, where better could you find a place that almost demands such contemplation?

Many of these founders of religions wandered without food or water for extended periods in the desert before they began to observe what they thought they saw. A few found or at least sought visions. Some talked with bushes or went off their meds and then heard the voices. Others fermented grapes in goat stomachs or beer in the wash tub, or they nibbled on peyote buds or Jimson weed to expand their awareness, and fine tune their synapses. So they were, shall we say, receptive to wandering about in their heads. Maybe this is how they concluded from all this that there must be a God, or several lower-case-g gods, running the whole thing, because they sure weren't.

I was a bit sleep deprived, hadn't had breakfast yet, and was more than half way through a Grande from Starbucks, so I wasn't in my right mind either. I knew I was watching something I considered beautiful and exhilarating. And I could recognize those feelings generated in my nerve endings. I have a passing familiarity with the physiology and know that there are physical reasons why I felt so good, and thus I couldn't credit a desert god pouring a bucket of rapture over my shoulders for this thrill. So I had no interest in starting a religion out of gratitude. But I did wonder if those nerve endings came about due to some random natural selection that favored an ancestor who enjoyed happiness in pretty places, of if just maybe a god put all that wiring in there as her gift to us lucky folks. So I caught myself thinking stuff that could get me into an argument with many different folks.

And right then that Simon and Garfunkel song slipped out of our radio, and I did the flashback. To 1966. I barely knew the girl who gave the valedictorian speech at our high school graduation. It was a small graduating class, but was clearly defined by its divisions, and I was relegated to one of the others. My group was small, insignificant, unwanted. So when this girl used that song as the theme for her speech, and she argued against the teen angst desire to become a rock and an island in defense against the unfairness of life, I figured she should shut up and go away.

And I remembered how I felt at the beginning of that commencement ceremony, for all those gathered in the gym were expected to enjoy a prayer, and I had no use for that, either. I had just turned seventeen, so I figured I knew everything. I had things figured out, for when that girl's favored social group was out having fun, I was spending time wandering about the inside of my head, concluding stuff. Among all the other stuff I knew without a doubt, I knew that there was no God. So why should I waste any more of my time with the trappings of religion?

I'm a bit older now, and hopefully some smarter, and I've opened my mind to some other thoughts. Mostly, I've noticed that I have fewer answers and far more questions than when I knew it all. I guess I'm allowed to play around with my questions when I wish. And I'll admit that I now don't know if there is a God, or gods, or just how this whole thing works.

Someone far wiser than me once wrote that if there were no God, people would invent one. Most people, if they give this notion a thought, would have to agree. The there-is-no-god crew would suggest that every god or God people have come up with is an example of such a fabrication. And the my-god-is-the-only-true-God people would simply conclude that the fools who know other gods all brewed up theirs. Somebody out there may be right, but how might you tell?

This conundrum often reminds me of the, "Do flying saucers exist?" discussions. Some people fervently believe in them. Others tend to wonder if those people who believe in flying saucers are a bit off. I always figured I would believe in a flying saucer when I actually saw one for myself. Up to then, I'll be skeptical, but not religiously so. For how, in the end, do you prove the negative?

Meanwhile, if I sometimes wonder about the wonder of it all, while watching the sun rise over the Mojave or a thunderstorm booming from the top of some mountain, please lose no sleep over it. 'Cause if I do finally come to some absolute truth for me, it still won't matter one whit to anyone else.

> *And the Colorado Rocky Mountain high,*
> *I've seen it rainin' fire in the sky*
> *You can talk to God and listen to the casual reply.*
> John Denver

Or not.

Novemer 29, 2011

Man, The Toolmaker

Homo hobilis, the "Handy Man" of prehistoric earth, began making tools back in 1.8-1.4 million years BC, that rocking time we now call the Stone Age. Not long afterwards, but well before "Tim 'The Tool Man' Taylor" hit the airwaves, my father in law, Rex, built a rifle. Like *H. hobilis* before him, Rex didn't make his tool from scratch. Back in the Stone Age, the locals picked up a rock that was already there, that had the right shape, and then they worked it into better shape, usually by sharpening it. Most often, they then attached a handle to the sharpened rock, a piece of wood, and it became a weapon.

Of course such tools were also very handy when these guys needed to gather up a mastodon or two for the weekend barbecue. Over time, these stone tools were improved. Eventually, the sharpened rock weapon tools evolved in one direction, and the hunting tools in another. But a family resemblance remained.

Rex built a hunting rifle by improving a weapon rifle. In 1917 and '18, manufacturers in this country built Enfield rifles chambered in the American service cartridge, the 30/06. They had been making Enfields chambered in 303 for the British earlier in the war, because we liked those guys. In World War I these rifles were sent across the Atlantic to help the Brits who were fighting the Germans, Austria-Hungarians, Ottoman Empire-ians and Bulgarians. When we sent homemade Americans across the Atlantic to help the Brits who were fighting the Germans, et al., we sent along rifles chambered in 30/06. We wanted to send Springfield rifles chambered in 30/06 because this was an American rifle, albeit one "derived" from the German Mauser (some would say stolen from the German Mauser). But we couldn't make enough of those, so we made some two million 30/06 Enfields, an English rifle "derived" from the German Mauser, and sent them along as well.

The German Mauser was not the original rock somebody sharpened, but it was a good one and folks still build rifles "derived" from it.

Attached to each of these rifles was a piece of wood that was designed to make these tools better weapons. They weren't very pretty, but they sufficed. When the next big war ended, a bunch of those Enfield rifles were still in government storage, and since the government wasn't yet obsessed with taking guns away from its citizens, people could obtain these old weapon tools, and if they wanted, they could turn them into hunting tools. Cut a piece or two off the weapon, bend another, refresh the bluing, mount a telescopic scope, and pretty soon they had converted a weapon tool into a hunting tool. A family resemblance remained, but now it served its new job better than the old mass produced one.

The biggest difference between the weapon tool and the hunting tool the people created was that piece of wood attached. Where the weapon tool had utility, the attached wood was not pretty. But the people building the hunting tools specialized in attaching the prettiest wood they could find.

Rex was very active in drum and bugle competitions after WWII. A friend on a competing corps gave Rex an Enfield rifle the team no longer needed. So in the very early 1950s, probably '51 or '52, Rex took a 30 year old weapon tool and turned it into a beautiful hunting tool. And much of that beauty came from the block of wood he carved and shaped and sanded and finished, which converted a mass produced weapon into a one-of-a-kind hunting rifle. And Rex turned it into a piece of art.

Now, the story doesn't end here. For when Rex had completed converting his rifle, save for that coating of finish that would highlight and protect the wood, he carried it into the hunting field. And as luck would have it, in the dark woods of Vermont, at a time when deer were far harder to find than now, the largest, most antler-endowed buck Rex ever saw wandered in front of him. But as luck also had it, the wood of the rifle had gotten wet the day before, and when it swelled and warped, it compromised the action, and when Rex pulled the trigger on that buck, the rifle wouldn't fire.

Other rifles came along in subsequent years, most lighter and easier to carry in the woods, and they put deer into the freezer for Rex. But to this day, 60 years later, the sporterized Enfield he built has not fulfilled its destiny. It's still as pretty, and Rex is very proud of his work, but this rifle has not yet helped to fill a freezer. And as Rex recuperates from some medical problems at the tender age of 96, I don't believe he figures it ever will.

But wait...

In two weeks we will drive to South Dakota, and we will bring back a bison for the freezer. I won't insult this beast by calling this endeavor a buffalo hunt, for I certainly know where the bison will be, and the usual exertion associated with a hunt ain't gonna happen here. But a rifle will be used to take this bison, and it's gonna be Rex's hand built Enfield rifle, which is now a treasured family heirloom. I don't know if you can make a rifle happy, but I think I know how to do that trick for Rex. He deserves to know that the tool he made so many years ago finally had the chance to do its job.

December 18, 2011

Deep Roots And Respect On The South Dakota Plains

Hi all,

Just back from a bison "hunt." I don't actually refer to this effort as a hunt, for I knew in advance where the bison might be. More a bison shoot. The ethics of which I shall address someday.

Brilliant sunlight bored into my eyes. This far up the map, the sun hangs lower in the sky than I am accustomed. And it lends less warmth. The wind arrived unimpeded by that five strand barbed wire fence, a few miles north and out of sight on the other side of the low ridge. Not one tree stood in the way. By local standard, it wasn't much of a wind that day. Just enough to qualify for what they call a chill factor on the TV weather. It found its way past my collar, right there at the back of my neck. By local standard, it wasn't cold either. Somewhere in the high teens. Shoulda been below zero this time of year. They are having a mild winter so far, but that will change. Still, my hands stiffened faster than they used to.

South Dakota prairie grassland extended to the four horizons under a seamless, intensely blue sky. Last summer had been remarkable. More than enough rain, at all the right times, and warmth that didn't cook everything to death. Everything grew beyond reason. The old folks just nodded, and said, "Don't get used to it." Next year, this could be a brown wasteland. But for now the bison stood knee deep in grass in January, and they weren't complaining.

A small herd of bison cows and calves fed in front of us. Behind them, on the slope rising to the north, six bulls lounged in the sun. They were built for a Dakota winter. Their ancestors thrived here for millennia despite four foot snows and wind fresh from the Arctic, bringing with it sub-zero temperatures. They are large enough to hang onto their heat. Their coats grow dense this time of year. And they can plow aside the snow with their huge heads, finding grass for their calves and themselves. They no doubt enjoyed this mild weather, but I'm sure the old cows just nodded and said, "Don't get used to it."

Bison and mankind have shared this land since the glaciers melted away a few years ago. Primitive man stumbled in after crossing the Bering Land Bridge, and found the bison here, shortly after the mastodons, saber toothed cats, and giant bears went away. Or maybe after the mankind hunters killed them off. When the White folks showed up, the Sioux and assorted other native tribes wandered the land, dependent upon the bison for sustenance. Several groups of natives predated the Sioux, each supplanted by the next, more ambitious or talented or nastier tribe. The Sioux were doing well when the Europeans arrived, but they couldn't compete. Not with those evil nasty Europeans. Evil nasty nasty Europeans. Shame on them!

There… we've gotten that politically correct self-recrimination thing out of the way. Don't want anyone to think that success should pass without an appropriate amount of blame and guilt.

We spent some time with the descendants of those White conquerors. They've put in enough time here so you can assess how they are doing. First off, they've set down roots. Deep ones. Like the cottonwoods that survive the climate there. Deep roots come in handy when times turn tough. The people here are inseparable from the land. They know they cannot live without it, and that they must not only care for the land, but also give thanks for it. And they don't wish to leave this place, even though other places might carry more glamour, or simply an easier life.

The folks with whom we stayed are a mite different from most around our home. They tend toward quiet, and modest. And they go about all that needs doing without protest or complaint. Work for them starts with the dawn, and stops when they can't see anymore. Their faith comes easily to them, kinda like breathing and eating. They simply do it and live it every day. The sun comes up in the east, and their faith is there to greet it. And they plug in the truck each night so it will start in the morning, regardless where the thermometer ends up, 'cause ya still gotta do your part, too.

The animals need care. Morning and night the people go out and break the ice so the calves can get water. Most years, the grass is thin by now, so they roll out the hay for the herd to eat. See a coyote stalking the sheep? Get rid of it. That's why the rifle lives in the truck. Loaded. For the coyotes. They can trust their neighbors, so the front door isn't locked.

When we were ready to leave, and the truck was packed, they gifted us with something precious to them. And this gift tells much. We left with a photo of their family, four generations, twenty-three people from 92 years to two months of age. Precious.

I was taken with the similarities, with how much the folks living on the prairie of Dakota these days resemble the Sioux and their predecessors.

The land and the weather and the bison defined the Sioux. These things defined the Sioux because they provided the sustenance needed by the Sioux, and also the challenges the people met to survive. And the faith that sustained the Sioux derived from these conditions.

Not much has changed. The weather and the land still define the place. The animals may be mostly Angus or Hereford now, but the bison are starting to come back. They still do well there. And the faith of the people blends into this land, too.

Historians like to say that when the Sioux killed a bison, the only thing they wasted was the grunt. They feasted upon the meat, and preserved what they could of the rest. They tanned the hides to build their shelter and provide their clothing. Bison horns served as spoons and cups. Various innards could be used to carry water or cook food. And bones could be turned into weapons, needles, and toys for the children. So when they felt the need, they used it all. Certainly, the bison filled many a need for the Sioux.

The historians conveniently overlook those times when the Sioux killed a few dozen too many bison, and they took the tongues and left the rest for the magpies and coyotes. But ya must do this to make the Sioux look good, and thus make their conquerors look bad. I don't think the Sioux were perfect, but I don't feel the need to condemn those folks who took over after them, either. The earth abides, and the people adapt, regardless who the people may be.

For my part... I chose from the herd that morning a bison cow with no calf, which meant that she would have gone to the butcher soon out of economic reality. My rifle was chambered in 45/70, an obsolescent cartridge once popular with buffalo hunters. She was quickly dispatched, and then loaded onto the flatbed pickup. The meat cutter turned her into nearly 300 pounds of meat. And we are having the hide tanned for a robe, and the skull cleaned and bleached. We didn't save the bladder to carry water, nor the rumen to cook in, for we have other things that fill those needs. So I suppose we weren't as frugal as the Sioux. But somehow, I don't suppose the Sioux would prefer a rumen if they were also offered a microwave.

January 8, 2012

Ghost Towns Reveal Our Humanity

"What a piece of work is man."

Shakespeare
Hamlet

Ghost towns are fascinating places. We headed for Bodie, one of the best. This eclectic collection of old wooden buildings nestles in a wide valley some 8,000 feet up in the treeless hills north of Mono Lake.

After weathering 100 years in that harsh climate, some might call it dilapidated, but I suggest Bodie is aged to perfection. A few of the buildings lean a little in the wind, but most have been reinforced or re-roofed to preserve them. The state park system guards the place now, so the human scavengers won't strip away all the goodies, but everybody knows that the best protection comes from a curse that follows any soul foolish enough to steal artifacts from the place.

So the town preservers, a slice of the late 1800's suspended in time, that we can experience vicariously.

Most visitors eventually browse through the cemetery on the little knoll above the town, wondering about the people memorialized by brief descriptions cut in stone. They quickly get a sense for the difficulties these people experienced. The hopeful converged on this mining town from all over the globe seeking their fortunes, only to die there from disease, accident, or violence.

We passed through on a holiday weekend. The parking lot was packed, so we just kept going on the rough gravel road. You can't find any ghosts when there are too many people there, anyway.

The road soon deteriorated into a nearly impassable, rocky obstacle course. Crossing into Nevada, we bounced along beside a small creek, through a spectacular gorge, and finally up the hill to the former site of Aurora. We passed a large rusting chimney, a crumbled mill, and then the huge open pit of a mine that seems to be consuming the whole area, modern man's answer to the problem of extracting mineral wealth from the ground.

Twenty rough miles from the crowds at Bodie, we had this ghost town to ourselves.

Aurora sprang up out of nowhere following a gold strike in 1862. In just a few years it had 10,000 residents, two newspapers, five mills, and the occasional saloon. Like Bodie, its neighbor down the road, it was a rough, often lawless place.

They scraped a few hundred thousand ounces of gold and silver out of the surrounding hills, made and lost fortunes, inspired Samuel Clemens to give up mining and take up writing, and then packed up and left before the turn of the century, when the veins finally played out.

Hardly anything remains from this ghost town but the most durable of wreckage. Anything worth taking was scrounged by folks building new boomtowns in other parts of the desert. The larger commercial buildings were torn down so post-war Los Angeles could have homes decorated with used brick. The cemetery however, is still there, and I wanted my wife to see one grave.

Aurora's cemetery is smaller than Bodie's, but more poignant. In that place and time, children died young, and mothers often did not survive childbirth, so these tombstones mostly commemorate young women and little children.

Horace and Lizzie Marden left behind three tombstones in their family plot. Two remember sons, aged eight and 18. The third lists four children, one on each side of a marble obelisk, who ranged in age from two to eight years. Pearl, Daisy, Dick, and Frank. These four all died between Feb.16 and 26, 1878.

We stared at that tombstone for a while, the big lump growing in our throats. Four babies, eleven days, nothing to be done but comfort the dying, console the living, and then wrap up the tiny bodies in this God-forsaken lurid town out in the middle of an uncaring arid wilderness.

Although I'd seen this grave before, it humbled me as if it were the first time. How could anyone be unaffected?

Imagine the tragedy of the Marden's lives, yet they stuck it out in Aurora for years.

What struck me at that moment was the resiliency of mankind. Our ancestors were hunter/gatherers. I guess we could have stayed that way, but soon people made their first metal tools from meteorites found on the ground. Then they learned to farm the earth, mine it, and travel all across it. Civilizations rose and fell, not unlike these ghost towns, often leaving little for us to know them by.

The primitive mining techniques of the late 1800's pale beside the massive operations of today, where an entire mountain is disappearing into the crushers just down the hill from the cemetery.

Good old mankind. How far we have come. How much has changed. We have mastered and scarred the earth far more than any other species before us. Not all of what we have done is good, or bad, but it is impressive.

We look at these ghost towns, with their faint records of lives lived and lost, and we grieve over babies dead a hundred years, and we realize, though mankind has greatly altered the earth, people really haven't changed all that much. Criticize man all you wish, but this comforts me.

June 13, 2002

When It's Time To Carry Your Dad

His cat's name is Diamond, but she apparently likes Kitty Cat better. Most good cats earn nicknames, and Kitty Cat is a good cat. Dad got her for Mom, he says. She used to keep Mom company. They were good friends, and Kitty Cat still goes to the door and looks into the garage whenever the car comes home, because that's where Mom would come into the house. Mom doesn't come into the house anymore, hasn't for several years and won't ever again, but the cat still looks for her. Every time the door opens.

Now Kitty Cat keeps Dad company. Took her a while, but without Mom around, Dad would do. He had always fed her and kept her box clean, so he was useful. Now she watches him eat and helps him read the paper. She is Dad's shadow.

Kitty Cat will run and hide whenever anyone else enters the house. Shy around strangers, she would say. After a while she'll come to investigate, but only from a distance. She prefers her own person. This morning Kitty Cat walked up to me and said, "Hi," and then rubbed her chin against my leg. And she let me pet her. I've known her for ten years, and she has never before asked to be petted by me. But her bowl was getting a bit low, and I guess she figured I could be useful for such things, so I put fresh food in the bowl, and she ate.

I don't know if Kitty Cat knows that Dad is in the hospital. I don't know what Kitty Cat knows about anything. She's a cat, so her thoughts are hers alone.

Every morning, Dad turns on the hose in the back of the house and fills the birdbath so the outdoor neighbors can drink. Then you get to see the quail, doves and woodpeckers as they stop by. And Dad cuts the grapefruit in half, the ones that fall from the tree unused since he no longer can eat grapefruit because they mess with his meds. The scattered halves of grapefruit on the ground feed the birds and bunnies. And the birds and bunnies feed the coyotes, for that is the way of things. Three coyotes stopped by for water the other day. There is no sign posted to keep them away, so that's how it is. Where water is concerned in the desert, everybody shares.

So this morning I filled the birdbath and cut up some grapefruit. The job must be done. And I pulled some of the weeds from around the barrel cactus, cause Dad asked me to do that the next time I visit. And I guess you can call this a visit. And I cleaned the filter for the air conditioner, and put more slices of my meat loaf in the freezer for when he comes home and he wants one for his dinner. Then it was time to go to the hospital and see that he eats his breakfast, and ask the doctor if they know any more about Dad's future.

I'm an optimist. Not completely without justification, because my Dad was doing really well before he fell, and he is no quitter. So I'm operating on the premise that he will come home, to his cat and his outdoor neighbors, and his future.

But I've never before had to pick up Dad in my arms and carry him out to the car to deliver him to an emergency room, so my hands shake just a bit as I type this. And I don't know what tomorrow brings. I like things better when I know what happens next. Always hated surprise exams. No time to cram. No time to get ready. Just show up and deal with it, for that is the way of things.

That I can do. But it wouldn't be my first choice.

May 16, 2012

Witnessing An Awe-Inspiring Homecoming

My phone plays a truly horrid tune when I set the thing on alarm and it goes off as directed. Nauseatingly horrid tune. It does achieve the desired result in that it will awaken me. Five thirty in the AM. Slide open the curtain.

Overcast. Breeze through the window smells of the sea. Cool breeze. Very fresh cool breeze.

A very few joggers and dog walkers are already out. The homeless guy is still there, sacked out on the cement, using the railroad tie as a pillow. Just beyond him is quiet water. The sun is up somewhere, and I can see just fine. The overcast flattens the light and confuses the distances. Some minor clanks waft up from the back door of the deli below. The hum of an air conditioner fan somewhere. A rare car drives past. But the sense is of quiet.

The square sails of the moored museum ship hang limp. A seagull makes small circular waves that soon fade to nothing. A scatter of lights across the bay. The jump of a fish.

I don't generally do cities. Cities are too big and they leave too small of spaces into which I can retreat. Too many people, buildings, cars… and the fears rise in my throat and it's time to leave. Now, please.

But somebody put this city in a nice place. On this bay next to that ocean. And as long as I can cling to only this thin slice of the city and kinda pretend that the rest of the city lurking behind me isn't really there, I can do this for a bit, and even enjoy it. I'm enjoying the early morning when this city is here for me, and the others can have it later.

San Diego. Been here four times before over the years. Once was pretty much terrible, save for the zoo visit. Dropped the girl off for her first year of college another time, and that was bitter and sweet. Did two conferences here, and they were tolerable. And discovered the bay and the joy of hanging off the balcony and just looking at the thing, and I could do this again. So here we are.

Another conference, and this has been a good one. The time spent on the balcony has been the highlight. Lunch break from the lectures, and back in the room. Sun out now and the light defies belief. This cannot be possible. The water sparkles. Every detail sharp and clear. The fresh cool breeze. Boats crisscross the bay. The walkway along the water is packed with walkers. The smell from the seafood restaurant. Navy ASW helicopter roars past on turbine driven rotors. And then I saw it.

I've seen pictures of this. I know they do it every time they come home. I just wasn't expecting to ever actually see it.

The *USS Makin Island* (LHD-8) sailed into the bay, made the slow starboard turn around the point of land occupied by the naval air station, and then passed by heading south toward its berth. I don't get to see an amphibious assault ship every day. This was my first, actually. The navy has eight of this class. They look every bit an aircraft carrier, only truncated at 840 feet long and 40,000 tons. The flat top can launch helicopters and Harriers. And then down below the various hovercraft and amphibious vehicles wait for the marines the ship carries, and heaven help those folks trembling ashore.

This ship has been out there for seven months, doing the sort of things for which we all should be thankful. Those of us who wish to see this country survive should be thankful, anyway. The rest who maybe don't know how thankful they should be, well I hope you never find out what could happen if you got your way.

Anyway, when an aircraft carrier comes home, the sailors in dress white line every edge of the flight deck, all the way around the ship, and they stand there as the ship sails into port. They did this for us today. I'll tell ya… if that sight doesn't put the lump in your throat, you been gone far too long. We have pictures. But even without, we won't ever forget.

Guys and gals aboard… Thanks for your service.

June 22, 2012

The Touch Of Evil

> *Bob and I have arrived at almost the same place in our careers. And I think of this every day, praying that God will spare my staff or myself the horror that will surely ensue should I be placed in the position of having to defend our little corner of the planet.*
>
> Harold Jones, DVM
> *friend and colleague*
> *reflecting on the column you're about to read*

I always figured I'd feel badly about it if I killed someone.

I'm sorry. I mean, wow, what a statement to spew out, to be tossed amid unsuspecting folks. But bear with me. I have my reasons for bringing this up.

I suppose this is a rather odd thing to introduce here, the first sentence on a blank computer screen. Who would write such a thing? Who would even think it? Reasonable people don't go around killing other people. It's rather an uncommon action. So why would I even contemplate my own reaction to this? It's not like I figured on ever learning how it would feel.

But my mind does wander into varied places, and I have actually found myself wondering about such a thing. The Vietnam War offered up an opportunity. College kept me out of the draft for years, but I faced one year in the lottery after graduation. And in those days it was not unusual for the candidates for canon fodder status to consider their options.

For instance, the wife at the time had told me in no uncertain terms that I would not be reporting for duty if invited. Nope, we'd be moving to Canada. But in spite of her dictates, I did consider the possibility of attending, doing my duty, testing my immortality in war. So I mulled about in my head the various consequences of such a decision.

Dying came to mind, as did living on with various body parts missing as a side effect of combat. And I contemplated the taking of life. War excuses many of the behaviors we avoid most days at home. In war, killing folks is not only accepted, it is mandated. So I suppose that contingency would make it all just fine. Strike down a few of them other folks, and then come home and take up my life again as if nothing had happened. Don't give it a thought.

But I gave it a thought. Several, in fact. Missed out on any real experience, for my lottery number didn't come up, but I finally concluded that I'd probably feel bad about killing someone if I was compelled to do it in war. And I didn't feel wrong for that.

I've been around for several of the more significant episodes of civil unrest in the last 50 years. I saw civilization suspended following Dr. King's murder and again when the disputed verdicts came down following Rodney King's arrest in Los Angeles. I saw the videos of the enraged mobs in the streets, the beatings and the attempted murders. I watched neighborhoods looted and I've witnessed blocks of businesses burned to the ground.

And I have sat in my little business here, feeling vulnerable and threatened by possibilities with those images in my head. And I've wondered, when faced with such a mob, if I would defend my life's work, and also my family and my employees who are both friends and family to me. Or would I simply run away and hope to survive, and take the loss of everything as just the price of participation in history.

I brought the rifle to work on the day the O.J. Simpson verdict was read, for I wondered what that night would hold for civilization. Would the mobs be in the streets of my town this time, and would the buildings soon be burning around me? Didn't end up needing it, but that old question was again in the front of my mind. Would I feel bad if I had to kill to defend that which was important to me, or would I instead choose to run away in terror, or die rather than kill?

We received the news via the internet. The young woman arrived at work at the veterinary hospital in Florida early in the morning to care for the animals and get things ready for the day. The practice owner arrived an hour later and was greeted by carnage and gore. The walls were splashed with blood, the floors flooded by it. The woman had been viciously beaten to death with a fire extinguisher after the savage had raped and tortured her. He was a twice convicted sexual predator, but of course he'd been let out of jail early both times, for someone didn't want to keep a man like this away from society. That wouldn't be fair.

The owner of that practice has a concealed carry permit now, and she is armed always. Her practice is located in a marginal area where crime is common, a neighborhood into which criminals are often released from prison to prey upon the decent folks, kinda like my place.

We hear of the doctor nearly beaten to death in his own hospital in Southern California because he annoyed a client, and of the strong-arm daytime robberies of veterinary hospitals for the few drugs found on the premises. And yeah, I know of all the armed robberies and those several murders that have been committed in the businesses just around the corner from my clinic. So yeah, that haven we call our clinic isn't all that safe a place after all.

We have contingency plans in place, and ready access to weapons in the clinic, and I acknowledge that it is not a stretch at all to consider that I might someday be faced by that old question again. And no... I don't want to be put into that untenable position.

I resisted the assignment to jury duty last month, for I did not wish to be inconvenienced by closing my clinic for five weeks. But I did sit in the jury box for a short while to be questioned by the judge and the DA before a jury was selected without me. And I spoke briefly with the murderer who was serving as his own attorney. It's not fair perhaps, to judge a man prematurely, particularly when charged by the judge with the notion that you must only consider his guilt or innocence based upon evidence presented later at his trial, but this man was a sociopath.

Twice I watched him walk across the hall to enter the courtroom while a gaggle of others wasted time in the hall. He walked tall, quickly, confident… or was it arrogant? But when he got up from his chair to question me, the potential juror, he was bent over, limping, smiling, shucking and jiving. A simple, humble man, trying to pull wool over eyes. But I also watched him as the attorney from the public defender's office tried to offer advice, and he transformed into the monster, flashing anger and hatred and that look in his eyes as he ripped into the man who tried to help him.

He dripped with anger, narcissism, thinly veiled unspoken threat, and no suggestion of a conscience. Simply watching him for those few hours was instructive, for I am a trusting person, and a tad naïve. And he had killed trusting, naïve people.

So I missed experiencing the murderer's day in court. The internet yielded the details, of how he gloated and abused his moment in the limelight of his own trial, and enjoyed being the center of the universe, even though that universe extended only to the limits of the room. He taunted his accusers, insulted his jury, and hurled pain and hatred at the families of the two he had murdered, screaming at them, torturing them, enraging them for his own amusement. He was glad to be alive, and utterly dismissive of those who were dead by his hand. No remorse. No second thoughts. No cares for anyone but himself. Capable of harm to anyone he chose.

He is the sociopath I had spotted in the first moments. He is a monster, but in his mind, he has done no wrong at all.

There is not even the suggestion that he feels badly about killing someone.

He is the kind of un-human that every person in that courtroom, having witnessed his evil and felt the touch of fear in their heart when looking into his eyes, likely would consider for a moment seizing the opportunity to kill him on the spot. But yeah, they would all feel badly after.

That jury now is deciding his fate, choosing between the slim chance that California would eventually abruptly end his wretched life, or simply gifting him with a life sentence without parole, which he referred to as his "retirement."

And I am left to contemplate, with the likelihood perhaps increasing every year that someone with this murderer's eyes will one morning barge into my clinic armed and angry and conscienceless, that I'll have to face that choice that I've dodged for all this time.

November 11, 1012

You Gotta Be Grown Up To Understand

I love it when a plan comes together.
Col. John "Hannibal" Smith
The A-Team

Arguably one of the least plausible series in a decade of forgettable television, *The A-Team* showed up weekly for five years during the '80s. Hannibal Smith and his small collective of Vietnam era expatriates fought evil dictators, corrupt corporations, and oppressive governments to rescue fair maidens, or the innocent relatives of fair maidens, in the name of truth, justice, and the American way. No wait, that was another show. Anyway, you get the idea.

In nearly every episode, Hannibal and his buds would somehow let themselves get talked into taking on seemingly impossible missions. They would endure hardship, double-crosses, deprivation, and disappointment, especially right before each commercial break. Jeeps flew through the air, rockets decimated guard towers, and thousands of rounds from automatic weapons sprayed all over the set, never hitting anybody unless it improved the plot line.

Finally, somewhere in the last five minutes, some totally implausible solution surfaced and the "A Team" managed to pull it all together to complete their mission. And Hannibal would smirk, emote his signature quote, and then stuff his cigar in his mouth as they all rode off into the sunset.

It dawned on me the other day that graduations feel different now than they did a few decades ago. I didn't get very excited when I graduated. I think I went through a ceremony when I finished grade school, but I don't really remember it. High school graduation was a blur and I didn't even attend my college commencement. They gave the license exam out here in California on the same day as graduation back in Illinois, and that was a lot more important to me than some silly tassel and robe.

Watching the kids graduate is another story. Somehow we got talked into taking on the seemingly impossible mission of rearing children. We endured hardship, double-crosses, deprivation, and disappointment, all without any commercial breaks. We got through term papers and tests, transfers and broken hearts, and the look of sheer terror on their faces when we dropped our kids off at some distant campus. Somehow, right at the end, it all came together in time for them to walk up and receive their diplomas.

My daughter's high school graduation was a revelation to me. I was excited. When she finished up at UCLA, I was thrilled. Even the ex and I got along long enough for our kid to have her day.

Then I got to sit beside my wife as her two sons graduated from Boston University and Swarthmore. She darn near exploded. The older boy got his Masters this year. Her feet didn't touch the ground for a week.

My stepdaughter finishes up grade school this year, so we are joining with the parents of her friends and classmates as we all celebrate. This is a lot more fun than when I was there.

Last June my daughter graduated from UC Davis with her veterinary degree. We were all there. My ex was crying, my parents glowed, and my wife carried the Kleenex. My folks saw me sitting there beaming and they had to mention that I didn't give them that satisfaction when I skipped out on my own veterinary school graduation. Sorry about that--I know better now.

When her class stood in unison to take the veterinary oath, the veterinarians in the audience were invited to join them. Since I never went to my own graduation, I had never actually recited the oath. Standing there watching my kid, I got most of the words out, but it wasn't easy. Thank goodness my wife carried the Kleenex.

My wife started college over twenty years ago. She has spent much of her adult life tutoring kids, helping them get through school, but it was only in the last year that she finished up her own baccalaureate. She couldn't get away from her students long enough to get to her own graduation, which was on the East coast, but she watched the ceremony online. I could see the goosebumps on her arm when they read her name and her academic awards. The big grin was on my face.

I didn't recognize the importance of my own graduations because as a kid I never realized that graduation isn't an ending, but really a beginning. You just put in all that time and all that work so you can move on to bigger and better things. I finally figured it out when it was my turn to watch.

Sitting through an eighth grade graduation the other day, watching the fathers stumble over each other taking pictures, and the mothers' tears, I realized one thing. I love it when a plan comes together.

June 14, 2001

Glorifying Copycats Becomes Self-Fulfilling

One of several reflections following the Sandy Hook tragedy. More can be found on pp.141-166. (RG)

A friend of mine is an avid reader concerning religion and how it appeared deep in the history of the human race. From time to time he discovers some event or factoid that lends question to what he recalls learning when studying his own family's faith as a child. Not willing to sit on these inconsistencies, he generally confronts his rabbi with questions at the earliest opportunity hoping to see some resolution to his frustration over this. He cannot help himself, and I'm certain his rabbi is amused and enthralled with his interest.

Some several years ago, I happened to mention that moment back at the beginning of time when Cain slew Abel by smacking him with a rock. Shows my ignorance. My friend hastily corrected me. Turns out, according to his reading, that Cain actually used a weapon known as a smiter (spelling unknown, at least to me). Now, you might wonder if anyone gives a care whether Cain used one or the other of these, and you would be right.

The story of Cain and Abel appears in several versions of the early writings penned by at least two major religions, as an object lesson presumably, to highlight one of the essential characteristics of the human. Many have used this as the second but most telling lesson we should learn about the human condition.

You remember Adam and Eve. They were the first two humans on earth, placed in Eden by God in his image. Cain and

Abel were their two sons. Adam and Eve were driven from Eden and into the nasty real world when they disobeyed God over some silly apple. Life for these two went downhill after that. That disobeying God thing would have been lesson number one, and it does show something of the human condition.

The murder of one son by the other gives some clue into the anger and inclination to murder that, along with all we do well, has to be included in mankind's makeup, in the bad category. This is the second lesson.

Others followed.

As an aside... when Adam tossed Cain out into the cold in his anger over the murder, Cain went to live with the bunch of other humans over there. You know, that bunch of humans those old stories never seem to account for. I figure those are the humans that descended from apes. And yeah, they have the evil in some of them too. Which settles the old argument between the creationists and the Darwin folks. They are both right. So they can stop fighting amongst themselves.

Now, you all know that this is about the unfathomable tragedy last week. And probably you are wondering how I can make light of this. Am I that delusional? Do I not care? Should I in turn be taken out and shot?

For the record, I am sick, scared, enraged, confused, frustrated. Kinda like everybody else. That slaughter of tiny innocent children by one evil man has affected me more than any other malevolent act that I can remember. I didn't live through most of the genocides inflicted by men upon humanity, but I know of them. I've seen many horrid things over the course of a lifetime. But right now I'm sitting here and I'm shaking and shaken. To the core. And like everybody else, I'm seeking some answers that might make it all better in my head and my heart. And I'm not finding all better.

I am not making light of this. I merely hide in the writing.

I am trying to put some pieces together in my own head even if they don't quite add up yet. I have reached some uncomforting conclusions.

I am not going to get all better. This tragedy will stay with me forever, and only time will allow me to put it somewhere so that it doesn't dwell always in the front of my brain.

I am watching the people who we chose to be the leaders of this country, for better or worse, fall all over each other trying to appear most concerned while they plot to use this to further their own power. Spare me this, please. Let the dead be put to rest at least before you start running for re-election. Don't milk the anguish of so many for political gain, for in a piece written to talk of the faults of humanity, guess where you are placing yourself.

I don't wish to discuss the weapons used by a madman, for I see no reason to think I'd feel any better if he had used some other. When Cain murdered Abel, the ground was littered with rocks and sharpened sticks, and boundless other methods of killing. His choice of a smiter over a rock could not be more irrelevant to the discussion. The action was the evil, not the tool.

I would like to know why this man did this thing. Everyone does. Somehow, if we knew why it could help. Perhaps such knowledge would prevent this horror from happening again. But of course it would not. This is wishful thinking only. Every evil murderer had a reason, and each reason was different.

I'd like to think that someone out there could act to prevent this from happening again. Perhaps we could outlaw something. That might work. Problem is… except for that notion in the Ten Commandments that thou should not commit murder, a rule that no one has ever violated, most rules we make to keep us safe are flaunted by the evil. Yeah, I know…

I considered asking the government to put uniformed armed guards in every school, on every street corner, walking behind every person to protect us. Somewhere safety lies, if we just put the government in charge of everything. We can trust the government to protect us if we just turn all of our freedom and convenience over to them.

Nah, I think I'll steer away from this notion. It's that, "Who knows what evil lurks in the hearts of men?" thing. Evil, too, often lurks in the hearts of government.

I believe we have created a population of evil that has learned that the way to worldwide notoriety is to copy the mass murderer. Surely a way to report such news can be found which evil people won't use to celebrate and magnify their acts. Right now the network news agencies are encouraging and milking the evil for profit.

I believe that the lesson found in the early writings, that Cain had anger and the willingness to murder, is still relevant. The human has not changed. All humans have anger, and some are capable of murder, and some thrive in this. This is a horror, but it is inescapable.

We all seek comfort and a solution so that children will never again be murdered by a madman. I'll offer comfort, but I offer no solution. No one has changed the human since Cain.

Too many who claim to offer solace and sure solution will be the next to deliver evil. Evil is opportunistic. So watch closely the most eager, which right now are the people hurrying before the cameras. History does not lie.

Don't know who said this but I'll end with, "You cannot hide from evil people. You can only confront them when they appear and strike them down before they do harm to others."

We all must do our very best at this, for we are what stands in the way of evil.

December 16, 2012

Dude, You're Pissing On My Wall!

> *Do what you love, and you will never work a day in your life.*
>
> Confucius

Confucius was a wise fellow 2,500 years ago, back in the days when China was a great nation, a nation that was busy figuring out a bunch of stuff that those uppity folks in Europe wouldn't ever discover if given a million typewriters and a million years. You know... stuff like macaroni and gunpowder. China had its affairs going so well that they could afford to have guys hang out simply to think of things.

Apparently, Confucius did well at this thinking predilection, because if you do a search on the sayings attributed to the guy, you can stay busy for some considerable time, and you will feel like you haven't really thought of anything first when you finish.

And you will be doing this many centuries later than Confucius. This guy did his thinking 25 centuries ago, but human nature being what it is, what he figured out so long ago still applies when applied to humans today. Confucius was real good at recognizing the good in the human condition and also spotting the bad. Not much has changed in the human condition. We still have the good, and the bad. But unlike Confucius, we aren't supposed to talk about it.

I was behind the clinic, airing the dogs, when I noticed the two guys behind the bushes. The little black dog barked at them. It was about one in the afternoon, and my usual assortment of homeless folks didn't generally show up until after dark, when the clinic was closed and I wasn't around to hassle them. So I wandered over to discuss with them their situation.

Ya see… I have a problem with the detritus left behind by the folks who indulge their addiction to alcohol on my property, for they have the annoying habit of leaving the dead soldiers lying about. I pointed this collection out to the two drinkers, and suggested they move on to sully someone else's turf.

The deal we eventually struck was that they would clean up the place if I'd look the other way while they enjoyed a beer each afternoon behind my bush. And surprisingly, I went with it. In the past I likely would not have.

I've talked with one of these men on other occasions since that day, and found out that his wife won't let him drink beer at home, so he indulges his hobby behind the bushes on my property most every afternoon, and from time to time he asks for a plastic garbage bag to clean up the mess to keep me happy. The guy loves drinking his beer. And apparently, he is free most afternoons.

As Confucius said, he does what he loves, and never works a day in his life.

I'm not sure this is what Confucius had in mind, but I've learned that when times change, you're supposed to change with it. I guess.

So when I pulled into the parking lot of my clinic, again at about one o'clock in the afternoon on a weekday, and I found one of the usual homeless guys urinating on the front wall of my clinic, near the front door, in broad daylight, and right there where every client will walk their dog to get to my door, I mentioned my displeasure to him.

"Dude! You're pissing on my wall!"

Now, you have to realize that I've grown accustomed to men relieving themselves on that other wall of my clinic, the side opposite the doors, behind the bushes, where only I can know what they are doing onnacounta the window in my office on that side of the building. That side of the building is apparently the designated outdoor toilet for the folks on foot in our city. That's where I once caught a guy talking on his cell phone while wetting my bushes. Multi-tasking. I had planned on yelling at the guy, because I'm that kinda stubborn about my property, but I was so dumbfounded at his behavior that I simply stood there in amazement. And the guy yelled at me for watching. I'm now a pecker peeper. Try saying that three times fast. He was angry with me because I caught him peeing on my property, and he thought I enjoyed the moment.

And I've grown accustomed to washing down the wall of the building after one of those guys uses the wall for a backrest when he, ah... poops. I know it's always the same guy, even though he doesn't sign his work, but I know him from the consistency of his, you know. It kinda runs down the wall, and what with the viral hepatitis and other concerns, I really enjoy pulling out the hose and cleaning up after him. But I can't be calling out the hazmat folks for every streak of diarrhea I come across. There simply are too many.

But I have drawn the line, and my side of the line doesn't include pissing on the front of my clinic at one in the afternoon. So I yelled at the guy urinating on the front wall of my clinic. He looked at me as if I were a completely unreasonable person.

I guess I'm just not progressive enough yet. But I should get partial credit, for I am working on it.

Ya see, I've relaxed my normal standards to accommodate people who live their lives somewhat differently than I. That's what you are supposed to do as you go through life if you are progressive. That's 'cause just because you have been taught right from wrong, this doesn't necessarily mean your right is the same as some other guy's right. That apparently is no longer reasonable. I am learning to live with that.

But to be progressive these days, you are expected to expand your horizons a bit further.

I'm now expected to welcome with open arms the homeless people nesting on my property, and accept the garbage, broken bottles, little wildflower tufts of toilet paper scattered about the land. I'm not to judge them harshly, simply because they have chosen a different path than I. I was taught right from wrong, but that was then, and this is now, and I guess there is/are no wrong(s)... only different. So I leave 'em be.

OK, so I'm getting used to this. The inevitability of it all helps. I cannot stop them from nesting back there, lest I annoy them, or trample upon their rights. Such is no longer allowed if you wish to be progressive. So I shall get over it.

And I won't use disparaging names, like wino or bum, for that throws these different people together into an artificial bag unfairly. They all have their reasons, and I should not be arrogant nor dismissive of their human variability.

We have learned to accept the frequent break-ins of our cars in the parking lot in broad daylight. Those poor unfortunates who break our windows to steal whatever they can find in the cars deserve accommodation, and understanding. For we don't know just what in their lives drove them to such deeds. It's not their fault.

And I'm working real hard, now that it has been pointed out to me, to not judge the gang members in the various neighborhoods in cities around our flawed nation. It's not their fault, you know. They've had it tough. Nothing besides food, housing, education, medical care (after they've been shot), has been handed to them. They are completely abandoned, on their own, unlike the rest of us who work time and a half so we can afford our lavish lifestyles.

They are merely coping in their own way with the discriminations that life delivered at their doorstep. So if in desperation they start killing people when they are 13, and they don't stop until they are killed at 22, it's not their fault. Heck, it's probably my fault, for I've had it easy at their expense... somehow. Anyway, that's what they tell me.

I should be more progressive. And I should get off their case. I should be less judgmental. I should be more understanding. And if for some demented reason, I object to this disruption of what used to be right or wrong, just what the heck is the matter with me?

February 10, 2013

A Requiem For A Rogue

Clyde is part of our blended family, a big, gray cat who thinks he is a dog. Clyde would rather hang with the dogs than do the usual cat stuff; he sleeps on his back and watches TV upside down, and he looks at us in complete disdain when he catches us bad-talking cats, if he thinks we are including him.

This is not to say that Clyde doesn't like us, for he delights in bringing presents into the house and leaving them around for our pleasure. He specializes in the perfect gift for every occasion.

Wednesday, it was the gopher he left at the front door. Last week, he strategically placed the back half of a roof rat at the entrance to the master bath for my barefooted enjoyment.

My wife says the mouse he dropped on the bed next to her the other day as she was putting on her makeup was an interesting surprise.

You gotta love the guy for his enthusiasm and originality. Clyde is laying low, right now, because his latest little present hit about 10 on the Richter scale.

I was pretty comfortable in my chair in front of the TV, but experience has taught me to attend when my wife lets loose with a bloodcurdling scream in the bedroom, so I trotted on back.

When I got there, she was cowering in the corner in her birthday suit, shaking, and pointing to an innocent-looking bathrobe lying crumpled on the bed. And she had a few unkind things to say about Clyde.

Not quite sure what to make of this, I picked up her robe and out dropped about five inches of seriously annoyed blue-belly lizard.

It turns out that a lizard inside one's bathrobe can produce rather interesting sensations as it runs up your back, and when it is your wife's back, it's time to remove the lizard. So I wrapped up the little guy and returned him to the bushes outside. In parting, I told him it might be best to stay away from big gray cats.

Poor Clyde can't figure out what he did wrong.

A short 10 years brings us to today, and I'm still trying to write a good column, but sadly, now I have to do it without Clyde's help. The old rogue has left us. It's just not the same without him — they broke the mold with him.

Say what you want, but Clyde was always his own man. He got something out of living with us, else he would have moved on. He didn't intend to amuse us, but I guess he didn't mind.

He ate our food and slept on our bed if it was cold, and then he melted into the yard to do his own thing, as he chose. We buried him back in the trees, his heaven, before the devil knew he was gone.

July 21, 2010

Some Animal Lovers Are Becoming People Haters

I used to call myself an animal lover, but I'm not sure I want to be known by that tag anymore. Once an animal lover might have been a little eccentric, a bit off center in an otherwise indifferent world, perhaps a trifle soft headed, but at least you could pass yourself off as well intentioned.

There was a time when animal lovers always put the animals first. They would feed a stray dog, rescue a cat, or provide a home for an old horse that could no longer work.

These folks made small sacrifices to help animals because they had a warm spot in their hearts.

Well, it doesn't always work that way any longer. These days, some people who claim to love animals have a completely different agenda. Instead of doing things out of love, now they seem to be mainly motivated by hate. In the name of helping animals, they hurt people.

For instance, some militant animal rights folks, who happen to be vegetarians, are celebrating the deaths of a hundred people in England and Europe. These people died from mad cow disease, a particularly unpleasant way to perish, but this radical group couldn't be happier, because this unfortunate disease forced a large segment of the population to temporarily forego eating meat. The hundreds of thousands of animals that were slaughtered to stop the disease in its tracks, I guess, were just collateral damage. That part doesn't seem to bother these animal lovers at all.

Another group of so-called animal rights activists bragged that they deliberately tracked through the quarantine area in England hoping to spread foot and mouth disease into the rest of the country, and thus have many thousands more animals slaughtered.

In this country, a spokesperson from People for the Ethical Treatment of Animals (PETA) has been quoted that she hopes the foot and mouth epidemic spreads to the US. Of course this would lead to the slaughter a few million more domestic and wild animals. Now that is a real animal lover for the new millennium.

These radicals claim that they only want to put the meat industry out of business so no one will be able to eat anything other than a vegan diet. I guess they figure a few million dead animals is small price to pay for all the future animal lives they will "save." And they sure don't care how that might impact the rest of us.

Just a few weeks ago, other members of PETA invaded a supermarket in San Francisco in order to attach stickers to tomatoes directing purchasers to throw said tomatoes at anyone they found wearing fur. Now that sure is a mature approach to a controversial subject. Sure makes me want to join up with them.

Meanwhile, two hundred sick inbred cats sit in a shelter in Petaluma, CA, thanks to someone who considers herself a cat lover, but who never learned the concept of the kitten stork. This irresponsible woman allowed a small population of cats to breed unchecked among themselves until she ended up with an incomprehensible disaster in her house, a house reeking of excrement, rotting food, and half eaten corpses. Apparently this woman was so consumed with her own distorted reality that she was blind to what was really happening in that house.

And heaven help the folks who had this catastrophe dumped into their laps, the cops and animal control officers who must clean up the mess, for some anonymous coward who also calls himself an animal lover has threatened their lives. He promises to set bombs if they humanely destroy any of these poor cats, even the sickest, craziest, and most miserable of the bunch.

Distorted reality seems to characterize many of these so-called animal lovers. They are so aggrieved by the injustice they perceive the animals suffer in our world, that they are perfectly willing to hurt people in their attempt to change things. Sorry, but if this is what it takes to be an animal lover, I'll pass.

June 21, 2001

I Must Get Old, But I Do Not Have To Like It

> *Old men like to give good advice in order to console themselves for not being any longer able to set bad examples.*
>
> François de La Rochefoucauld
> <u>Reflections; or Sentences and Maxims</u>

I never really thought that I would get old. Aging of course, was inevitable, but not getting old. I was cruising along as the years passed by, while the music changed, the fashions changed, and the cops got younger.

For a while I enjoyed the music the kids listened to. I tapped the steering wheel to the new beat, sang along with the lyrics, and thought I was still just as cool as ever.

I didn't change my wardrobe to match the new styles, but I have never been much of a clotheshorse, so that wasn't an issue.

In the last few years, I was surprised to find myself on better terms with the police. I thought this was a good thing, since I carried a little resentment toward the boys in blue in the baggage I brought along from the Sixties. Back then the police always seemed to come by just to keep us from having a good time.

Then I worked for a few decades and managed to accumulate some things, and suddenly I didn't want other people coming along and taking them from me. Thus, I developed a healthy distaste for criminals, and I am now glad to have the police handy.

When the Beatles' music showed up in the elevators, I found myself amused, for I remember being sixteen and arguing with my folks about how long rock music would endure. They never got it, because that music just annoyed them, but those tunes are still around; in fact they are mainstream, and they're still mine.

Then all of a sudden the kids descended on me with rap music, and those pants you could hide an infantry squad in, and spiked hair, tattoos, and pierced this and that. And I found myself reacting with discomfort at this effrontery.

I squirmed when my windows rattled as they drove by with their angry, obscene music blasting out of those industrial strength speakers. And I fumed when they sashayed in front of me in the crosswalk, deliberately obstructing traffic as they stopped to pull up those ridiculous pants.

Implausibly, I woke up one morning and discovered that I had become old. It happened when I realized that all the things the kids did to annoy me, actually did. I hadn't reached some magic number of years, but my youthful state of mind was irrecoverably lost.

Ok, so now I'm old. I'll learn to live with that, but I don't like it.

My beard turned gray a while ago. I tell people that I grew the silly thing back in my twenties so I could look older. Now, it is working. I hope a silver beard makes me look distinguished, which I figure beats extinguished.

I've also developed a few creaks and groans. Our dogs look at me kind of funny when I hobble out of bed in the morning. I think the noises this old body makes bother them. They can hear sounds we humans can't, ya know.

Of course I don't hear as well as I used to. My wife keeps telling me I must have developed a case of selective hearing loss, because I often sleep right through the stuff she is trying to tell me.

I forget things too, except for all those old stories I keep telling over and over again.

Bob Hope said that middle age is when your age starts to show around the middle. Mine does.

I gave up on the gym. I used to spend an hour a day on the stair-climber machine trying to peel off some weight, but it never helped much. I passed the time by looking around the room at young men who weren't wasting their effort on aerobic exercise. They were there to pump iron.

They transformed themselves into impressive physical specimens, with muscles where I don't even have memories anymore. They strutted around in front of the mirrors, posing for the young ladies, who in turn made sure to strain their lycra right back at them.

Sweating away on my machine, I was a little intimidated by all that muscle, so I would appease myself by recalling the long list of things I have accomplished over the years. I remembered the marathons, the backpacking trails, and the mountains climbed. Then with smug self-satisfaction I looked over at the young jocks and muttered to myself, "You guys come back when you have actually done something, and then we can talk."

Of course, they still had all their things to look forward to; I have to be content with my memories.

The worst part was when I was leaving the gym, and the little girl at the desk said, "Good night, Sir."

"Sir?"

I really hated that.

June 11, 2002

Takes A While To Get In Christmas Spirit

I have been accused of being a "Bah Humbug" kind of guy. This is, of course, totally unfair.

Granted, I acknowledge a certain lack of effusive enthusiasm for many of the usual trappings of the holiday season, but that doesn't mean I cannot get into the spirit of the thing eventually. It just takes me a while.

Christmas means many things to many people. Originally a pagan winter solstice celebration, it was taken over by the Christians because they needed a day to celebrate the birth of Christ, and since no one really remembered exactly when that took place, this day would surely do.

A few centuries later, the strictly religious proponents of this time of year started getting shoved to the side by certain commercial interests. Pretty decorated trees and houses, Santa Claus, and the chaotic scene of stockings and wrapped presents began to demand equal billing.

So now, instead of a one-day celebration, those of us of the "Bah Humbug" persuasion have to deal with an entire season. It takes that long to get one day celebrated these days.

You can tell I'm an old fogey, for I can remember when folks didn't start thinking about Christmas until after Thanksgiving. Friday after Turkey Day got its reputation as the biggest shopping day of the year because it was the kick-off of the Christmas season. That's when decorations and wrapping paper, carols on the speakers in every store, and the fat guy in the Santa suit first showed up in the mall.

A few years ago, they started pushing the season forward, a few weeks at a time. Pretty soon all the Christmas stuff was on the shelves even before they cleaned up the Halloween mess.

Now, in many places, the Christmas paraphernalia is in stores before summer winds down.

I remember joking with the teller at the bank shortly after Easter, the Christian celebration of the resurrection of Christ that has also largely been usurped by commercial interests. I said I half expected the Christmas goodies to turn up on the day after Easter, and thus the commercial exploitation of the holidays would be complete.

And I figured that would have Jesus spinning in his grave… if he was still in it.

Anyway, I'm not ready to do Christmas in May, or October, or even mid-November. I don't want to decorate. I don't want to listen to Christmas carols. I cannot even start thinking about what present to get who quite that early. I've only got room for so much Christmas in my life.

Now, before you write me off as the most hopeless Scrooge the late Twentieth Century may have spawned, hear me out.

I actually like Christmas.

Christmas morning thrills me.

I love watching little kids empty stockings and open presents. I think it is cool to watch them squirm when you make them wait until the older folks are done opening theirs.

I love it when I manage through some miracle to find the perfect gift for a loved one.

I love it when I see people go out of their way to be nice to the strangers they encounter on the street and in the stores, when they drop some cans into the food bank box or a check into the homeless fund. I think it is great when the season is enough to make us act human again.

I love Christmas music on Christmas morning. And I can watch one of the Tiny Tim vs. Scrooge movies each year, before I turn the football game on.

Sometimes I even take a moment to contemplate the original reason we have this holiday. I'm not a proponent of any one religion, but if there ever was a guy who preached peace, generosity, and goodwill among men, maybe we should celebrate such a thing once a year. We certainly don't do enough of that the rest of the time.

I'm going to celebrate Christmas *on* Christmas this year. I will see some of my family and think of the rest. I will watch the sunrise and hope yet again for peace on earth. I will try to feel good about my fellow humans, even if they don't deserve it.

I suppose I should apologize to all those people who think I am a Scrooge in the weeks and months leading up to Christmas. I'm sorry I cannot stretch the thrill out that long, so I just want to be let alone.

I still enjoy the day, and I hope you all do as well.

December 25, 2003

Birds' Familiar Tune Brings To Mind Our Own Chaos

I pulled out all the bird books last weekend. We have a few pretty yellow and black birds flitting around the trees behind the clinic. I figured them for Bullock's Orioles, but of course I wanted the good color picture to show to my wife. The best picture was in Stokes Field Guide To Birds. Anyway, I spent the bulk of that evening leafing through the pages of three bird books, looking at the pretty pictures. And you wondered what we do when we aren't working.

That's when I stumbled across the Brown-Headed Cowbird, *Molothrus atar*. This is one bird that will ruin every nice thing you ever thought about birds. Ya see, this species doesn't bother to make a nest and raise its own hatchlings. The female simply finds a nest of some songbird, like an Oriole, and it lands there, kicks an egg out of the nest, and lays one of its own eggs in its place. And then she up and leaves. The birds that constructed the nest end up feeding this interloper, as if it were their own. The larger cowbird baby often out-competes the other babies for food or actually boots them out of the nest. Nice, eh?

But wait… listen to what the Audubon Society Field Guide to North American Birds has to say about this species:

> Cowbirds are promiscuous; no pair bonding exists.
> In late spring the female cowbird and several suitors move into the woods. The males sit upright on treetops, uttering sharp whistles, while the female searches for nests.

The various field guides have other less than flattering things to say about these cowbirds. There is one reference to the males' song, which is described as similar to the sound of an un-oiled swinging gate. Another describes the courting male as, "delivers a variety of high, squeaking whistles and gurgling notes accompanied by head-throwing postures." That unconscionably vicious judge on *American Idol* couldn't have been a harsher critic.

According to my bird guides, when cowbirds parasitize songbird nests, they threaten the successful reproduction of these desirable species. Although a large percentage of cowbird babies don't survive to adulthood, their population is still expanding at the expense of other birds. And the proliferation of suburbs, with a disruption of forest and wildland, facilitates this expansion.

Now picture a flock of strutting suburban or urban males, chasing down promiscuous females to the accompaniment of sharp whistles and ear rending music. No pair bonding exists. These females then abandon their babies to be raised by others, but still most of these babies don't survive to adulthood. And this whole corrupt process ends up wrecking the families of the bonded pairs that try to do things right, to the detriment of all involved.

Cowbirds do some good in the world, by picking lice off the backs of cows. But as I watch the chaos that follows in the wake of all the human babies that are left to others to raise, or simply left on their own on the streets, I feel little but despair. Gangs and violence, ignorance and drugs, and the disruption of civilization is the consequence of such irresponsibility. And it is just getting worse.

May 17, 2009

Part Two:
The Commies and
The Fascists

For Last Resort Only

I keep one in the treatment room of my clinic. The treatment room is the center of things, and you pass through it to get anywhere else in the clinic, so it makes sense to keep it there. I spend much of my day in the treatment room, so yeah it makes sense to keep one there.

It has been in the same place for over forty years. I check on it every month out of habit, making sure it is always well maintained and loaded. And then it just sits there. Never once have I actually needed to use it, which is a good thing. I suppose one might question the need to keep something like this handy when one has never actually needed to use it. But there is always that small possibility that someday I might suddenly need it. If that time comes, I'd rather it be there than not.

I concede that it is not one of those deals where everything is always positive when you keep one of these around. I know of one very tragic case where we think the young lady tried to use one of these to save her life when the twice convicted violent rapist attacked her in a veterinary clinic much like mine, and he took it away and used it to murder her. So there is that side to the argument that I hear often.

I have one at home, too. This one lives in a closet, but it is always in the same place, waiting, ready, and easy to access. There's one in the truck too. For that just-in-case moment when really... nothing else will do.

For some reason, the politicians aren't trying to prohibit me from keeping it around. I guess they don't see the political potential here that they see in, oh, my guns for instance. And they fail to see the benefit of, oh, my guns for instance. My guns also hang around on the off chance I might need one to save my life and property in an emergency. And they harm no one in the process of waiting. Still, the politicians seek to take away my guns.

But the politicians have no problem at all with my fire extinguishers.

January 26, 2013

First Column After Termination

Bob didn't stop writing after his time with the Contra Costa Times. *Instead, he used his blog,* drbobssundaycolumns.blogspot.com, *to reach his loyal readers. His second blog post follows. (RG)*

After ten years writing for our local rag, I outlived my welcome, and my editor canned me. This is the first column I wrote for my email followers, which includes the column the paper rejected, for content.

On those long days when my energy runs a bit low, I sometimes wonder if I'm losing my sense of humor. Then I have a day like last Wednesday, and I'm sitting there laughing, and I know I don't have anything to worry about.

I've noticed one of those human nature things in my line of work. In the middle of the afternoon a young man comes in with his dog. The young man is fresh from his workout at the gym, where he spent hours building up his upper body, but not his legs, 'cause it's pecs and biceps that impress the other young men, so why seek any balance between upper and lower body? Oh, and they think it works with the ladies, too.

His dog is a large breed, a Rott or a Dobe, male, complete with testicles and a Harley-Davidson collar. The dog is not well behaved, maybe even a little dangerous. The young man struts when his dog barks and intimidates unsuspecting strangers. The dog is what we call a surrogate penis on a leash. It makes up for any perceived shortage in the young man's, ah, lower body.

I've been at this work long enough to see these young men grow older, like my age, and now they show up in my clinic with their new dog. It's a cute little dachshund or poodle, and he is clutching it to his chest. This is what maturity does to us guys, I guess. We change.

I can remember back about 40 years ago, when long-haired scruffy me was standing defiantly in front of those riot police on our campus after the Kent State students were shot down by confused national guard troops. I wasn't too fond of cops back then. So I can only imagine what I might have said then if you told me that I would get fired now from a ten year old gig writin' for the newspaper because I wrote a column in support of our local police officers. Heck, I'm having a hard enough time wrapping my brain around this development as an old guy.

I cannot say that I was surprised when I got the call from my editor. He has been annoyed with me for a while, cause I just can't seem to shut up and toe the line. And if I was all that concerned about keeping this job, I probably should have. But I didn't. In fact, I am probably guilty of deliberately provoking him with this latest column.

Someday I may sit down with my collection of weekly columns. There are over 500, so this will take some time. Many have concerned subjects that somebody would call controversial. Some of these columns were pure intellectual exercise, and others frankly sprang from conscience. Some subjects were arguably the oxen of the liberal left, and others the conservative right. I thought I might sort them into two categories, labeled the commies and the fascists, in deference to the folks who disagreed with me, and just add up whether I actually favored one side over the other more often. I think I gored a pretty even number of oxen over the years, and up until lately, I sent these columns in to editors who mostly just gave me my head.

With the arrival of the new administration in Washington, the paper lost its tolerance. And I began to hear from my editor whenever I questioned that administration's actions. Suddenly, I was told that my columns should be limited to local interest, whatever that is. I was told to change sentences or whole paragraphs, submit new columns, or live with having my work rejected because the paper didn't approve of what I thought.

I noticed that they never said a word when I had criticized the previous administration. But suddenly I was charged with being too conservative, of spouting Tea Party propaganda. I guess that was the worst source of point of view they could think of. And since there was no one in the section of the paper in which my columns appeared writing columns in opposition to my thoughts, I was told it wasn't fair. And no, they never once offered to move me to some part of the paper where opinions might have been more appropriate.

In short, on Wednesday my editor phoned and told me I was just too much trouble, and so he dropped my column. And I sat there for a moment after hanging up the phone, laughing.

Anyway, this is the column that got me fired. During my career I have cared for police dogs from eight departments. I have enjoyed working with these dogs very much and I enjoyed getting to know the officers handling these dogs. I admire these young men and women, and frankly I have adopted a very protective attitude toward them. Long term readers may remember some of the columns I have written after police officers have been killed in the line of duty. There have been too many of those columns. And apparently for the paper, this was one column too many for them to endure.

> *I'm not qualified to have an opinion on this kind of thing. Not officially, anyway. I'm not a psychiatrist. I'm not an attorney. No police agency wants me to be a spokesperson, and I haven't heard from any criminals*

hoping I might champion their side of the story. I'm just an opinionated guy.

I feel strongly about this. I'm wearing the t-shirt right now, and I'm not taking it off for anybody. Call it team colors, if you wish.

It was a dark night, 2:30 AM, in Tampa, Florida. The car didn't have a visible license plate. Cars without license plates at 2:30 AM, in addition to being illegal, are often driven by drunk drivers or criminals. Cops know this. It's their job to protect us from such people. They stopped the car.

Two police officers. Two people in the car. The only witnesses who survived were the killers. The two cops don't get to tell their side of the story.

The gang member arrested for this crime is only 24 years old, but he has the "long criminal record." Just got out of prison three months earlier. I suppose we will have to wait a few years for this case to go to trial, so I cannot actually say he killed these two police officers. That would not be right.

The suspect is charged with pulling a gun, ambushing and fatally shooting both officers a close range, before they could defend themselves.

The memorial t-shirt is from a citizen group raising money to help out the families of the two murdered cops. Two widows and those innocent little children. We ordered four.

Another dark night, 2:30 AM in Concord. This time the police confronted a man, a suspect in many armed burglaries in our area. The early reports suggest this man resisted arrest and then pointed a pistol at the officers in the dark. They had to fire their weapons at him, and he fell seriously and possibly permanently wounded.

Only later was it learned that his pistol was only plastic. Imagine the sickening feeling when the officers discovered that the gun was a fake. They opened fire thinking their lives were threatened, and now get to live with that reality.

I figure they had no choice, and I lay the blame entirely upon that misguided man. He had choices to make leading up to his injury, and in my mind he made bad choices. And I hope the next cops in that situation don't hesitate to defend themselves because of this.

I don't want to buy any more t-shirts.

July 5, 2011

Some Things Never Change

I was riding shotgun in a Sheriff's Department patrol car, sometime after midnight on a weeknight, cruising the dark streets of an unincorporated area near here, and the dog was barking right next to my left ear. I cannot remember the dog's name, but it was twenty plus years ago, so I hope you can forgive me. This tour was called a ride along, and the cops will sometimes do this to give us naïve civilians a taste of what the dark of night feels like to them. The police dog was a patient of mine, a rather cranky fellow, and his bark was deafening. The officer had been a client for years and I think he enjoyed showing me around. I spent most of that night with the two of them, cruising streets I thought I knew, but feeling very different about them from that unique point of view.

The area we patrolled that night was not one of our finer neighborhoods. The locals used to claim that those two rundown bars on the main drag near the east end were so rough that if you showed up without a gun or knife, they would issue you one at the door. These same locals took a certain pride in the bad reputation the area had. It was a badge of honor they wore proudly. Most were decent enough folks who simply didn't worry much about the traditional ways of keeping up with the Joneses, but there was a significant criminal element there, too, who made ya want to lock your doors when you drove through. At night the Sheriff's Department stationed two cars out there, usually one at each end, and they stayed in touch constantly in case one or the other needed back up.

Most of the time each officer was alone, so if he had to deal with more than one of their customers at a time, it could get interesting. The dog evened things out considerably, but you couldn't bring him out of the car to munch on folks for the minor things, so that officer learned other tricks to control multiple troublemakers. He said that the pair of handcuffs he left dangling from the push bar on the front of his patrol car was just the thing for when he had to restrain more than one person at a time, since he certainly couldn't park a perp in the backseat with that dog, tempting as that might be. He said he never did actually drive off with one of those troublemakers chained to the front of the car, but he did claim to have mentioned that temptation to some of the big mouthed ones, from time to time. It functioned as something of a deterrent.

Did I mention it was dark? Most of the streets had no streetlights, and it was as dark as Hillary Clinton's heart. I sat wedged in between a bank of radios, a laptop computer mounted to the officer's right, and a pump shotgun, with the wire screen between me and that perpetually angry German shepherd in the back. The bulletproof vest I wore was a smidge too small. The two-way radio competed with a scanner that helped the officer keep track of the highway patrol frequency, and other police and fire/emergency departments. Slowly, we motored through the streets, pretty much just watching and waiting for folks to make things go wrong in the world.

The narrow backstreet was lined with mature trees. There were no curbs or sidewalks. The homes were small and old, a few well cared for and the rest dilapidated and a bit ominous looking in the cone of light from our patrol car. About halfway down the block, a house on the left slowly came into view. Parked in front, across the street, and in the driveway and the middle of what once was a front yard were half a dozen cars. People stood around in the dark at one o'clock AM like it was a yard sale on Saturday afternoon, and then scattered like cockroaches when the light hit them. The dog was going nuts, barking and growling. My officer slowed as we passed, window open, dog barking, cockroaches distressed. He made no attempt to silence the dog as we passed.

We were just showing the flag. It was a drug house, and this was how you let them know that you know that what they were doing there was no big secret.

Somebody else on some other night would raid the place, but for this night apparently our job was just to annoy them a bit. Someday they would all get chased down the street and arrested, and the dog would probably get to bite a few, which he really wanted to do, and then the dog would sniff out the drugs from their hiding places and somebody would go to prison for a while and the drug house would move to another dark street, and the game would start all over again.

I remember thinking that somebody in there was working hard enough, buying and selling drugs, and probably fighting for the turf and rights to sell there, and he was going to "work" all night every night, and he was probably working harder at this nonsense than if he just went out and got a job. And I wondered briefly, *why would ya even bother?*

I'm older and wiser now, and perhaps just a bit jaded. I don't ask that question as often these days. For one thing, in a perverse sense this guy was following the American Dream. He prospered from working with his own hands, being his own boss, sinking or swimming by virtue of his own initiative. He hoped to earn more working his own racket than he could make working for someone else. He was an entrepreneur.

And he probably would have been very annoyed if, instead of arresting him, the government came along and put him out of business by taxing him to death so it could use his money to set up its own program to pass out free recreational drugs to the needy. Then, if this guy thought about anything other than skin color, he would probably vote against Obama.

The politicians have us common people all stirred up these days, arguing over just how much we should ask not what our country can do for us; ask what we can do for our country. One bunch of politicians says they are going to limit the negative impact of government upon free folks, and the other would turn government loose to fix any and everything wrong in the world that impacts needy folks. Both are worthy goals I suppose, but they run at cross purposes. Hence, the need for these arguments.

I have long contended that the best of what comes from the human species results from the things we do as motivated individuals, and also what we do as a well-intentioned group, and the worst that comes from the human species is that which comes from the selfish individual or the misguided group. The history of our species, going back to that first monkey that stood on its hind legs to reach for a piece of fruit, or those first two in the garden of Eden who did the same, is nothing more than this.

The yammering of politicians would suggest that we can change this equation by simply putting one group of politicians out of work, and another in. For they would claim that it is the fault of that other group for whatever harm befalls us unfortunate citizens, when in simple truth, this is really the fault of our species' reality.

Cleverly hidden in plain sight lies the truth. When one group of politicians says we should throw out the other set, what they really mean is we should instead substitute them for the other. Somebody talks us into putting them into power instead of the other, and they get what they want. Which is not solutions; it is power.

What we get is more of the same. We get we the people, and the people never change.

But if you wonder why Obama, or whoever your favorite whipping boy might be, was running for re-election even before he was elected, just remember. This is never about fixing the mess. It is always about who's in charge of the mess.

Autumn, 2010

Bison Diaper Wisdom

We recently visited Wind Cave National Park and Custer State Park in South Dakota. Wonderful places. I suspect most of you have not heard of these two parks, because they don't receive near the publicity as Yellowstone or Grand Teton. I suppose I should hope that they never attract the hordes of tourists these more famous parks endure, 'cause that would wreck things. I'm selfish that way. We had both parks pretty much to ourselves, except for the animals, and they were great!

We saw hundreds of wild animals in their original habitat, all acting uninhibited and natural. The grass prairie was peppered with herds of massive bison and thousands of tiny prairie dogs. Margins of the wooded areas revealed grazing mule, and whitetail deer, and elk. Pronghorns stood out in the sunlight, highlighted by their vivid colors. And hawks soared above it all on thermals of joy.

No fences kept the animals off the roads or the people off the prairie. And although most of the human visitors were house trained, the animals clearly are not. The roads were conspicuously decorated with bison poop, which can best be described (you aren't eating now, are you?) as five pound plops of soft serve ice cream. Bison weigh in at one to two thousand pounds, and they recycle grass in prodigious amounts.

You can miss some of these road pies while driving around, but the law of averages catches up to everyone, and so you can plan on hosing off the bottom of the car when you get home. Which brings me around to my latest fantasy...

Historically, sitting presidents travel about the country in those last few weeks before elections kissing babies and wrapping their arms around the shoulders of their party's candidates, hoping that something good will rub off to collect a few votes. Popular presidents significantly improve a candidate's poll numbers simply by showing up. But when a disaster president visits, it can be the kiss of death to an election campaign, if some of the horrid performance adheres to the candidate.

Guess what is happening this time around?

It seems that the few candidates our current president will visit in the coming weeks have such large leads that the desperate man hopes to receive a boost for himself, rather than the other way around.

South Dakota sent a young congressperson off to Washington a while ago, hoping for good things from her. Folks in South Dakota have their feet firmly planted on the ground, and if you have ever experienced the wind there, you would understand this. So you can imagine how outraged those honest hard working people became as they watched their young congressperson voting with Nancy Pelosi time after time. Many in South Dakota farm the land, and they recognize bull "bleep" when they see it. The congressperson's re-election campaign is in trouble, and you won't see the current president dropping by to help this young lady, 'cause he's really not welcome there, or most anywhere anymore.

But I understand that the Democrat party is sending the first lady out on the stump, trying to prop up some failing election campaigns, 'cause they can still find a few people in this country who don't dislike her. So she just might show up in South Dakota in my fantasy. And of course, she would have to do the obligatory photo op at Mount Rushmore.

Now, I doubt Michelle or her hubby have much use for Mount Rushmore or those four dead white guys on it, 'cause those men are hardly relevant to the direction they want the country to slide. But they are savvy enough to realize that a few of us old fools still like the monument and what it once stood for, so if they have a chance at conning folks again in this election, they have to keep up the pretense.

So after the usual speeches and interviews in Rapid City, in my fantasy Michelle would enter the long black armored limo, and with the seven black armored Suburbans in line, she would head up the hill to the visitor center to stand before the cameras, and those four faces. And after that staged show, she might also be shuttled around the mountain to visit Custer State Park and Wind Cave National Park. 'Cause this all would look so good on the six o'clock news.

And if my fantasy comes true, Michelle steps out of the limo at a particularly scenic spot, and plants her size 13's into a still warm and fragrant, perfectly sculpted plop of bison poop. And she like-totally ruins a brand new pair of Gucci's. She will be *distressed*!

This story could end here, with what many would consider a happy ending, but not in my fantasy.

No, I'd like to see where this would go given the current climate in Washington. The minions inside the Beltway would swing into action before the last dollop of putrid poop dripped from the toe of Michelle's shoe. Something must be done to rectify this horrid situation, left over of course, from the Bush administration.

This is a perfect "shovel ready" project. So I have no trouble believing the current administration would come up with this solution: diapers.

We need diapers, in extra giant size, for each and every bison in those two parks, so that no American will ever again step in bison poop. And we will need to change those diapers, several times daily, on each and every one of those hundreds of bison. Every time a diaper becomes soiled. Lots of diapers.

And rubber gloves. A change of rubber gloves for each diaper.

Goggles, too.

And those heavy duty respirators to guard against the occasional methane leak. Got to keep OSHA happy.

PETA will want baby wipes. Scented ones. With lanolin. Don't want no bison diaper rash.

This problem will require study. Grants must be granted. Audits of course, 'cause this all must be transparent. And supervisors. Lots of supervisors.

We will need to hire people to change diapers. Lots of 'em. Three shifts a day, plus replacement workers on weekends and holidays. Overtime. And a union.

But therein lies the beauty of this. Jobs creation. We'd be creating jobs! Good Democrat voting jobs. And they say the president hasn't created jobs. Well eat your words, you skeptics. Bison diapers is a growth industry.

Funding might be a problem, since this will cost millions, if not billions. We will have to make allowance for this crap in Stimulus Three, or is that Four? There are lots of future generations coming along who will need to pay for this, but they don't vote now. The President isn't concerned; he will be retired on Maui, or maybe Indonesia, years before this chicken comes to roost.

There's a lot of bison poop out there, and it needs to be properly disposed. But who knows more about spreading "bleep" than our federal government?

October, 2010

That Piece Of Fan Mail

Received this e-mail in response to my column from last week. I believe this cancels my statement that the folks who think I am an idiot have stopped reading my stuff.

> *Pull out your Merriam-Webster and look up the powerful word "Reification." And no, you don't know the meaning based upon your... columns.*
>
> *That will clarify for you the real problem in this country. One example: the Supreme Court's decision to make entities out of corporations.*
>
> *Yes, the country appears doomed. But only because "you people" (isn't that Limbaugh's expression?) thrive on ambiguities and abstractions.*
>
> *Soon the division between the super-rich and the rest of us will become obvious to you, but by then it will be too late.*
>
> *Fortunately, being in the final stage of COPD, I won't be around to witness it.*
>
> *And unfortunately, you're too deeply ingrained in a tea-bag mentality. What a shame. I'm sorry to see a fine mind that has gone wanting.*
>
> Friend

So I wrote back...

> *Sorry, but I've not had my coffee this morning, so if I seem a bit dense just chalk it up to a caffeine deficiency. In response to your critique of my latest column... I'm not real sure what your point might be. I expect you know what you wanted to say. I'm just gonna have to fake it here, and trust that you will set me straight, as usual. That said...*

I don't listen to Mr. Limbaugh and have very little knowledge of, nor interest in, the tea party folks. Curious how any criticism of the nonsensical rush to bankrupt the country is always met with the same attacks. Isn't anyone allowed to question the direction we are headed without being accused of being a dupe of some talk show host or Sarah Palin? I got that nonsense from my editor, and another columnist (who should have stayed in East Germany) when I was still with the paper. Who sets out the talking points for this?

I do sometimes toy with abstractions, but attempt to avoid ambiguities when possible. I am aware that the law recognizes corporations as individuals in certain contexts, but I don't see how that relates to my last column. I have few people I would describe as rich in my circle of friends, and even fewer super rich, but I think I would know one if I saw one. Whether you refer to that rabble of overpaid actors and athletes or to the crooks who brought us the latest credit crisis, you certainly know that I have no use for either. And I don't care whether it's the Democans or the Republicrats that are overspending my taxes to corral power and perpetual re-election. They both suck.

I once had to look up the word iconoclast before I replied to Joie's personal ad in the newspaper, 'cause I didn't want to come off as a complete idiot if I didn't remember it completely. So yeah, I looked up reify before replying to you. And this refresher perplexed me for a moment, for I saw no connection with my column. So I did a search, and way down at the bottom of the page I found reference to the writings of Karl Marx. Apparently, he liked to use the word, and those apologist self-proclaimed intellectuals who have tried to clarify his theories in the wake of the many failures as folks tried to live those theories, and in the process simply clutter up the language with unnecessary jargon, seem to love it.

Wow. I haven't read Marx in thirty years. History has kinda run off and left him in the dust some time ago, as the carnage of once great nations still smokes following the disasters his thinking brought about. So I pay him little heed. That said, even Marx must have realized that a government that continues to overspend far beyond any hope of repaying its debt is going to crash some day. Certainly, the communists learned that lesson.

Marx would have raised taxes to balance the budget, at least on the folks he didn't have to kill to gain power. To fund his utopian society, Marx would of course milk the wealthy first, to punish them, and shortly thereafter the rest of us until all were equally broken. But once he had bankrupted a nation he would have had to resort to government oppression, just like all those other folks who took his theories to heart. For once the government goes broke and begins to disappoint the gullible who fell into the trap of trusting it for their every need, they get cranky. And they, too, must be punished.

Socialism sounds great in the abstract. All them folks sacrificing for others out of the goodness of their hearts, and all leaning into the harness for the good of society. Problem is Marx never took human nature seriously. He never admitted that the people he claimed were so terribly victimized were just as selfish and crooked as the ones who squatted at the top. He attaches all the evil in man to the wealthy, and thus ignores the reality that every other life on earth walks around with that same evil.

Like Rodney King, Marx and his apologists wondered "why can't we all get along?" But that is a naïve, childlike expectation. Each time folks tried to live his theories, they failed, and they ended up crushed by the operational arm of the left, communism, or some other form of totalitarianism (consider the Nazis), to keep the righteously angry folks in line. And what a joy that was.

Marx's notion that folks are too stupid to see when they are being duped into working by their very freedom, which I guess sorta sums up his whole reification theory, won't wash. For they are far less anesthetized by promises than are those others who expect that all should come to those who merely sit and wait (while drinking).

I'd like to see some solution to our credit problems without having our nation end up living under martial law, but I don't have much hope for that. This country thrived and its citizens fared better than in any nation in history for two hundred years. But that success stemmed entirely from the ambition and hard work of a bunch of free people, not by the interference of government and its oppression, or by those who would sacrifice all to an overreaching government because they find that easier than striving to succeed on their own.

Once people fall victim to total reliance upon government for their every want and need, societies and economies grind to a halt. Ambition, despite its obvious drawbacks, moves society forward. We are *losing this virtue in our nation, and we are trading it in for a lowest common denominator, mediocrity. And this is a shame.*

August 8, 2011

Demonstration And A Hammer

> *I call it the law of the instrument, and it may be formulated as follows: Give a small boy a hammer, and he will find that everything he encounters needs pounding.*
>
> Abraham Kaplan, 1964

A disorganized mob composed mostly of young people poured into the streets. They were not in a good mood. Their country was engaged in an unpopular war. The world economy was seemingly forever trapped in a downswing. They had been promised much, but in their minds they had received little. They were disappointed. They were angry.

Some of these demonstrators seemed a bit out of place. They were college students like many of the others, but were much older. Instead of graduating in four years and getting on with their lives, they were on the 14-year plan. They took the occasional class at the university, but spent a disproportionate amount of time drinking coffee and smoking in the student union building or in neighborhood dives, talking among themselves, a Greek chorus of like thinkers. Somehow their majors kept changing, so they never graduated or got on with their lives. Many needed a shower. All were smarter than anyone else, just ask them, and they eagerly pronounced that they had all the answers, if only folks would listen.

Randomly distributed through the protesting crowd, a smaller collection of people attempted to direct and incite the mob. They all seemed to have the same assortment of talking points, as if they had been prepped for this role, and although none had any visible means of support, they were well funded from somewhere. When these people were done shouting into the microphone, the mob may not have known exactly what they wanted to say, but at least they knew which slogans to chant in unison.

On the outside of the demonstrations looking in, the old folks scowled in silence. They had seen tougher times than this and they had simply rolled up their sleeves and got on with things. To them, the mob of young people were spoiled, over-indulged brats. And they wondered about the future of a world they had worked so hard to improve, that they would soon turn over to the care of these naïve whiners.

Meanwhile the mob railed against their ineffective government that seemed unable to fix all their problems, and they railed against the great corporations and Wall Street, for they had been diligently educated to think that corporate greed was the source of all the world's problems, and therefore the cause of their current disenchantment. And they watched themselves on the television at night and felt important.

And the people who worked got up each morning during these demonstrations, and they quietly went to their jobs, and they quietly prospered, and they watched the news each night, too, noted the demonstrations, and shook their heads in disbelief and frustration.

I was in some of those demonstrations many, many years ago, and I saw how it worked. And as long as I was completely surrounded by like thinking people, I dutifully fell into step with them. But I won't be attending any of the demonstrations that are "spontaneously" breaking out these days, conveniently timed to influence the coming election. Perhaps I'm simply one of those people who gets up and goes to work each day and has no time for such things, or maybe I'm just an old codger standing off to the side scowling. But I don't see much difference between these latest demonstrations and the ones I attended.

Again, the aged college students on the 14-year plan are in attendance, and they are smarter than everyone else despite complaining that no one is listening to them. Many are in need of a shower. They are still spouting the same tired old slogans they borrowed from Marx. Those few people who are directing and inciting the mobs look much the same. They are, again, well-versed in their talking points and well funded from somewhere.

And the bulk of the mob are college students or recent graduates who continue to think like college students. They feel they have been promised much and yet delivered of little. They were told that they could do more with their lives if they obtained an education, and they interpreted that to mean they were entitled to everything, and when that everything didn't instantly land in their laps, their entitlement sense became incensed. Instead of going home to watch themselves on television, they now pull out their latest model 4G phone or tablet computer and watch themselves demonstrating live. They may be impoverished, and terribly oppressed, but they are doing it with all the toys.

The *why?* of these demonstrations isn't quite clear, but those involved obediently vent their anger against the great corporations and banks, and Wall Street in general with predictable vehemence. And most seem distressed that their president and his side of the congress cannot yield their mighty hammer and fix everything they think wrong with the world.

You remember the hammer. That's how this piece got started so very many words ago. The president wants to use his hammer to pound every problem into submission. Apparently, it is the only tool he has, so every problem is now a nail. The president's hammer aims to drown our problems with money. Your money. More government spending. More government jobs. More manipulation of folks with government money and hence government control. Government fixing everything and then everyone will be so grateful that they vote the president and his party into power again. And individuals will fade away and government will be all.

Disregard the cost. We should simply raise the debt limit. We should raise taxes, just so long as somebody else has to pay them. Tax the rich, because we have all been taught that it is the rich we should hate for all the harm they bring us. Leave our grandchildren in debt for eternity while we disassemble a system that has improved the lives of each generation as it took its turn.

The president makes his proposals for massively expensive government projects that never work, but he says will solve our problems, and his opponents vote them down. And the president's minions in congress and the media cry out, "OK, vote down our president's genius, but where are your proposals for how government can solve all our problems? Let's see them."

So hung up are these folks with the hammer that they see no other way into the future, other than government control.

Perhaps we need different tools. Or perhaps we simply need more perspective. What if reality states that things go good and then bad in the natural course of things? Economies go up and down. Climates warm and cool. Great nations rise and then fall. What if the notion that you can fix this is the myth?

What if we realize that although government can surely screw things up, it rarely actually fixes anything? Where does that leave the president's hammer?

And what becomes of all those entitled whiners marching in the streets when the reality settles upon their shoulders that somebody else will not be fixing their problems for them. And they better get busy working on it themselves. Do you wonder if America still has what it takes for us to do this?

October 16, 2011

What To Expect From Uncle Sam

> *Frank made a few appearances in columns over the years, and while his only inclusion in this project follows here, there's enough to bring you up to speed on his philosophy and relationship with Bob. (RG)*

You recall Frank, my n'er-do-well friend who has frittered away his adult life fruitlessly waiting for his ship to come in. Well, he called the other day, and in the course of our conversation I mentioned how pleased I was to receive a bigger refund due to the recent cut in income tax rates. Frank was incensed. Turns out he didn't get a bigger refund, nor any refund at all, and he thought that just awful.

Now, you have to remember that Frank doesn't exactly have a job, and therefore he has very little income and pays no income tax. So an income tax cut does him no good at all. He did inherit a house, and he dutifully pays property tax on that. His house has increased in value, and his property tax didn't go down. In fact, it went up. He figures this to be patently unfair.

Frank likes it when the government gives him stuff. He would love for it to give him more. And he knows that for this to happen, someone has to pay taxes. He just doesn't want it to be him.

I have to sort-of agree with him here, for I don't want to pay taxes so the government can give things to Frank, either.

Frank and I are among the 292 million people who live in this country who argue over how much the government should give to people, and how much the rest should be taxed to pay for it. Opinions on this matter range all over the place.

We argued such stuff when we were still in college, as we sat on the floor of our apartment, drinking screw top wine at two in the morning. And some of the most interesting minds in academia argue such things today.

Take Peter Singer, for instance. You may have heard of him. He calls himself an ethicist, and he is a full professor at Princeton, spending his days passing his vision on to the future leaders of America.

Mr. Singer has some interesting ideas. He made his reputation in animal rights, for instance. He doesn't think you should eat meat, and he would gladly change the laws to force this upon us all. And he says he would sacrifice his own child to any disease that might be cured by using animals in research, since he argues we have no right to misuse animals in this way.

And of course, he would not let any of us benefit from such research, either. He is an ethicist after all, so his ethics should extend to everyone. That's why he teaches at such an important school.

Some people argue that his ethics go a little too far when he suggests that parents should be allowed to kill any newborn child up to 28 days of age, if said child is born with sufficient defects. But that discussion must wait for another day.

Singer also proposes that we, as a wealthy society, have a moral obligation to feed all the poor of the world. He thinks we squander far too much on personal luxury that should instead be given to the less fortunate.

He produces studies that prove the average middle class family can subsist on $30,000 a year. And he figures if you make any more than that, you should gleefully give the rest of what you earn, all of it, in taxes to feed the world.

Now, I don't know about you, but when presented with such an idea, I said more than, "Huh?"

Singer is no fool. He knows that "humans are not by nature egalitarian" and we might object to such largess. He suggests we achieve "equality of wealth" by "fairly stern authoritarian measures." That's the part where the arm-twisting to encourage your altruism comes in.

When asked, Singer admits he currently contributes far less than this personally, but he promises he will match the rest when we all join in.

You might be thinking that this column is a waste of newspaper ink, since we voters obviously will never go for such a plan. Perhaps not, although Singer is not the only one supporting such ideas.

But consider the arguments against the recent income tax cuts. These cuts are after all, intended to help only the rich, or so I have heard. The loyal opposition is proposing that they will indeed raise the taxes on the rich once they regain the throne after this year's elections.

You might want to read the fine print, however. One number they toss about to define when you get to call yourself rich would equal the sum of the salaries of a firefighter married to a public school teacher, right here in the Bay Area.

Is this the rich that you were thinking of when you figured you wouldn't mind passing some of your taxes on to someone else?

May 20, 2004

Looking Back With The Luxury Of Time

One of the few advantages to growing old is the opportunity this presents to realize that the events we watch unfolding in real time will someday be a history that folks will evaluate, argue over, and likely rewrite time and again to suit their new realities. I remember my own internal debate when the start of the second Gulf War rolled around, and I thought the timing was all wrong. I figured we'd need to fight that war at some point, for Saddam would eventually do something to us that even the worst of America's critics couldn't excuse. Only then would going to war have been the "right" thing to do.

But nobody ever gets credit for a preemptive strike, because if successful, the ever-vocal critics will always claim it was unnecessary. I knew that anyone who could recite, "It's Bush's Fault," would never agree with his decision to start that war, even though they would be the first in line to condemn the man when Saddam did finally attack us. Their criticism was the only completely predictable element at the time.

I remember most of these same arguments during my generation's war, Vietnam. We thought we had it all figured out back then. We got our information from some pretty reliable sources, and all of that information told us the war was wrong, that our country was wrong, and certainly that the men sent there to fight were really, really wrong. So I had it all worked out. America was unequivocally wrong to fight that war.

Some time passed before I realized that the information I had used to form my opinion on that war was a bit slanted, because the pretty reliable sources I relied upon were reliable only to the degree that they always criticized this country. They were not reliably correct, but merely consistent in their opinion.

In the four decades subsequent to that war, I've noted other opinion, and viewed previously unavailable information, and I've also had time to think. For myself.

For example, that 1972 Pulitzer Prize winning photo of the crying Vietnamese girl burned by napalm, walking naked down the dirt lane, black smoke plume behind, has resurfaced for its 40th anniversary. We all remember that photo for it was the personification of all that America did during that war that was wrong. That photo of that little girl proved that America were the bad guys and everything America did was bad. And the pretty reliable sources all proclaimed this, and we took their cue and criticized our country.

The story that follows that photo evolved over the decades. Now we know that Phan Thi Kim Phuc, the nine year old girl injured in that attack was treated for about a year in a South Vietnamese hospital before returning to her home village.

After the communist takeover, she wanted to go to school to become a doctor, but the government wanted her for propaganda purposes so they forced her to quit school and recite their monologues for the cameras.

Later, she traveled to Cuba to continue her education. She now relates talking with the photographer who took that photo while she was in Cuba, and she describes how careful she needed to be because the government was always listening, and she feared punishment.

She married, and while flying from Moscow back to Cuba, she fled the plane during a refueling stop in Canada and asked for asylum. She later became a Canadian citizen.

So the poster child for the enemies of America finally was able to flee communism and sought freedom in the West. And those nasty Americans, who fought that war to try to stop the spread of communism around the world, to help people like Phan Thi Kim Phuc find freedom, still face the criticism of those who would like to see more people living under communism. All of this makes perfect sense, looking back on the history.

I have stated that we shall not have a true picture of the value or harm of the second Gulf War until decades have passed. Those who have led the criticism of Bush's conduct of the war, the liberal professors, mass media, and deceitful politicians who would sell out anyone to keep themselves in office, are the same pretty reliable sources of information they were back during Nam. If we are listening to them now, we won't much like what our nation does in that region. But what will we learn in the next 40 years about this latest attempt to preserve our freedom? Might be, this country could turn out to be "right" after all.

June 3, 2012

Programmed Stupidity

I have in my small collection two 50 caliber cartridge cases that I found lying on the ground in the Mojave Desert. The headstamp on one has a W and A, and the number 43. I've always figured this identified the manufacturer and year made. And since I knew that General Patton trained his troops in this area before sending them to Africa and eventually Europe in 1943 and '44, I guess we can conclude that the rounds were fired around that time. So I found them more than 50 years after they were used in those exercises.

I was with a small group hiking the open desert when we came across a track on the ground left by an armored vehicle. An old track. You can tell when desert soil has been undisturbed for a long time. It gets this patina called desert varnish. Walk across it and you crack it. The varnish blending the old track with the rest of the surrounding soil was unbroken.

Shortly, we found an old field telephone wire stretching across the land, and then a scatter of rifle cartridge cases on the ground, and these two larger ones. I had become the resident expert once I began identifying these things for the group, so they were brought to me when found.

One lady on the periphery of the group had missed most of this, and when she caught up she asked what was happening. I smiled and held out my hand, holding a cartridge case, and I told her what it was.

The poor lady screeched, and ran away in abject terror. I tried to calm her, explaining that this cartridge had been fired 50 years earlier and thus represented no harm to her or anyone. I was wasting my breath, for this object had something to do with guns, and thus in her mind it represented a lethal threat to her.

Any, even the most superficial knowledge of firearms would have negated this fear, but this woman was utterly uninformed in this subject. So for no rational reason, this harmless object terrified her.

Now, let's step back for a moment and study why this last paragraph is totally erroneous...

This woman was not ignorant regarding firearms. She was in fact, thoroughly and effectively educated about firearms. Indoctrinated might be a better description. Since she was a babe in arms, she had been taught to fear and loath guns, by her parents and teachers, her political leaders, and her news and entertainment media. She knew all about firearms. They kill ya. They were to be feared. So she ran away from a harmless piece of 50 year old brass, simply because it was associated with firearms. Just shows to go ya that you don't have to teach the truth in order for the teaching to be effective.

Now, the temptation here is to call this woman stupid. One 50 year old cartridge case does not represent a threat to anyone, and reacting as if it would climb out of history to harm this one woman does fail the likely test. I've a bunch of friends who would call this stupid. And I can assure you this woman has a bunch of friends who have implied that I am stupid because I harbor some notions they have been taught to disregard.

I'm a rabid proponent of our Second Amendment rights, and it does toast me when most of the opposition arguments are tainted by misinformation. But that is how things are done in this world. Nothing new here, folks... keep moving.

I've grown tired of being called stupid just so someone can disregard my arguments. But it's gonna happen. I have enough faith in my own brain and my own arguments that I don't fear losing these rights due to better arguments. But I do wonder how to counter all the lies and misrepresentations, and the indoctrination of so many. A lot of people want me to lose those rights. And a few of the others.

With an election looming, the stupid word is flying around, sent from both extremes toward the other, and it is getting old. Both extremes are out to reduce our rights, so they should be recognized and opposed.

The first rule in debate is to address the issues, and not to denigrate the arguer. I'm tired of hearing that Bush was stupid, or Obama is stupid, or pick one. Stupid is what you pull out when you cannot counter an argument with a better one of your own. Why cannot we argue the issues, on their own merit, honestly, and leave the stupid word to those grade school bullies who have grown older, if not up? They still want to ruin our lives, and we don't need to let them.

August 5, 2012

Considering Integrity

The following four columns were written after the Sandy Hook Elementary School shooting in December, 2012 (p.83). This tragedy, and the conversations that it prompted, made a big emotional and philosophical impact on Bob, and he vented via his 'puter. (RG)

I'm not from New York. I do know where it is on the map atlas. I know there is that big city, and then the rest of the state. I've driven through parts of the rest of the state, and other than noting that the folks there drive much faster than me, it seemed almost pleasant. And I've driven past that big city, nicking one corner just long enough to sense the insanity endemic there, and that was close enough for me. As you no doubt recall, I don't do big cities.

Because of the entertainment media and the news media I do know a fair amount about the big city. Large portions of the entertainment and news media live and work there. From outside looking in it seems that the people who habitate there pretty much think it is the center of the world and the whole rest of this country is something else, something less, not worthy of attention. This is a view no doubt fostered by the entertainment and news media, for they clearly act this way. And those of us who live elsewhere just kinda throw that whole lot who live in that big city into one big hopper, and we ignore that too.

I wouldn't know a Bronx from a Queens if presented with one. This makes me something of an idiot to the people who live in their world, but then they might not know how to paddle a kayak down the Snake River. Maybe that makes us even. So when I heard about *The Journal News* it didn't register with me.

But I'm sure those folks living near the big city are familiar with it.

What little research I've done suggests *The Journal News* is an insignificant wannabe struggling to survive in the suburbs of the big city, in the shadow of the media giants, kinda like the paper I used to write for. They clearly have their point of view, which they endeavor to deliver to their readers. And I'll venture they wouldn't print my stuff either, for I stubbornly annoy editors who don't tolerate the way I think.

Anyway, it was *The Journal News* that thought it important to print the names and home addresses of every handgun permit holder in some of those counties bordering the big city. Don't know which counties, but for this discussion it really doesn't matter. Some have asked of the paper why they might do such a thing, and their response seems to be that they think the folks in the area are interested in knowing who living among them might own a firearm. And since they are rabidly opposed to nice folks owning guns, this is no surprise.

One issue that pops up here is the simple reality that many such permit holders are judges, district attorneys, retired cops and others who might not want to let certain people know where they live, what with the fondness certain people might have for exacting revenge upon the civil servants and their families who did their job by putting said certain people away for a bit after certain people committed their various crimes.

It's harder than heck to get a handgun permit in that area of the country. Ya practically have to be married to the mayor to get one. You certainly have to prove you might need one because your life is at risk without one. You can bet the permit holders have been vetted thoroughly before such permit was issued. In other words, it's likely they are not a collective of dangerous criminals.

Maybe, just maybe, these people on the list whose lives have now been put at further risk... they might object to this list being published.

But the way I see this, it doesn't seem like *The Journal News* cares about this part. No, I expect they simply thought they could get some of the locals stirred up, have them mark those homes of their neighbors, maybe picket with signs, throw rocks through their windows, write letters to the editors, and of course nag their politicians for further gun control, for once this Megan's List of gun owners gets out there, panic will spread through the community as those poor vulnerable people realize that they have been living under the unfathomable risk of a nearby firearm.

You remember Megan's List. You can go on-line to that list and find out where the rapists, sexual predators, child molesters, and kiddie porn addicts live. You know, all those folks who shouldn't be out in public but are because like so many other violent and nasty folks, our system of justice likes to simply let them go to prey upon us at their leisure. Decent people like to know where such vermin live.

What you see happening here in New York is real simple. Law abiding upstanding un-threatening handgun permit people are now cast by the media into the same light as rapists, sexual predators, child molesters, and kiddie porn addicts. *The Journal News* appears to suggest that they are just as dangerous. So the paper is simply warning their neighbors of this horrible risk.

And... if you are even half as paranoid as me, don't you wonder if this newspaper would be delighted if some judge or retired cop they outed gets murdered in his home, in his sleep, simply so they could say... "SEE! Keeping a gun in the house didn't make him any safer!" For of course, like the vast mass of media in this country, this paper fervently believes it must teach the people that guns in the home are inherently evil, so the paper likely has systematically sensationalized criminal misuse of guns and yet has actively hidden any evidence of successful defense of one's home and life with those nasty handguns kept in the good people's houses.

That's how you influence public opinion if you own a newspaper, you know. By manipulating that which you choose to report. And I'm betting that like most of the media, they don't want the opposition to be able to answer back when attacked about gun ownership. They might paraphrase and then ridicule the opposition point of view, but they rarely allow anything approaching equal time to rebut their attacks.

I've told this story before, but it is illustrative. Picture the arid desolation of Nevada. I was with a small group of desert aficionados camped amid the quiet beauty, and the subject of guns came up. That NRA decal on the window of my pickup sometimes does this. It's kinda the red cloak in front of the liberal bull.

One woman asked if I had brought any firearms along on this trip and I assured her that I had, and that they were securely stored out of harm's way. She admonished me, "Keep your guns away from my car, for I don't want my car to blow up."

I didn't want to let on that I didn't figure my firearms were going to climb out of their cases in my truck and start shooting her car when I wasn't looking. But I did mention that the only time people firing guns causes cars to blow up in massive fireballs, flying in slow motion through the air, was in the movies. Many things happen in movies that are not real, or even possible. But maybe this lends some insight into the minds of those movie stars who think our benevolent government should confiscate all the guns. It certainly was well ingrained into this woman's mind by the entertainment media.

Another well programmed woman on another desert trip ran away screaming when she saw the cartridge case from a fifty caliber Browning machine gun that we found in the Mojave Desert in an area where Gen. Patton had exercised his troops before they left to battle the Nazis in North Africa. That sixty year old piece of expended brass was no more dangerous than an empty coffee cup, but it had something to do with guns, and thus it terrified this poor woman. Not sure what level of indoctrination had so modified this woman's brain, but it certainly worked. No doubt the media had a hand in this too.

And there is no question whatsoever how fervently these two women would want to see our caring politicians clear the country of the menace of citizens owning firearms.

I can remember well the wind up to the last "assault weapons" ban. Every TV network had their input. They'd do a voiceover about the horrors of these mythical weapons, and then they'd show a video of a machine gun firing a few hundred rounds on full automatic. I believe this is where the fanciful notion of "assault weapons" spraying bullets came from. Or maybe it was those movies where the guy with an Uzi fires off a few thousand rounds from a thirty round magazine, and he never has to reload. You know, kinda like a garden hose. None of this had the remotest relevance to any discussion of the guns our government eventually "banned," but it did influence a lot of people to favor the ban.

I've yet to discuss the "assault weapon" issue with anyone who didn't ask me why I thought people needed a machine gun. (Machine guns have been illegal since 1934. None of the firearms these folks now classify as an "assault weapon" are machine guns. That's just one of those little lies the media and certain politicians need to resort to in order to sway public opinion.)

The Media has also spread false notions about "Saturday Night Specials," "cop killer bullets," "sniper rifles," "plastic guns," "high-powered military style weapons." Such vacuous titles are designed to demonize firearms, to make them seem far more dangerous, and to single out each class of firearms in turn in the incremental process intended to disarm the nation.

In the wake of the Newtown, Connecticut, tragedy, a fresh media attack on the 100 million firearms owners who are not criminals has surfaced. Now, according to the media, the blame for the slaughter of innocent children by a madman belongs to every law-abiding firearm owner in America. It's time to demonize you and me. We are on the new Megan's List for gun owners.

The last "assault weapon ban" lasted ten years. It was so cleverly worded that it did not take a single weapon off "the street." All those "assault weapons" were still out there, not killing anybody. Because of the "ban," a handful of firearms could no longer be sold to supplant those already out there, but they had previously been purchased in such small numbers that this hardly mattered. Many other manufacturers simply changed one or two cosmetic features that did not affect their firearms' function, and these remade no-longer-assault-weapons continued to flow into the marketplace due to their popularity with the decent law abiding folks.

Senator Diane Feinstein (D-CA) likes to claim that the former ban lowered murder rates, but her logic is a mite flawed. Hard to imagine how no reduction whatsoever in the number of firearms that she would call "assault weapons" might lower the murder numbers, but I'll take that as a fail on her part. In reality, the cosmetically legal firearms that continued to be sold by the thousands to law abiding enthusiasts didn't mess at all with the murder rates that had been falling before the "ban" and continued to fall despite the addition of thousands of these guns to the population.

Oh, and when the "assault weapons" ban expired in 2004, nothing changed. The predicted bloodbath out there in the streets has not happened.

So of course, Sen. Feinstein is ready with her new "assault weapons" ban. This one, among other nonsense, will turn my little 22LR target rifle into an assault rifle, because of the way it looks. When I stop laughing, I'll have to fight her on this one. My rifle hasn't even been fired on the range yet, but she is out to get it. Because of the way it looks.

The media will support this. They always do. They support this with distortion and outright lies, and by stifling any notion that firearms in the hands of the decent people do far more to suppress crime and violence than they do to foster it. There is considerable evidence to support this statement, but you won't see any sign of this evidence in the entertainment and news media. You have to search out this truth on your own.

All this is in the shadow of the horrible tragedy in Connecticut. The media doesn't care that none of the gun control laws they support to date would have stopped this madman. The media doesn't care that this madman could have used any number of common household tools to kill six year old children trapped in a room in the ten to twenty minutes he had to play with before the police could arrive to stop him. The media doesn't care that had one teacher broken a stupid law and had carried a firearm to work that day, she might have stopped this pathetic loser before he could carry out his heinous task. Such has happened before, but of course most have not heard of this. The media suppresses almost all of these notions. They refuse to report it.

"Whenever there is a shooting, somebody always wants to punish the people who didn't do it." I didn't make this up. Don't know off hand who did. I merely stole it because it is so very true.

No, the media views its job here to be fanning the fear and loathing of people beyond any reason so that when the politicians try to disarm the citizens of this country, the well-indoctrinated sheep will urge them on. Which explains why *The Journal News* is printing the Megan's List of the names and addresses of legitimate gun owners. Like the individual classes of firearms, this newspaper is attempting to demonize all of these people.

I'm approaching a loss for words here. I guess if you want to see lies and distortion drive this country, then you will reap that which you sow. I'll be arguing the other way if you need to ask. For most every gun control law that has come into being in my lifetime has either done absolutely nothing to inconvenience criminals, or it has actually raised crime numbers. "Reasonable gun control" does nothing to deter or render harmless a criminal. It simply punishes the good folks.

Don't know how you feel about this, but I don't see it as a good thing. The media, on the other hand, is trying its hardest so you don't find out about how often they distort reality. If you are interested in the truth, perhaps you should seek out other sources of information that are not as corrupt as our mass media.

By the way… the "journalist" responsible for publishing that list of gun permit owners is a fellow named Dwight R. Worley. Somebody dug up his address and posted it online. I won't be doing that, for that would be a despicable thing to do.

Oh, and some have reported that ole Dwight owns a .357 magnum revolver, with a gun permit. Presumably for his own protection. No fool here, but if this is true… Can you spell hypocrite?

I'm sending this to *The Journal News*. Not that they will appreciate it, but because if you are going to take a shot at somebody, they have a right to know. I like to think this involves a degree of integrity. I don't know what they might consider integrity.

December 30, 2012

The Great American Novel

I grow weary of discussing gun control. I truly do. I started back in the 1970s when I was the rabid liberal and thought all guns should be taken out of the hands of the public. I took it up again in the '80s, with a somewhat different perspective and conclusion. And by the '90s I was completely caught up in the controversy along with the rest of the good folks in this country. This debate has continued, with some increase and decrease since then, with a considerable growth in volume and ferocity. And in case you haven't noticed, the subject has surfaced again.

I've learned some things along the way. In these past 40 years I'd hope I learned something. I've been taught a few things, been indoctrinated about a few others, and have sought out information when it has been available, not being one to always believe that which others have wanted me to think. I don't claim any absolute truths here. One thing I have learned is that there are few absolute truths in this world. In fact, the most important thing I have learned is that when an absolute truth is presented to me, I'd best check it out, for guess what... absolute truths often have the very least truth attached to them.

Going back to my mind in the '70s, I see an optimistic, sheltered, reasonably well-educated and socialized young professional who watched and read the news, and discussed issues with friends. Presumably I was an asset to the community. For instance, I voted for Dianne Feinstein a couple of times, for the Sierra Club liked her, and she had pushed through the preservation of large tracts of wild country I thought worth saving. And she had argued for a handgun ban in San Francisco, and everything I had heard from my friends and seen in the newspapers and on TV had taught me that handguns were pure evil, and of course they should be banned.

Only much later that I learned that Ms. Feinstein had a concealed carry permit in those days, and this was because she felt she was entitled to protection. Then later when she got those armed guards, those armed guards that she still has, I began to wonder again about her honesty. For she was trying to disarm people who thought they also needed protection, but these were those who could not afford armed guards and didn't have the influence in government to get most anything they wanted, like the people in the ruling elite. People like Ms. Feinstein.

Later, I discovered that that bit of land in Utah that Ms. Feinstein managed to preserve from mining, scenic land that I wished protected, just happened to hold a precious mineral much in demand in this country. Imagine my surprise to find that the mining company in Southeast Asia that supplied this mineral to our country was owned by her wealthy husband. Excuse me for being human here, but I kinda lost faith in the lady senator's honesty around then.

Back in the '70s it was expected that if you were a liberal, you were opposed to handguns in the hands of regular folks. Handguns were just for killing. No other purpose. They were more dangerous than most anything on earth. Kids picked 'em up and blew their little brains out every day. Only idiots and savages owned them, and all the rest of us were put at risk as a consequence.

Heck, when Barney Miller came home from the police station on TV, the first thing he did, before kissing his lovely stay-at-home wife, was to unload his service revolver and lock it in that little drawer way up by the ceiling, and then lock those nasty bullets in the other little drawer way up over there, because even though they had no children, no grandchildren, no day care children in their apartment, and he didn't get raging drunk every night and beat his wife, the TV made it clear that a handgun was so dangerous that if you didn't lock it up unloaded, somebody was going to get killed, and that really hurts.

Politicians, like Ms. Feinstein told me that handguns were worthless and dangerous. So did the TV news, the newspapers, my friends, musicians and movie stars, and my teachers. And there was not a voice within hearing that even suggested any other view. This would be the indoctrination part. It was very effective.

I voted once to ban handguns in California. I thought that "Saturday Night Specials" should all be rounded up and melted. Imagine, an inexpensive killing machine like a "Saturday Night Special" could still be bought in California, and all it was good for was killing people.

It was only later that I learned that the proposed ban on "Saturday Night Specials" was essentially an attempt to disarm poor Black people down in the bad neighborhoods. It was little more than another example of the institutional racism I had thought I had been fighting for all those years.

Ya see... there was a piece to the puzzle of life that I had missed out on for many years. It's a little known fact, mostly ignored, or suppressed, depending upon one's view of life I guess, whereby the use of a handgun to defend against crime is actually a common event. You won't hear about this in the newspapers or the TV news. The politicians won't mention this. Movie stars and musicians often pass right by this notion. Teachers will argue against even the thought. And your friends will look at you in total disbelief if you so much as mention it. Heck, somebody will email me tomorrow to take them off this weekly little gab session because I bring this up.

But some people actually think that a handgun in the house is more likely to help you defend yourself from a crime than it is to harm you or anyone you know.

Blasphemy!

This is a minority view. I'll concede that. The Department of Justice, the federal version, who keep track of the misuse of firearms by criminals and have a long history of downplaying any positive aspect of firearm ownership, estimated that firearms have been used to prevent crime as often as 110,000 times a year. Other than the usual, "Zero times," you are likely to get if you ask the Media, or the likes of Ms. Feinstein, this is about the lowest estimate you can find. One guy set out to survey random people to prove that defensive use of firearms is a myth came up with a result he didn't expect, an estimate of defense against criminal attack... 2.5 million times a year. This on the plus side in case you are wondering. This author was surprised. Others with different methodology came up with only 0.75 million.

Don't look for this information in the Media or from Ms. Feinstein.

They will argue against it, and have. Shortly after such numbers have been released, the Media and politicians have asked all the gun ban organizations to get their take on these numbers. Each and every one of the gun ban organizations has lambasted the conclusions of these studies. They are so sure of themselves that they rejected the conclusions often without even reading the studies.

I know, my paranoia here, right? Well... look into this. Read Gary Kleck and John Lott. Then check into the responses from the gun control advocates. It's rather shameful. Then come back and tell me I'm paranoid. Sure, we can argue the numbers, just how many times the good guys win, but the numbers are pretty solid that it's mostly the good guys.

The next time a gun control issue shows up in the Media, such as the coverage of the recent school murders, take quiet note of the number of gun control advocates consulted and quoted in the stories. Note the slant of the story itself. Note the horror in the tone of the Media content. Note the Media editorials. And then notice how any opposition to the gun control stance is handled. If any shows at all, it will receive fewer words in print, less time on the air, and often you will not hear much more than a soundbite or two, and then a synopsis of the pro-firearm stance by one or more opponents of such a stance. Our Media consults the opponents of firearm ownership to paraphrase the arguments that they oppose, rather than presenting to the public those arguments.

Notice the nearly total absence of reports of crimes prevented or stopped by citizens with firearms. Note the near complete absence of reports of mass murders prevented or stopped by citizens with firearms. And try to avoid the temptation to disregard this request with some response that you have never heard of such defenses. You have just made my point.

You will notice that I am no longer the gun hating liberal I was in 1972. And for some reason, I am far more skeptical of politicians and the Media.

Consider the discussion about "cop killer bullets" some time ago. Two guys invented a bullet intended for law enforcement use. Normal handgun bullets often deflect when fired into car windshields and doors. A denser metal bullet would penetrate better, and in the hands of the police could prove useful in urban settings. Somebody asked the developers if such a bullet might defeat the body armor that the police were beginning to wear, and from this the notion of a "Cop Killer Bullet" was born.

Politicians and the Media smelled blood in the water, and turned a non-issue into the next great threat to civilization. NBC, I believe, decided to televise a special intended to raise alarm among the general public, and over police protest, proceeded to give a primer to criminals on how to kill a police officer in a gunfight. The cops were thrilled. Politicians took the nonsense and ran with it, demanding a ban on every cartridge in America that could defeat the body armor of the day. In other word, virtually every hunting rifle cartridge. Some people objected to this draconian measure. They were of course, vilified in the Media. Hunters were all branded as cop killers.

The argument raged between people who saw this as a way to render so many firearms worthless and the citizens who thought this unnecessary. Eventually, a law limiting the actual armor piercing bullet in question to use only by police was written. (In case you care, the dreaded demon known as the NRA helped congress write this sane law, which passed easily.)

Oh, and after all the fuss, the sum total of police officers killed by "cop killer bullets" remains at zero. And they haven't been manufactured in years.

Mel Gibson used a "Cop Killer Bullet" in one of his movies a few years ago, after they were no longer made. Blew a hole through a bulldozer blade to kill the bad guy at the end of the movie. Clever trick, if a bit exaggerated. Mel doesn't much like guns. He has made a fortune misusing them in his movies, but he doesn't want us citizens to own any. He talks often of disarming all of us. Imagine that.

Mayor Bloomberg mentioned "Cop Killer Bullets" the other day, too. He thinks we should ban them. He doesn't care that they do not exist. He has a few billion dollars and the ear of the Media, so he can say anything he wants. He presumably gets along well with Ms. Feinstein as long as they are trying to disarm people.

Mel has used and misused machine guns to make a fortune in his movies. In one particular movie the bad guy with an Uzi sporting a thirty round magazine hoses down the neighborhood for a minute or two, in slow motion sometimes, burning up a few thousand rounds without reloading. The bad guy generally holds the Uzi with one hand while cradling his beer with the other. Mel fires back with an automatic rifle holding twenty rounds, launching back a few thousand bullets, blowing up cars and chopping down buildings.

I'm pretty convinced this is where the notion of "spraying bullets" came to be attached to the "assault weapons" ban idea. From stupid nonsense in movies. I've fired an Uzi. Legally I might add. I have some firearms experience, and yet I could not make a thirty round magazine last more than a second. It goes empty that fast. Course I didn't try, for if you use that weapon like a hose, the recoil causes the muzzle to rise to the ceiling if you really don't know what you are doing, and really knowing what you are doing doesn't include holding the weapon with only one hand. "spraying bullets" from a machine gun is a movie myth. And by any definition, "assault weapons" are not machine guns.

The last "assault weapon" ban was kinda funny, looking back on it. Ms Feinstein is deadly serious with her "New Assault Weapon" ban. But we have to see what will come of this new one.

The last "assault weapon" ban left us gun owners a bit confused. I know a bunch of people who are extremely educated in firearms, and yet not one has ever owned, used, or seen an "Assault Weapon." At least they don't think they have. Sounds a bit weird, but firearm owners didn't invent "Assault Weapons." The Media and the politicians did. Maybe these folks know what an "assault weapon" might be, but the rest of us don't.

Mostly, it appears that this new "assault weapon" ban will again be a "whatever we want it to be" definition reminiscent of the "cop killer bullet." And since the Media will be educating the public on how they should view "assault weapons" this will become interesting. And since Ms. Feinstein is pushing the deal again, honesty shall not likely rear its ugly head.

Last time, the Media chimed in with their usual distortions and lies. On the TV news you could watch discussion of the "assault weapon" ban with machine guns firing in the background and the spokespersons from all the gun ban organizations talking about how horrible these mythical weapons are, how they are the guns of choice among the gangs roving the inner city neighborhoods, the source of the pile of dead gang members clogging the streets, and the scourge of civilization. And the gun ban folks got to paraphrase the argument they expected back from the spokespersons opposed to the "assault weapons" ban, like they always do. All while we tried to figure out just what firearms they were talking about.

Ultimately, they settled on a buffet of firearms, some grenade launchers that were already illegal, machine guns that have been illegal since 1934, and a variety of models judged solely by what they looked like.

The Media propaganda blitz continued for a while. Pistols became "high-powered" even though they weren't. "Military style" became style, for like the models strutting down the walkway in designer gowns, appearance was everything. Suddenly a black colored rifle was more dangerous than it had been the day before. Twenty-two caliber rifles also became "High-powered," and if they had magazines that "nobody needs in order to hunt deer," we had to remind them that such caliber rifles were not legal for deer in most states because they are not powerful enough for that.

The "assault weapons" ban didn't remove a single firearm from the street. It did limit the sale of some for a short while, and some were no longer sold, but everything they called an "assault weapon" that existed before the law passed was still there when the law expired ten years later. In fact, virtually identical firearms continued to be sold throughout the ten years of the ban. Lots of them. A few cosmetic changes made them legal, which suited the spirit of the law. It was all about appearances, after all.

Ms. Feinstein is making the rounds as we speak, touting the reduction in crime brought about by her first "assault weapons" ban. And presumably she is talking up the carnage she claims has washed across the nation since the ban expired. Ms. Feinstein has an active imagination, but her pronouncements are echoed by the Media and those spokespersons from the gun ban groups.

Crime rates, including murder rates, which presumably would be influenced by an "assault weapons" ban have been falling steadily since the very early '90s. The number of firearms in the hands of American citizens has climbed consistently since then. The number of firearms identical to the banned "assault weapons" grew by the thousands each year of the ban. An estimated three million are in private hands. And crime rates and murder rates fell. Most city police department don't track the numbers of crimes committed with "assault weapons" because they see so few. Which hasn't changed since the onset of the ban, and hasn't changed since the ban expired in 2004. But Ms. Feinstein shouts that the ban has been so very effective, and its expiration an unmitigated disaster. Ms. Feinstein is a bit full of it. But I guess you don't have to believe me. I admit that I have an agenda.

As before, it is difficult to get much information from the people opposing the new "assault weapons" ban. It's not that we don't have much to say, but it definitely is in line with the influence of Media and politicians. Control of information is critical to the passage of the next "assault weapons" ban. And if anyone wants an opposing view, they will have to work to find it.

I was completely indoctrinated back in the '70s, and today I argue with people similarly "educated." To them, I am an idiot because they have never seen or heard anything that opposes the point of view they've been fed. They point to the fall in crime and go... "*See!*" Dianne was right!

Well, lots of things probably resulted in the drop in crime. A ban that never actually happened doesn't seem to be one of these. And heaven help ya if you mention all those statistics that suggest that concealed carry permits in all those states just might have contributed.

Oh, I know. We're right back to how nasty those handguns are, and how they shouldn't be in the hands of citizens. The studies quoted by the Media and politicians show that those guns are a bazillion times more likely to kill the baby in its crib than to defend the people in the house. *Everybody* knows this!!!

OK sorry. I'll go back to my corner and put on the dunce cap. I've other statistics, but the folks who run the gun ban organizations all say these aren't true. The Media echoes them, and the politicians prattle on.

Thirty nine states now have concealed carry. Some for twenty years. Five million carry permits have been issued. Crime and murder rates go down, faster than the trend already mentioned, and the numbers all began changing at the onset of the CCW permit laws, and continue to this day as more permits are issued. States without CCW don't see the same changes. Not one state has even considered rescinding the permits. The number of accidents involving permitted people is nearly zero. The number of crimes committed by permitted people is nearly zero. The number of murders is so much lower than the general public that it would amaze and confuse the Media and politicians who predicted a slaughter.

The gun control groups have looked at these statistics, and a rare few have actually acknowledged their results. Mostly however, they have chosen to attack the messengers rather than address their message, or to cherry pick and cook the numbers to suit their preconceived notions, rather than let the numbers speak. Liars can, it appears, figure.

I won't suggest that CCW permits are the sole source of the improvement, but I will suggest that the chaos and carnage predicted for states that adopt CCW by the Media, politicians, and gun ban spokespeople have not come to pass. And I will suggest that those Media, politicians and gun ban spokespeople might prosper from looking at the rise in crime and murder that seem to accompany most of the gun control measures they have foisted upon the citizens. For that would be kind of embarrassing.

Of course, when a gun control law fails to do what it was intended to do, the Media, politicians, and gun ban groups have a predictable response. They need more laws. And as long as the indoctrination succeeds, they will get them.

The numbers are there, but you will have to do your own work to find them. Subject to interpretation, certainly. I'm not talking absolute truths here, but guess what... the Media, politicians, and gun ban groups all spout absolute truths. And the best way to swallow absolute truth is not to ever question it. But is that the best way?

January 06, 2013

Calling for Reason

I cannot imagine a greater tragedy than the death of a child. To have one snatched away in a violent act, the consequence of the irrational hatred of a madman, must be the most painful. Who wouldn't do their best to prevent such a thing from ever happening again? Vice President Joe Biden states that our president promises to do whatever it takes so this never happens again. Not one more child. Not ever.

This is an ambitious statement, but heck, not one more child would be worth whatever it would take, whatever it would cost, right?

I'm not going to make light of murder. I'm not that callous or stupid. But I've been watching the response to murder, and it lends itself to some head scratching.

We are experiencing an epidemic of shootings in schools. That's what they are calling it these days. Those of us trained in medicine use a different definition for the word epidemic, but this situation clearly demands a little hyperbole, so I'll let that go. One murder is too many, and there have been far more than one.

In the last twenty years, 484 kids have been killed in shootings in our schools. It was way worse back in the early '90s than it is now, for the gang warfare had spilled from the streets into the schools. They didn't call it an epidemic back then. And it's slowed down considerably since '93.

But since the mid '90s, a few crazies have discovered the nearly everlasting notoriety they can gain by murdering innocent people they catch defenseless in shopping malls, theaters, and schools. They choose to become famous for murder, and garner weeks of 24-hour-a-day cable news coverage, their pictures plastered over the TV screen and in the newspapers, their life stories broadcast, with all their grievances aired as their reward. All this publicity turns their heinous crimes into something almost heroic in their demented minds.

So now we have madmen killing kids in schools.

Four Hundred Eighty Four kids in only twenty years... A big number. A national disgrace. A horror. An epidemic.

Why, this is a bigger number than the 200 kids killed every year by drunk drivers.

It's even a bigger number than the 250-425 kids murdered by their own parents every year. And it is parents who have always been by far the biggest murderers of kids. So yeah, this number of kids dying from shootings in our schools is too high.

What to do, you might ask? This is a question on every set of lips these days. How to protect our children from mass murders.

Some have suggested stationing a police officer in every school. We have 55 million kids in PreK through Grade 12 to protect. This sounds like a good idea, but there are only 800,000 police officers in the entire country, and we have 130,000 public and private schools to guard. The other criminals out there in our society, the bunch other than that handful each year who want to commit suicide by killing a group of innocents, might take advantage of the artificial shortage of cops this would create. And who could guess how much harm they'd do with this opportunity.

Senator Feinstein mentioned using the National Guard to, uh, guard the schools. We have roughly 500,000 Guard soldiers, but many are already occupied, so I don't see that working.

Likely the president has other ideas. He is an idea guy. One of his oldest, firmest ideas is his desire to disarm the entire American population. He's been talking this up since he was a teacher of Constitutional law at the University of Chicago. Presumably, the president figures if he begins taking all the firearms away from all the people, starting with the easy people, the folks who obey laws to a fault, and then slowly working his way through the people who might "forget" to turn in their guns, and then investing the effort to disarm the really stubborn bunch who will simply refuse to turn in their guns without a fight, he might eventually, finally, get to the psychopaths and criminals we'd all like to disarm.

Let's see, that would be about 95 million law abiding people before he gets to the bad guys. That won't take long.

For this the president will need all 800,000 cops, the 500,000 National Guard soldiers, and likely the rest of the military. Things will surely change around here for the better, once 300 million guns are confiscated. The psychopaths and criminals will be the last to give up their guns, of course. Oh, and that bunch of formerly law abiding productive citizens who actually revolt against this annoyance will be a fly in the ointment But eventually, the president's dream might come true.

This disarming the good guys to eventually disarm the bad has never actually worked in any other country, but this is America. We know how to do things right.

The president did promise to protect all 55 million kids. Every one of them. So after the smoke clears, it will be worth it.

So I'm also waiting for the president to announce when he will take all the children away from their parents, to have them reared in safety by the state. You know, onnacounta that bunch of crazy parents who kill their own kids. Can't let that bit slide, because not one more...

And when will the president order the destruction of all the motor vehicles? Without vehicles the drunk drivers cannot kill another kid.

Most likely, the president won't get the chance to remove every firearm from America. And he is unlikely to suggest anything remotely like the last two paragraphs. Which is fine. The ideas in those last two paragraphs wouldn't save every single child. Losing video games and violent movies won't do it either. Somebody somewhere, some angry crazy person with a hammer or a 2X4, will eventually kill another child. Or a roomful.

The numbers won't change much, but they already hover right around lightning strike. Can anyone make the promise of not one more child? Nope. Not even a president. Do we need to change everything because of this?

Nope.

Won't help.

January 13, 2013

Letter To An Assemblywoman

Susan Bonilla represented the 14th District, including Contra Costa and Solano counties, in the California Assembly from 2010-2012. (RG)

It's time to write to Susan Bonilla again. I dropped a line a while ago with the simple request that Ms. Bonilla not support any of the bills that contribute to the avalanche of gun restrictions that have surfaced in the wake of the horrible murders of school children in Connecticut. My request was simple and direct, for none of the proposed restrictions would have any impact upon criminals or upon the insane folks who choose to murder a classroom full of tiny children. These restrictions will merely, by fiat, turn good citizens into criminals, punish the innocent for the crimes of criminals, and infringe upon our Constitution and our rights.

Ms. Bonilla was kind enough to respond, although what I read was merely a prepared script. Her response suggested a need for common sense restrictions imposed upon the law-abiding folks due to the rising tide of gun violence and the epidemic of mass shootings. Wow!

That's interesting, for how can one describe the remarkable decline in the rates of murder by firearms and in the rates of violent crimes committed with firearms, a twenty year decline to levels not seen since the 1960s in this country, as a rising tide, an epidemic?

And what an amazing coincidence... These are the exact same phrases repeated endlessly by your president, multiple US senators and representatives, various governors and a few state representatives, and just about every other politician with a 'D' behind their name. These are the politicians responsible for hundreds of proposed laws, all designed to punish the law-abiding people and to restrict their Constitutional rights under the guise of common sense. But rather than acting with common sense, each and every one of these new laws is senseless, useless, and onerous. And every single one has been proposed by a Democrat politician.

Your president's recent ignominious defeat in the Senate, due entirely to the roar of irate citizens, was called by that president a dark day for Washington. He claimed his opposition was driven by those seeking political gain. Yet the impetus for this voter revolt was in fact brought on by the Democrat party itself, which has been seeking short-term political gain at the expense of our freedom. And sadly, while America mourns the deaths of little children, it is the Democrat party that *celebrates* these incomprehensible and monstrous murders as an opportunity to promote their political agenda. This is offensive to anyone with a shred of moral character and makes me want to puke.

So I figure I'm entitled to some explanation if Ms. Bonilla chooses to support or votes for any of the oppressive and unnecessary gun control bills now working their way through the morass that is Sacramento. These would include, but not be limited to SB 47, 53, 108, 293, 299, 374, 396, 567, and AB 48, 169, 180, 187, 231, 500, 711, 740, 760.

None of these bills would reduce crime or prevent mass shootings. They would however negatively impact thousands of honest citizens, turning many into instant criminals. So while my government is increasing violent crime by releasing criminals from prison to prey upon the citizens of this formerly fine state, our politicians busy themselves with plots to harm everyone else.

Simply reading from the party script won't cut it any more in this discussion. Any drone can do that. I would hope that Ms. Bonilla might learn something about firearms so she will not simply parrot the same old lies. I would hope Ms. Bonilla could familiarize herself with the current state of violent crime in this country and make some effort to keep the people responsible for that crime behind bars, and leave the rest of us in peace. Please Ms. Bonilla, give this some actual thought, and then decide if short-term political gain is worth the cost to the freedom of the people you are supposed to serve.

May 30, 2013

Make That Cheese Easy To Find

Consider this fable before I attempt to describe California.

A scientist put a laboratory mouse in a box with six rooms. The mouse soon learned the cheese was in room three. Therefore, it always ran directly to room three upon being put in the box. One day the scientist put the cheese in room five. Upon entering the box, the mouse ran directly to room three. "Hmmm... no cheese." The mouse looked around. Tried room four. No cheese. Tried room five.

"Ah-ha! Cheese!"

What would a human being have done? He or she would have continued to return to room three again and again and again -- expecting and then demanding cheese. "Where is my cheese!? This is where it has always been. It's supposed to be here! I want it NOW -- GIVE ME MY CHEESE!!! I have rights, you know. Blah, blah, blah." And so the complaining was heard through the night in the now-dark laboratory. Meanwhile, the cheese remained in room five.

So what is the difference between mice and people? Mice get their cheese. (author unknown)

I don't know why we study rodents to try and figure out why people do what people do, but maybe it is because sometimes it works. Behavioral scientists who do all their studies on actual human populations tend to look down their noses at their colleagues who work in "rat labs," but much of what has been learned from watching rodents solving a maze actually translates into how we behave.

We know what happens to a rat colony for instance, when the occupants reproduce to the point where overcrowding forces them into new behaviors. Formerly smooth functioning colonies revert to savage societies, with outbursts of inappropriate and gratuitous violence and the abandonment of offspring by their own parents.

You know, like we now witness in human cities.

But, we also see that sometimes people and rodents don't follow the same patterns. The fable above illustrates just such an example. The humans deprived of their cheese should turn out to be as resourceful as their rodent counterparts, but often they are not.

Now, to be completely fair, if you put enough people into enough mazes you would find that some go out and find the cheese. Human society would have ceased to exist a long time ago without that kind of initiative.

What the maze in the fable shows, however, is how predictably some people cope with a change in their maze by whining rather than by making the appropriate changes. And if the cheese does eventually show up as a consequence of the whining, those folks don't head out looking for room five. And thus we create a society of whiners, incapable, or at least unwilling, to take care of themselves.

With the state deficit hovering around a bazillion dollars, some folks are whining like crazy now. The rumor is we may need to cut down on the cheese in room three, and that isn't sitting real well.

No one has touched the cheese yet, but they might. These people are whining on spec. It has started in anticipation.

California voters tossed out a governor because he got blamed for playing a shell game with the cheese. And the legislature hasn't had a clue about the reasonable management of cheese for decades. The new governor promises to clean up the whole cheese mess, but so far he is just suggesting a new shell game.

Remember the lottery commercial, where the winner was staggered to realize he could "like totally afford all this cheese?" Well, we haven't won the lottery. We can't afford all this cheese.

California hasn't been able to pay for the cheese for the last few years. This has come as a shock to many. Years of budget surplus artificially generated by a flush economy led to the erroneous belief that room three was a bottomless resource. Now that the economy has cycled back down, government can no longer afford to put as much cheese into room three.

Room five still has cheese. It is a little harder to find, and people have to work for it, but like the mouse, many can still get cheese if room three turns up empty. The whining merely confirms how conditioned the rest have become.

Maybe we need to learn a different lesson. Maybe society never could afford to put too much cheese into room three. Maybe it was a mistake to try.

Some politicians still argue for more cheese. But let's not forget, that is how they got elected in the first place, and they want to stay elected. They don't care if society can afford the cheese. They don't even care if the cheese helps people.

They actually like the whining, and stir up more when they can. That is just the sound of job security to them.

Date Unknown

Film Comes A Long Way From Cowboy Stereotypes

From IMDb: Brokeback Mountain (2005); The story of a forbidden and secretive relationship between two cowboys and their lives over the years. (RG)

"I'm not gonna hit ya!... I'm not gonna hit ya!.... The H*!! I'm not!"

John Wayne
McLintock, 1963

Pow!

I stopped watching cowboy movies about the time John Wayne stopped making them. Near the end of this flick, Wayne just had to punch this one guy out. That character truly deserved to get punched out. Everybody in the audience wanted him punched out, and they all knew John Wayne was going to punch him out. And so he punched him out. He was as reliable as the sun rising in the east. And we all cheered.

Cowboy movies were all about stereotypes. You had the good guys and bad guys, the settlers and Indians, and the cattlemen, sheep herders, and sod-busters. The nice thing about stereotypes is that all these folks acted pretty much like you expected they should, and the movies had formulas that were as predictable as ants at a picnic. So you could count on feeling good at the end, and you didn't worry about bringing the kids, for other than the gratuitous violence and some thinly veiled sexual innuendo, there wasn't anything in these movies to hurt them.

Cowboy movies weren't good history lessons. I suppose they weren't really intended to be, for fantasy is generally more entertaining than history. And there was all that messiness about invading and killing off entire populations of Native Americans that so many of us are all embarrassed about these days. But, since the victors get to write history, I guess that lets them make the movies, too.

They don't make movies like that anymore. They make other kinds of movies. You might have heard of one of them, a feature called *Fractured Spine Hill* or some such. It is sort of a cowboy movie, supposedly set in Wyoming, and it is getting all kinds of attention these days. The critics love it, the Oscars will probably be headed that way, and everybody is talking about it.

The part where it's not really a cowboy movie, but actually a sheep herder movie got lost in the shuffle. This takes us to the stereotype thing again. Everybody knows about cowboys, and has preconceived notions about cowboys, and the two characters in this movie don't act anything like those stereotypical cowboys. I think the makers probably intended to portray this contrast, because this likely was the whole point of making and promoting this movie.

And I guess when these two sheep herders go to town together, unlike those stereotypical cowboys of old, the townsfolk won't have to lock up their daughters for safekeeping.

These two characters are who they are... that's all. And somebody made a movie about them. And that's fine with me. Like people actually say in Wyoming, "They can do as they like, just so they don't scare the horses." If this one sells, somebody will no doubt keep making similar movies, although I suspect they will even if it doesn't sell. I probably won't watch those either.

They've made a few movies where the Indians are portrayed in a more realistic light, and some of these were even worth watching. I suspect someone was trying to make amends for all that genocide we laid on the Native Americans over a hundred years ago. Those tribes were treated rather shabbily by our ancestors. Except for a few tribes that were relegated to reservations in wastelands that had that sticky black stuff oozing out of the ground, most of the surviving tribes have had it kinda tough.

This is changing these days. One way you can tell is that many tribes now have enough cash floating around to bribe senators and members of congress. We are not talking chump change here, for although they are as predictable as John Wayne, our politicians don't work cheap. But this is how the tribes got all those casinos built, where they are currently exacting revenge on the descendants of the folks that ran them off their lands.

A few of these tribes hired that lobbyist Abramoff to spread their graft around. A big fuss was raised over the news that most of these bribes went to Republican crooks this time instead of Democrat crooks. Some would suggest that the Republicans are bigger crooks.

I'm not sure this is true. I was thinking it was more likely that this was just because the Republicans are in charge now, and the Democrats aren't likely to replace them any time soon, so the tribes just don't want to waste their money.

February 19, 2006

Saying Proper Thanks To A Very Brave Man

Inspector Raymond Joseph Giacomelli was shot and killed by a recent parolee while conducting a murder investigation on April 15, 2003. Bob made clear on many occasions, including this one, how he felt about allowing criminals to chronically engage in criminal behavior. (RG)

The defense attorney ejected me from the jury panel. Excused for cause, I believe, was the jargon.

I had been invited to a criminal trial that was going to be resolved solely on whether the jury members believed the uncorroborated testimony of the defendant… or the police officer. The two sides of course, disagreed about certain things.

The defense attorney didn't want anyone around who might actually believe a cop.

This is the American system of justice, after all. Innocent until proven guilty. Better a hundred guilty go free rather than one innocent be convicted unjustly. This is the system that patriots fought and died to create and then preserve over the last two and a quarter centuries. I often argue that it is the best in the world, but I also sometimes regret that it is the one we are stuck with.

For this is the system that turns so many criminals back onto the streets to continue their depredation upon society.

The defense attorney asked each jury panel member whether they were related to, partied with, or in any other way knew any cops. I guess he figured if we knew even one, we might just believe something they would say. The defense attorney was looking for the rest, the ones he assumed would automatically distrust cops. He hoped to pack the jury with people he could con into releasing the defendant.

People don't really sort themselves into two distinct groups over this matter. Ask a random set of people about cops, and the approval/disapproval ratings range all over the place. But if you mention the OJ Simpson murder trial you get something of a litmus test. He is guilty, or not, based solely on whether you like or dislike cops. Sometimes it's as simple as that.

This defense attorney wanted nothing to do with me because I work with a few police dogs. I guess he figured I wasn't on his side. He was, of course, right.

I got the phone call shortly after midnight. It was a remarkably unremarkable night up to that point for me, but everything changed in an instant. One of the service dogs had been killed, and the cops needed my help.

One of Pittsburg's less stellar citizens got whipped in a fight and decided he was mad at the world, so he barricaded himself in an upstairs bedroom with half a dozen guns and took a few random shots out the window. He screamed to anyone who chose to listen that he was going to kill somebody. Nobody doubted him.

The ACLU didn't show up in the middle of the night to stop him. Neither did any defense attorneys.

Only the cops showed up.

The filthy, dimly lit house was cluttered with kids' toys, and it reeked of cigarette smoke and booze and death when they let me in to pick up the dog's body. The man killed the dog with a rifle that would have defeated the body armor the cops wore, so if one of them had gone in instead of the dog, we would have lost yet another officer in the line of duty.

Twenty years later the memory of this house still gives me the willies. I don't know where cops find the courage, but they willingly go into dangerous situations like this night after night.

A jury actually convicted this man, and as far as I can tell, he hasn't hurt a law abiding citizen the whole time he has been in prison. The officer who handled this dog was a good guy, but he got out of police work after this. I can't say I blame him.

Despite the danger and difficulty, another Pittsburg police officer, Ray Giacomelli, showed up for work for 23 years. He was part of the thin line of officers who stand between us and that group of people out there who just won't play by the rules. He went into dark, dangerous holes after the bad ones. He built the cases against murderers in order to send them away to prison, and thus gave us a world that was just a little safer for our kids.

I never met Inspector Giacomelli, but I imagine he felt the same frustration other officers have expressed when "the system" turned loose criminals that by all rights should never again see the light of day. It was one of these that ambushed him last week.

And I can only wonder if he sometimes questioned his role when he bumped into citizens who had no appreciation for the tough work he did.

I hope he knew that some of us do.

Thank you, Ray Giacomelli.

April 24, 2003

Part Three:
X Number of Mornings

Key To The City

Enjoy this edition of Bob's palpable love of our national parks. He also alludes to the government shutdown of 2013 that closed a number of the parks for a time. (RG)

I don't remember when I first saw a film clip of the mayor of New York City handing over the symbolic Key To The City to some famous person. I'm sure I was a kid, and all the pomp and ceremony probably confused me a bit. The actual symbolic Key was over-sized and ornate. Banners draped the podium. Bands played. Citizenry cheered. Folks wore formal clothing, and flashbulbs popped, and carefully practiced smiles filled the view.

The Key To The City opened every door in the place, the ultimate in, "Welcome to our city; it's yours to enjoy!" It was the finest compliment a city could convey upon a person who had done something so admirable that no other gift would suffice.

I don't expect to ever stand before a mayor to receive such an honor. Heck, I wouldn't know what to do with a Key to New York or Chicago or L.A. Sure, it would open every door, but I wouldn't know why. What does one do in a city, anyway? I don't have a clue.

But don't worry about me. I'm up for an award this Saturday that I worked long and hard to achieve, and it will open many doors for me that I will appreciate far more.

My award is called the "America The Beautiful - National Parks and Federal Recreational Lands Pass - Senior Pass." It's the ultimate, "Welcome to our parks; they're yours to enjoy." No mayor will be presenting. Neither banner draped podium nor noisy band, neither cheering citizenry nor pomp and ceremony will clutter up the event. And no one will need to put on a tie or practice their smile. I will be smiling, but I have no need to practice. It will no doubt come naturally.

Oh, and it won't be happening in some city. I get to pick the site, and it came down to two. One might have been more cherished than the other, but only by a smidge. But the first is a thousand miles farther away, which would make for a long weekend. So we will travel to Yosemite instead, and at the Big Oak Flat Entrance Station the trees will tower overhead, birds will flit through the shrubs, a deer may watch from the shadows, and I'll hand over my ten bucks and the driver's license that proves my age, and I'll receive my Key. And all I had to do to earn it was live for 62 years. Difficult and admirable, yes… but doable.

The View From Here

They used to call this award the "Golden Age Pass," but that made too much sense, so they changed it to that much more verbose "America The Beautiful-etc." Either will get me into every national park, national monument, and the other federal recreation lands for free for the rest of my days, as well as shave off some of my campground fees, boat launching fees, and a few other expenses associated with having a good time on federal land. Just flash the card and wander through the gate, and Yosemite, Yellowstone, Grand Teton, Rocky Mountain, Glacier, and all the rest of our national parks can be mine.

And as we stand in awe somewhere in Yosemite Valley this weekend, and the mountain light flashes off the granite and the waterfalls rumble and the river burbles, my heart will swell and my eyes will glisten. And this will happen every time I visit until I no longer can crawl that far. This will be a treasured gift that will last the balance of a lifetime.

Unless they close the damn government, and my parks with it. That will most likely really annoy me this weekend. You'd think if they can run the government trillions of dollars into the red each and every year (without giving reality a thought), and far worse than that if we keep that most recent idiot in charge, they could keep the parks open one more weekend just for me.

July 8, 2011

If Wishes Could Make It So

This ran soon after Bob left the paper and before he left on a vacation. (RG)

Well, I guess I don't have an editor anymore, so this is the director's cut.

When I was a mere lad, the Sears catalog was the size of a big city phone book, and if memory serves, it showed up several times each year. And it was full of *everything!* There was clothing for men, women, and kids. Tools, oh lord, there were tools. If you knew what you wanted and what you were doing, somebody said you could build an entire Model T Ford right out of the Sears catalog, one part at a time.

After the new catalog arrived in the winter, I'd find the toys right away. Tons of toys. And just in time for Christmas fantasy. I lusted for those toys. And you could buy a bolt action .22 rifle for just a few bucks. I lusted after those, too. And motorcycles! You could buy a motorcycle from a catalog! And when I got a little older, there was that *huge* section with nothing but lady's underwear, and that's a subject for some other essay, but yeah, I lusted after that once, too.

Sears doesn't send out catalogs anymore. Now I have a computer on my desk, and every morning before the workday begins I fire up that time and travel machine and go to bookmarks, and punch up codywy.org, and there live my webcams. And I get to look at downtown Cody, with no traffic to speak of on the main drag, and then down the page I go to Jackson Town Center with its elk antler arch, and then up to the return to webcams button, and I get to look at the Tetons through a bunch of different cameras, and then I look at Mammoth Hot Springs in Yellowstone where sometimes I can see bison or elk lounging about, and Old Faithful, and a bunch of other neat places, and I lust after it all.

A couple of weeks ago it snowed in the mountains of Wyoming, and I watched that on the webcams, and I went nuts over that. And now each day with my 'puter I monitor the onset of autumn color, as the cottonwoods and underbrush begin to change, and now finally the aspens are chiming in. And I lust after that. And I note that the color is late this year, and that means maybe, just maybe, we will find a lot of that color when we get to Wyoming next week.

I've got that anticipation ache in my gut just thinking about it. It's like getting the new Sears catalog. The options are not only endless, but they are all good. We get to go to Wyoming for a whole week! I have tags for pronghorn, and I'm hunting a good area, so the prospect for some fine wild game meat for the freezer are excellent. We should be able to get to Cody to have a cup of coffee on our property and say, "Hi!" to a few friends. We will probably get to see Yellowstone and Grand Teton again. And with any luck, I will have time to show Joie some really neat places, like Mt. Rushmore and The Badlands and Devil's Tower. I am excited beyond belief.

I'm hoping for aspen color at Angel Creek, just out of Wells, NV, which is our first night's stop. And there might well be color along the North Platte, where there should be lots of cottonwoods. And I want to see Teapot Dome, the source of one of the first of many major corruption scandals that set the precedent for the sad state of our current government.

Wyoming has over 500,000 pronghorns, more than the total human population, and 25,000 of them reside in my hunt area. Game and Fish offers over 2,000 tags for my area, and I have two. I have both rifles sighted in, the newer 7 magnum and the old 6 Remington that dates back to the early '50s. I've taken two pronghorn so far with the six mm, and it is my sentimental favorite.

I've made my lists and the gear is coming together. I checked the oil in the truck, and the windshield washer jug is full of the freeze proof cleaner stuff. Soon all I will need to do is plug in the GPS and the CB radio, and we will be backing down the driveway. I cannot wait. Anticipation is such sweet torture.

July 14, 2011

Entering Wyoming

If you have an iPad handy, or you're reading this near a desktop computer, dial up a map of Wyoming, and let your eyes wander back and forth from these pages to the map. (RG)

If you are so inclined, you can sneak into Wyoming without immediately seeing how beautiful the state is. Crossing the border after traversing Nebraska on I-80 might be a relief after 400 miles of sunflowers and those things so boring they make sunflowers seem interesting, but that entrance is not beautiful. Eventually, you get to the good parts, but I-80 from the east is not it.

But if you leave South Dakota and Mount Rushmore, and head west into Wyoming, you pass through the Black Hills, which is some very nice country, and you'll have Devil's Tower for an exclamation point that you won't soon forget.

Wander down from Montana, the Little Bighorn Battlefield and Custer's error in judgment, past the quiet, comfortable town of Dayton, with high plains on your left and the Bighorn Mountains on the right, and you can take any turn and the beauty is everywhere you go.

Gardiner, Montana is the northern gateway into Yellowstone, and I need say nothing more. If you cannot find beauty in that park, we have nothing to talk about. The town of West Yellowstone points you into the west side of the park, and that's even better. Meander alongside the rapids on the Madison River, past the young forests that are healing the scars left by the fires, and watch for moose in the shallows and eagles in the trees. If you only spot the herds of elk and a few bison on the road, don't feel as if you missed too much.

From Idaho you can hop over Teton Pass or meander through Swan Valley along the Snake River. The Teton Range is just around the corner, and you could spend the rest of your life trying to find finer scenery, and you will fail.

The first time you see these places, you will promise yourself that you will win the lottery, or scheme some way to live there somehow, and so passing through any of these entrances will always feel like coming home. You want to see them in the spring, summer, autumn, and winter, for each season brings new beauty to your senses, and you will anticipate the next trip every single day until you can do it again.

That still leaves I-80 entering the state from the west, and you don't want to miss this either. Just as you leave Utah, you climb into a pleasant canyon, with lush forest and inviting meadows on one side and a garish display of red sandstone cliffs on the other, with the trucks lugging up the hill in the right lane, and the trains chugging up their tracks alongside on the left, and you smile knowing you aren't in Kansas anymore, or California for that matter. The first time we came in this way was about five years ago, after using all those other entrances for over 40 years. Now we look forward to this one, too.

Eventually the canyon ends and you emerge onto sage covered plain. The horizon is suddenly a long way off, and the first pronghorns appear way out there on the right. In case you cannot tell, the wind reminds you... you are in Wyoming.

We entered the state this way a few weeks ago. Autumn color highlighted the canyon this time. I wanted to explore each and every side canyon, but we had many miles to go and that diversion would have to wait for another time.

A brisk wind pushed us across the high plain as storm clouds scudded across the horizon ahead. Small groups of pronghorns dotted the sage covered ground. We even saw a lone moose out for an afternoon stroll just east of Evanston. We didn't stop until

Rawlins, where pronghorns grazed on lawns and in vacant lots at the edge of town. Collapsing there for the night, we anticipated the morning drive, for it promised even better.

Sunday morning found us groggily sucking down coffee in a friendly local restaurant, where I indulged myself in one of those skillet breakfasts that I would regret later when reacquainting with the scale upon returning to work. Back in the pickup, I found NPR on the satellite radio, and the chatter of the Car Guys entertained us while motoring north. We crossed the Continental Divide twice, dropping into and the climbing out of the Divide Basin. Pastures on both sides of the road supported herds of Hereford cattle, and just about every time we turned our gaze left or right, we spotted more groups of pronghorns.

The occasional mountain loomed in the distance, and then numerous rock escarpments took over the scenery. Soon we were in one of those many gorgeous settings that Wyoming offers, with the Pathfinder Reservoir tucked into the valley to our right, with vertical rock walls rising above, and then the North Platte River dipped under our highway, lined by cottonwoods busily changing into their autumn wardrobes, and dotted by those perennial optimists and their flicking fly rods.

North of Casper we entered a vast grassland, preserved now under the name of Thunder Basin. Looking across this plain, I wondered about those many settlers who walked alongside Conestoga wagons through this eternity 150 years ago, putting in ten miles or so every day for months to get this far away from the East. And here we were knocking off 1,300 miles in a weekend.

I've often referred to Wyoming as a time warp, a place where we can return to an America of thirty years ago, a time I can understand far better than the contradiction we must now endure. The radio talked of some politician's scheme to raise money for the state by charging the tourists a toll to drive the state's roads. Said money would be directed to road maintenance, a plot that almost makes sense, even to a passionate tax hater like me. I like Wyoming so much, I'd probably pay it. Wyoming voted it down.

In California, as Herb Cane often observed, we are charged admission to get into San Francisco by the tollbooths on all those bridges leading there. Here we pay road taxes that never go to maintain the roads, but instead disappear into the morass of entitlements and government waste and corruption. We have the worst roads in the nation, and no one even questions this, as this confused state staggers into an uncertain future.

And I sit here thinking about Wyoming every single day, and it is worse now, because in a week we will go there again. I'm having trouble staying patient.

August 3, 2011

Lessons From The Truck

Notes from I-5, and beyond...

I could learn a lesson or two from the truck.

I was worried over nothing. It was one of my classic worries. Would we get to the campground early enough to get a site or would it be full already? My mind... it was too busy conjuring up what-ifs. You know, with my luck there would be only one campsite left on this three day holiday weekend, and it would be too small for the trailer and truck, or just too difficult to back the rig into because of one tree or a rock in the wrong place. And then I'd have to conjure up someplace else to camp and keep on driving when I wanted to stop, when I'd already be tired and cranky. I had my heart set on this place. Grumble, grumble... worry, worry, worry. You know how I get.

We pulled the trailer along with us to the clinic on Friday morning so we could leave right at closing time. Driving over Kirker Pass first thing that morning, I realized just how happy the truck was to be working again. With the truck it's all about the journey. The destination is not important. Destination is just another place to park while everybody else gets to have fun. Trucks have to be patient when parked. Nothin' else to do.

Now pulling a trailer... that's a worthwhile endeavor for a truck. You can tell he likes it. Driving daily, empty, back and forth to work and home is no trick. Heck, he can idle along in sixth gear to get us there and not break a sweat. Packing a load makes him happy. The trailer makes him happy. You can hear it in the suddenly joyful rumble from the exhaust. He was made for this. That gear selector is meaningless without a load, but when ya pack him up, all those gear ratios start to make sense. Set him to work on a long uphill grade and he leans into the harness and the grin spreads across his grill.

Heck, when loaded, the truck even likes long, boring I-5.

In the dark, in the rain, in the Central Valley, there's not much to see, but I can still notice things. Cruise control set on a few over legal, we plod along in the number two lane while the crazies wail past on the left, cut us off to pass two minivans on the right, and then zip back into the hammer lane in time to slam on the brakes again behind the next idiot who is only going fifteen over the limit. Maybe two seconds shaved off a six hour trip. The truck is a slow and steady kinda dude. Down the long, seemingly endless ribbon of asphalt he rumbles. Content just to pull.

That collection of fast food outlets, closed fruit stands that lean a bit in the wind, cheap motels, and peddlers of fossil fuel at each freeway exit is like one frame, where the miles of interstate highway filled with vehicles is the movie. It gives you a slice of the whole, frozen for the time it takes to fill a tank, a stomach, and a toilet. In such places you get to meet the people who infest all those cars you saw lined up, lights stretching to the horizon in the dark. And if you are not careful, or just a bit bored, you might draw conclusions from these brief encounters.

Like:

- Whoever coined the term "the dumbing down of America" was like, totally right. Apparently, even though the process of taking an order, nuking a burger, stacking the right stuff on a bun, and getting the correct collection of unhealthy food into the correct bag has been simplified beyond all reason, as a society we can no longer produce anyone clever enough to do even this rudimentary task in a timely manner.

- Nobody speaks English in this country anymore, and that includes the folks born and edjumacated here.

- Milling around in a colorful crowd in the confined space in front of the hamburger store counter, waiting ever so patiently for two hamburgers, fries and diet sodas, I looked around at my fellow travelers. Taking up two tables, a family of Southern California typecast, stamped from the mold just like everybody else, talked among themselves, oblivious to the poor lady calling out their number, two bags of burgers dangling from her hands. Back under the heat lamps the bags went.

- Save for the plastic people and me, everyone in the building was Hispanic, and most stood quietly, looking around furtively, waiting to get caught and sent back to whatever hopelessness they had fled, hoping to do better as slaves here. One guy was duded out in black cowboy hat, pearl button shirt, serving plate belt buckle and *tight* jeans, with his Saturday night boots on. He was skinny as a rail. Everybody else was fat, especially the too many kids and the moms with the blank looks. They waited patiently for their food. They looked like they have survived on patience for an eternity. They tolerated the wretched inefficiency of the place much better than I.

- The lady behind the counter called out #31 again, and this time Barb and Ken and The Kids heard, and he quickly fetched their dinner. By that point the pictures of the burgers on the sign likely would taste better, but they hardly noticed as they crammed rubbery burgers into their orthodontically perfect mouths.

- Remember the time long ago when the guy selling you gas could also fix your car? Well, don't try that now. That product of California schools behind the counter in the gas station mini-mall sold me well aged coffee, but when I mentioned the condition of the bathrooms to her, her blank face lost even more detail, 'cause that wasn't her job, *you know*.

California collects taxes on all that fuel you buy, specifically intended to keep the roads in some semblance of repair, but for years, in case you haven't noticed, they haven't spent much on road repair. All that tax money has gone into the general toilet, er fund, and the roads have been left to rot. And boy can you tell. I-5 is just a bit smoother than a slightly used minefield.

Back on the road it doesn't get much better. Really strange people call talk radio in the dark when you are trapped on that endless black ribbon in the rain. At first you shake your head in disbelief, but to change the station is the only true coping mechanism. Problem is, in the valley in the dark the only choices seem to be whether you get to listen to idiots in our language, or in Spanish.

Satellite radio helps. It offers some choice in the listening. We dialed up the Road Dog, the professional truckers channel on Sirius. Plodding along in the two lane pulling the trailer eventually lends itself to listening to the truckers as they complain about us. An item on their news broadcast: A professional clown was elected to the Brazilian senate. His campaign slogan? "What the heck, it can't get any worse." Along with the lady porn star who was once elected to national office in Italy, it would seem that we all get the governments we deserve, or at least that our choices in characters running the place are somewhat limited. The rest of the news simply follows from this.

We turned left at Bakersfield. Bakersfield is best done in the dark. It smells the same, but ya can't see as much. Consider that a blessing.

Surrounded by generica, the Walmart parking lot was dotted with parked RV's. Nice new rigs used by retired people who have nosed the grindstone, done well in their lives, and can now reap some of the reward, at least until the price of diesel destroys their lifelong plans, sat next to some less inspiring vehicles no doubt occupied by artists, writers, or similar bums. With our well-seasoned trailer, we are almost ready to blend in with that second group for our golden years. We joined them all for a few hours of sleep. Then in the early hours of a fresh day we gave the diesel its head as we trotted over Tehachapi Pass. Mike's Cafe waited for us in Mojave.

Breakfast at Mike's can happen all day long, and it's worth the price. Don't tell 'em, but they could hit you up for a cover charge just for the entertainment. The old pedal cars still line the shelf rimming the place high on the wall. We'd love to learn the stories of each of these treasures. They each made some kid happy on a birthday or Christmas, and those kids are now old or gone, and ya wonder if they remember those times.

Our harried waitress was a short, chubby, perky young Hispanic lady in a low cut blouse, with a red, white and blue American flag tattooed on the, uh, left one. The café was crowded, and the patrons kept her flag waving as she hurried about the room.

They have thin paperback books on the tables, humor writing revolving around coping with life's little trials. The book I was sampling was titled, "Things To Say To Idiots." Ben Goode, the author has much to tell and y'all could benefit from his observations. The one sentence I read while waiting on my pile of home fries, eggs, salsa, and spicy sliced beefsteak had something to do with folks who think like they have had their brains pierced, too. I figured I could use that description sometime, and I would be sure to give credit where due for this brilliance. (I wonder if Mr. Goode now lives in a tilting, rusting, seen-better-days RV?)

The loud, crude guy at the booth in the corner was complaining to his friends about how he had just been diagnosed with diabetes, and no he wasn't gonna do all that silly stuff they wanted to force him to do to take care of himself. His friends were trying to talk some sense into his head, but it would have been pretty lonely in there. Sometimes, I have learned, the less some people know about something, the louder they proclaim their ignorance. This guy did a splendid job with that.

The quiet, older fellow in the next booth got up to leave, and he turned to wish the mouth well as he passed. He hobbled in serious pain, thanks to his diabetic neuropathy, he said, and he now viewed a murky world through bottle thick glasses. He mentioned this to the loud mouthed lout, along with a statement that the narcotic pain meds he was compelled to take had just about wrecked his life. This fate, or worse, would be the stubborn man's own if he didn't listen to his (our, since we likely paid for them) doctors. The lout's only retort was that he had once been a junkie, so he knew all about that, and he didn't much care. Shaking his head, the gentleman left the mullet behind.

Mr. Tard was annoyed and annoying, but he soon got up with his friends to leave. Watching him, I believe he did have a brain piercing to go with his tats and backwards ball cap. I shook my head, too. He had been offered good advice, and it was nothing to get pithed about. He left the place clouded in uncomfortable silence, having wasted all that oxygen while he was there.

I-15 was like I-5, except the traffic ran much faster. It looked like all of Southern California was needed in Vegas, and they were all in a hurry to get there. We let 'em go on without us at a lonely exit, and traded crowded asphalt for a far more primitive path.

Three miles, plus or minus, of washboard gravel road. All the way up to third gear on the straight-a-ways. Enough inconvenience to keep most of the rabble out. Most everybody on the interstate was headed toward a city. We weren't. Nobody else was on this road, even though for a while you could see the cars on the freeway in the mirror, so we hadn't gone far. Fifteen miles an hour and still the fillings rattled in our teeth. Lovely desert desolation on all sides. Round the last corner and we could see the silver cantilever bridge where the railroad crosses the river, and the bushes where the Phainopeplas perch and chirp, and the campground. Nearly empty. All that worry for nothing. I felt better, but we disappointed our truck. Parked for a day of nothing but reading, writing, napping and looking. He will get over it.

Rain drummed on the trailer that night as we slept. The wind pummeled. A few trains rumbled past in the dark. Dreams came and went, odd dreams fueled by the crud dump happening in my brain as it realized it was free to do what was necessary to fix that which was bent in my head, out in the desert and the empty. You will need to reboot when the delete process is complete. And make a cup of strong coffee in the morning.

Morning quiet. Pink clouds. Wet ground. Slaked vegetation. A desert cottontail runs through the campsite. Someday, if he doesn't learn to stay under cover, he will make that hawk over there very happy.

It always rains when we go to the desert. This time it snowed on Mountain Pass, and the Joshua trees and yucca wore a mantle of white, which is kinda weird. Southern Californians stopped on the freeway shoulder to take pictures of each other in front of the strange white stuff. Brief stops, because they don't do cold.

Everybody on earth was in Vegas that weekend. I'm happy for the merchants. Even those, uh, affiliated folks who profit, win or lose, through the decades in this God forsaken place. Those prognosticators on the news who tell us the economy is getting better, or simply doomed, should see this place. It's either the mercury rising or the end of the world is at hand, take your pick, but the decadence is thriving. Crowds of wide-eyed tourists mobbed the Strip, a mass orgy of imitation fun, which will all stay in Vegas when they leave, along with piles of their dollars.

We left Vegas, and that was clearly the best part of our time there. I should learn from this. When leaving Vegas becomes the highlight of the trip, it's time to find another place to go to put in my time listening to those lectures I need. The oppression of the city spilled off our shoulders as we ran screaming away from that place. And right outside of there was the glory of the colored hills surrounding Lake Mead and the wonder of the new bridge at Hoover Dam, and short hours later we were camped in the desert again, listening to a babbling stream. In a land of improbably colored rocks, Saguaro cactus, ocotillo, cholla, and blue herons we found a flat spot, turned on the songs, and watched the sun course toward the southwest, and I found some words again instead of just the frustration of a blank computer screen. It takes so little with me. I should learn from this, too.

August 15, 2011

The Window Seat

I prefer a window seat. All those rumors regarding my alleged agoraphobic and antisocial tendencies notwithstanding, I prefer a window seat for the view from the airplane. So if you note that I sometimes open said window and stick my head out and scream, well that has nothing to do with how much I enjoy being *trapped* in an aluminum tube for any length of time. No, it's just about grabbing a bit of fresh air, and taking a peek around.

We did a touch and go to Germany last week. A United 747 carried us from San Francisco to Frankfurt, and the 777 brought us home, and I had window seats both ways.

We stayed long enough to watch the kids get married, and for me to eat all of the German food in that fair city. The local citizens were likely happy to see me leave, as they now face famine until the next crop of sauerkraut and schnitzel comes in. I can only imagine the horror our pilot must have felt as the end of the Frankfurt runway rapidly approached, and his aircraft was struggling to lift my newly acquired weight off the ground.

I enjoy the view of our earth from high above. I pull out the road atlas prior to any flight and imprint into my brain the landmarks that I will watch for as we fly over. I like to look for places I've seen from the ground, and for the big landmarks, like Half Dome and the Grand Canyon. Once I spotted a dirt road in the Nevada desert that I had bounced over in the truck years earlier. So I was looking forward to this aspect of the long flights to and back from Germany.

We took off headed north, veered to the left of San Francisco and quickly banked directly over the Golden Gate Bridge, heading northeast. Gorgeous as usual. And then we ran into the clouds. I already knew what clouds looked like from the inside, so this was no thrill for me. But the bigger disappointment arrived when the flight attendants asked all us window sitters to pull down the shades to darken the cabin, just in case anyone aboard wanted to sleep all the way to Germany to somehow help cope with those nine time zones in between. So except for those few moments when I cheated and peeked under a barely opened window shade, I couldn't watch much of where we were going.

During those peeks, I saw some Idaho mountains, and what I figured was North Dakota. Not too many large landmarks in North Dakota except the Missouri River. And then the water soaked center of Canada rolled by below us. In between movies, the big screen at the front of the plane showed a GPS map of our flight, and some pertinent facts relating to our progress. Over Ontario we enjoyed a 120 mile per hour tailwind, which nudged our ground speed up to 720 MPH. I snuck a peek out the window just as we left the sun behind, and somebody's contrail glowed pale pink just below us on the starboard side. And then it got real dark outside.

Somewhere over the Atlantic, between Iceland and Ireland, we found the sun again. I was sitting on the shady side of the aircraft, so I missed out on the actual sunrise, but the colors cast upon the clouds below did not disappoint. Remember the last time the washing machine overflowed, and those billowing puddles of suds spread across your new hardwood floor? Well, that's what these clouds looked like from above. Only ours were spread over an already wet ocean so they didn't wreck anything, and they were turning pink to red just for me, and the pilots, 'cause they didn't have screens over their windows.

The movie screen said we were at 43,000 feet altitude, and the outside temperature was -60°F, so I left the window closed.

Scattered cirrus clouds well above the cumulous puddles turned color first, and then the billowing ones below got the treatment. Another airliner, following a parallel path a few miles to the south, glinted silver when painted by the sun. Those poor folks who actually got some sleep on our plane missed the show. For their sake, I pulled down the shade again.

August 16, 2011

Winter Rains Scare Tourists, Bring Special Beauty To The Coast

The north coast is greener in the winter. There aren't nearly as many flowers, and I didn't see any goldfinches, so I missed those colors, but boy, was it green.

The grasses were green, as were all the other ground dwelling plants. Green moss painted the rocks and trees. The evergreen trees were even greener than they are in the summer. And those lichens that dangled from tree branches, looking like Spanish moss even though they weren't, were also green.

In summer, like elsewhere in this state, the coastal hills shimmer under a hot sun in shades of brown and gold. Now they are brilliant green, and the low-angle sun that strikes them when they are still heavy with droplets of moisture fires up the color and they glitter in the light. The sheep on the slopes are white; they look like marshmallows scattered on the velvet of a new pool table.

The green and those droplets of moisture are a consequence of the rain. The rain is a presence this time of year. You cannot be bothered by little things like storms if you wish to enjoy the Mendocino coast this time of year. Storms are the condiments that season this season, and the water brings the place alive.

Storms can be tedious if you are sleeping in a tent, and when viewed through the window of a motel a downpour is little different from what we see around here. But in our small trailer, with the drumming of a heavy shower on the roof and the gentle rocking induced by a nudge of wind, you can remain dry but still feel like you are part of the scene.

Rain fell on and off all afternoon and into the night. It was a hot chocolate, tea and good book kind of day. The sky tap shut off often enough to walk the dogs, so they didn't mind. And in the depth of the night, when the clouds cleared for a bit, the stars pierced a black sky with an intensity you never get to see down here in the light-polluted places.

Most of the tourists have gone south for the winter, so the campground and the roads were lonely, which is how we like them. Apparently the hawks from up north did a similar migration, for the telephone poles and fences posts were festooned with these big birds. Which is also how we like it.

The storms bring with them larger waves, which roared against the beach and exploded against the rocks. Kodachrome is no more, but these were such moments.

December 29, 2009

California Winter

A hint of winter scented the air. That got my attention. The dogs and I were outside the clinic, taking care of matters. The dogs probably noticed it before me, but I don't know what it meant to them, 'cause they just carried on. It meant a lot to me.

Each year the experts try to convince me that winter has something to do with the circuit of the sun around the earth (or was that the other way around?) or some date on a calendar. But they must be looking at things in a different way. For me... well I go out and sniff the air. That generally tells me when winter is at hand.

A day earlier, those cirrus clouds we call mare's tails went scudding by. That would portend a change in the weather, usually rain if you must know. And in California, rain almost always means winter. Standing there, waiting for dog requirements to finish, I noted the gunmetal ceiling overhead, and I smelled the cool damp. Definitely, rain coming. And I took my change of clothing out of the car and stashed them in the clinic, so I would not have to go outside to do it after the precipitation began. Clever me.

I don't usually need a change of clothing after work, but we were leaving for Wyoming when the day elapsed, and we both dressed for cold. The Weather Channel suggested it would be snowing on Donner Summit when we were planning on passing through, and I've tried that before on a Friday night, so I also packed emergency rations, sleeping bags, and the other survival necessities, just in case the short drive turned into an ordeal.

California doesn't cope well with weather. When things get hairy, parts of it tend to fall off. Californians do worse. Three-quarters of an inch of snow on the interstate leading up to Donner sends Californians into panic. Any more than that, and you'd think the world had come to its end. The game of bumper cars soon follows. Cal-Trans puts on the chain restrictions to slow folks down for those crashes, but tire chains do not make people smarter, and neither does buying a four-wheel drive SUV.

So after wasting too much awhile at the first chain control station, and then fidgeting for an hour at the second, we parked in our lanes in the middle of nowhere-in-particular, waiting while the wreckers and ambulance passed us on the shoulder and disappeared ahead. Another hour. And then they let us go forward.

We proceeded cautiously, trying to anticipate which Californians would do something fundamentally wrong on the slippery snow, and thus put their rides sideways in front of us. I managed to miss those who did. Meanwhile we enjoyed the snowfall, and the flocked trees, and the scent of winter.

Our boots crunched on snow and ice in the motel parking lot in Idaho on Sunday morning. The locks on the cover that hides the bed of the truck were frozen into obstinacy, and the windshield defroster faced a daunting task. Those new deerskin gloves I bought just for driving came in handy, and they smelled real good. When you need four-wheel drive just to get out of a parking lot, that is also a hint of winter.

My nose finally convinced me that winter was truly at hand as we stood atop that snowy ridge late Monday afternoon, binoculars dancing over the surrounding mountainsides seeking the elusive elk. The fire blazed away beside me, turning the wood we pruned from a dead snag into welcome warmth, and sending sweet smoke up to me. Campfire in the snow. Yep... winter has arrived.

The thermometer read -23°F at Wednesday dawn, and the intense blue of the sky bewildered my senses. Ground fog hovered by the base of the mountains, and half a foot of fresh snow as fine as volcanic ash cloaked my truck. But it was the light that captured me. I remembered the light from those below zero days when I was young. It was so intense and so pure that even as a naïve waif I recognized the wonder of it. And it was so good to experience it again.

September 15, 2011

Appreciating The Pioneers Of Mountaineering

I still have a couple of pairs of my old hiking socks. I pull them out only during hunting season, because they fit between my feet and the old heavy boots better than my newer socks. In my backpacking days, they were just the trick for coping with the rubbing and pounding of those long miles spent lugging a 45-pound load along rocky mountain trails. They are thick gray wool, with a bright, one-inch wide band of red at the top. That bright red band attracted the hummingbird.

We were taking a breather after we had crested a shallow saddle at about 12,000 feet, rounded the ridge, and then wandered up a wide valley to about 500 feet higher. Our backpacks rested on sandy soil off to one side while we leaned back against the softest rocks we could find, munching down granola bars. Brilliant high altitude sunshine bombarded us from an unnaturally deep blue high altitude sky. The valley dropped away to the west, past Big Brewer Lake and down Brewer Creek. If memory serves, that was the route taken by William Brewer when he first climbed Mt. Brewer, way back in 1864.

A flash of emerald green caught my eye. The hummingbird hovered next to the red band of my right sock. We froze and watched. A hummingbird was about the last thing we expected to see up there. He perched ever so softly on my ankle before flitting off. Hummingbirds don't weigh very much at all.

We thought that was pretty neat. The last trees were nearly a thousand feet lower on the slope beyond our feet, as timberline was about 11,200 feet. Except for a few columbine and monkey flowers near the rare watercourse, we had seen no flowers to attract the little bird. I suppose he was just passing through, and that red band on my sock caught his eye. There was no nectar in my hiking sock (no kidding!), so he didn't stay long. And then he flashed away.

The open slope upon which we sat ended above us in a jumble of rocks between Mt. Brewer and a peak called North Guard, both of which we planned to climb. Spectacular as it was, the place was a bit of a moonscape, with no significant landmarks close by. So although I carried the topographical map, knowing my correct altitude involved some guesswork.

Sure, I wore a digital watch that doubled as a thermometer and an altimeter. The altimeter ran off a pressure sensor on the side of the watch. The higher we climbed, the less pressure the column of air above us, rising to the edge of space, would bear on our heads. The watch's altimeter simply measured the pressure and then calculated our altitude. So as long as the weather didn't present a rise or drop in pressure, we could read an accurate altitude off that digital watch.

Brewer and his party had a similar problem when they climbed the peak. They had two of those big heavy wood and glass barometers that were all the rage in 1864. Sealed within each was a colored liquid that changed height within a glass tube in response to air pressure changes, so as they climbed, the liquid level also changed, and the marks on the glass told the men their altitude. Except... when the weather changed.

This was a survey expedition, and these were scientists as well as adventurers, so they wanted to measure the height of the mountain, and do this accurately. Since their climb took several days, they were assured that the weather would change and thus introduce inaccuracy to their measurements. So they used two barometers, one that they carried along on their climb, and a second that stayed behind at a base camp at a known altitude. Measurements were taken with both at the same times each day, and as the weather changed the readings of the barometer at the base camp, the readings taken with the climbing one could later be adjusted to the same degree, so its altitude readings would be more accurate.

Obviously, they couldn't get a mountain's measurements down to the inch this way, but looking back, they didn't do badly. Standing atop each mountain, they could look out at dozens of peaks of nearly the same height, and since they were hoping to find the tallest of the bunch and then climb it, and there were so many, they came up with another shortcut to judge height. An unpatched lead ball left in a musket will roll out of the barrel if the front of the barrel is lowered. So they would aim their musket at the peak of each nearby mountain, and if the ball stayed in their barrel, they knew that mountain was higher, and worthy of a climb.

These men didn't have any of the things that made our climb so much easier than theirs. We had a map of the area, guidebooks telling us where to turn, trails going to known places, digital watches with altimeters, nylon backpacks full of freeze dried food, and nice socks with red stripes around the top. We didn't feel like wimps, but I sure do admire the guys who did this long before we did.

September 19, 2011

The Wedding Back East

The events surrounding his closing the clinic, driving across the country, and spending quality time with his family was, judging by his writing, one of the highlights of Bob's life. That he took time to describe the day-to-day details that most of us would miss is a lesson we all would do well to learn. (RG)

Friday, the first day…

We stole out of work at noon, put air in the tires and fuel in the tank, and off we went. The Jetta was loaded to the gills but took to the road, like all its German relatives, with understated elan. I-80 was packed with folks heading for Reno. Lots of motorcycles, with slimy folks wearing leathers labeled with gang names. I was very polite with them, giving them more than their share of the road. The first thing we heard when we turned on the TV news at the motel later was the shooting between rival motorcycle gangs at one of the casinos. Glad they waited to take out their violence on each other rather than us boring people.

Dinner tonight was sushi scored at the Walmart in Fernley, Nevada. I don't think it was assembled in China, but I guess you never know. Anyway, we were motoring in a generally eastern direction at a sedate and sane 75 MPH on cruise control, munching down sushi as we passed through that scenic wasteland called the Carson Sink.

Once upon a time, the Carson River gathered its moisture in the Sierra Nevada Mountains southwest of Reno, and then wandered about until it ran out of steam in one of those shallow depressions you can find in corrugated country, where the water can get in, but not out. The hot sun eventually boiled away the water sitting there, that part that didn't simply seep into the ground, and left behind a large alkali flat, one of those pristine white pool table flat things that are fun to pedal across in a jet propelled land speed record breaking vehicle, but no fun at all to trudge across with oxen and Conestoga wagon back in the gold rush days. Folks died out there in that heat and dry, and it still feels like you really don't want to break down there even today. Which I have done, but that is another story.

Anyway, we passed through this gorgeous wasteland, with white playa over there and the purple-gray outline of distant mountains looming behind, and only the incongruous half crisp tufts of desert brush in the foreground, eating Walmart sushi. Surprisingly, it was nearly edible, and the sliced ginger and wasabi woke us right up. And we had baked Cheetos for dessert, as forlorn Lovelock appeared ahead past the curve in the interstate.

The sun fell behind, and the last we saw of it was that red glow on the horizon as it gave up the chase. When we reached Battle Mountain it was full dark. Don't worry if ya never heard of this place. It lives in obscurity halfway between Winnemucca and Elko, and if you don't know these towns either, just figure they are way out over there, and Bob and Joie sure enjoy going to weird places.

Saturday, the second day…

Dawn turned the eastern sky purple, and then pink over the outline of yet another desert mountain range. The Car Guys came on the satellite radio as we turned left at Wells. We saw our first golden eagle on a power pole just north of the Idaho state line. We were in Mountain Time by then, so the wristwatches worn by those pronghorns out in the alfalfa field were an hour ahead of mine.

Farmers were harvesting potatoes in southern Idaho, I believe, but at that distance it's hard to tell the spuds from the similar sugar beets. Everything else was still nicely green, so somebody got enough water this summer. More ice went into the cooler in Pocatello, because it was still hot in the Snake River country. Then we trended north again, climbed into the trees, and later slowed for the town limits of West Yellowstone. The trip odometer showed 960 miles about where we saw the small herd of elk next to the Madison River. Not too many elk left in Yellowstone, but I hear the wolves are still growing in numbers. They won't be when they have killed off all of the elk. But that is nature's way, after we have screwed her up completely.

Sunday, the third day...
28°F greeted us, with frost on the car. The windshield wash fluid froze on the glass as we drove toward another dawn. Aspens were changing into their fall colors all over the hillsides. The willow stuff down by the creeks and ponds had gone red. The roads were nearly empty of vehicles. Velly pleasant!

An osprey sat in a nest platform atop a power pole north of the park. Saw first deer, a whitetail doe, in a pasture just east of Bozeman, next to the interstate. The first bald eagle perched on the very top of a jagged cottonwood over by the Yellowstone River. Pronghorns outnumbered the people.

The day wound down as we motored the scenic route through Theodore Roosevelt National Park. The scruffy trees of that arid clime were about half autumn colored and green. Fat prairie dogs crammed more grass into their mouths, no doubt sensing the coming winter. Three mule deer, including a small buck, wild horses, pronghorn, and two bull bison completed the mammalian show. Ravens, LGB's, and meadowlarks kept company.

Bismarck, North Dakota, is larger than I expected. But it was kinda dark when we arrived, and so that's about all I can tell you about the place. It's a city, and we've seen cities before.

Monday, the fourth day...

Driving into the dawn, we enjoyed that weirdness that pink sky and low angle light provides. Cormorants draped all over spindly dead trees knee deep in small lakes, wings spread to gather warmth, all presented as silhouette, as were the windmills and high tension towers, and those few municipal water towers. Each detail was exaggerated for our pleasure, pink sky providing contrast.

Cross the Red River and the scenery changes. Progress into the state of Minnesota, and the trees gather, and soon each few hundred yards of highway provides another small lake, some right along the road, but the bulk filtered by trees much intent upon turning yellow, orange, or red.

A short detour brought us to Lake Itasca, the lake that provides the start for the Mississippi River. We marveled in the Indian summer weather, the multiples of color lighting up the forest, and the beauty of the lakes. Of course we hopped the rocks at the mouth of the lake, walking across a tiny river that does get a bit larger in time. There be fairies there, but they were back in the trees, what with all the tourists mucking about. My only two photographs before the batteries died in the camera: a baby in diapers sitting butt deep in the infant Mississippi River. The two of 'em, each just getting a start.

Just after the sun set on northern Wisconsin, two black bear cubs crossed the road before us, and I barely missed the second fawn that followed its mom and sibling across the pavement directly in our path. We got a really good look at them. Even as the dark grew, we thrilled at the colors of the trees lining both sides of the road.

Tuesday, the fifth day...

The cloud ceiling hung nearly to the ground, and the lake. Superior likely earned its name from its size, but it has the attitude too. It seems to know it is the boss around here. The old pier poking out into the lake sits unused now, decaying in the sun and winters. Eighteen hundred feet long, with three levels of railroad tracks that once held entire trains of iron ore that was quickly dumped into the holds of the ore ships, such as the ill-fated Edmund Fitzgerald. Ashland, Wisconsin, mines tourists now, and ships off only its children who find work elsewhere.

Miles followed miles of two lane highway burrowing through nearly continuous hardwood forest. The leaf colors defy description as we caught them near their peak for the year. Soft drizzle kept everything wet, which enhanced the colors. When the sun poked through for a moment, red through yellow inclusive reined.

Nearing the border we share with Canada, we faced a decision. Wander into another country in the dark with no idea where we might stay the night, or take our chances in our own nation. We headed south, over the eight miles of the Mackinac Bridge, climbing out of ground fog to the heights of the bridge, and then back into the mist.

Wednesday, the sixth day...

Low clouds and ground fog greeted the morning. A fine breakfast in a prosperous looking, friendly small town in upper Michigan. We motored south through more forest, the fall colors about a week behind that bunch we'd seen the day before. Wisps of ground fog muted and blurred the colors into soft focus. A hundred miles later we turned left headed towards a short-cut across Ontario. We were just beyond that invisible line that separates the glory of upper Michigan from the dread and depression that is the lower. The bags of candy on display in the truck stop doubled in price. And we made a point to lock the car when we went inside.

Canada will let you in after you tell them you didn't bring along your target pistol. They will ask each and every one of us who venture up there as if we all are gang bangers, motorcycle gangs, and drug runners. I guess they watch our TV news.

That government doesn't trust its own citizens to own firearms. And they don't trust Americans. That government will tolerate us in their nation, but they don't act as if they like it.

Along the roadside just over the border is a simple sign that reminds all to obey the traffic laws. Or else...

"Safety through enforcement." The government apparently doesn't want ya to forget who is in charge in that country.

The Canadian government has spent the last few years, and millions of those Canadian dollars trying to get its citizens to voluntarily turn in their hunting rifles, but the folks up there have quietly refused. The government seems to have given up on that issue for the time being, and apparently the government has also lost control of its drivers. My advice if you must drive up there... watch yo butt. Like dogs sniffing each other's tails, Ontario drivers have a profound obsession to tailgate. They like to rush up behind you, slam on their brakes once within a few feet of your bumper, hang there for a while and then pass hurriedly, inches from your fender. They do this with little cars, pickup trucks, and eighty thousand pound semis. I got used to it, but I don't think I could ever learn to like it.

I sat in the slow lane, cruise control set firmly on legal, and I let the locals fly by, after sniffing my tail of course. I was such a good boy. Made it safely to the Buffalo side, checked out the Niagara Falls, and then hurried over the bridge, back to where I belong, even if that happened to be New York State. Didn't get arrested even once, despite all that implied threat, much to my relief.

Thursday, the seventh day...

The Adirondack Park takes up a bunch of room in upstate New York. We wandered about the southern end in the rain. Some early fall color lit up the trees. Hills, a few muddy rivers, and a Dog Patch collection of run down aged buildings filled the windshield for a while, and then we ran into the upscale parts that hung on the fringes of the lakes to the east. Small lonely highways zigged and zagged their way into Vermont, and we got lost on purpose and found some very neat places scattered around that state.

Western Massachusetts entertained as well, and then we were at Joie's dad's house, and we rested.

October 2, 2011

Sierra Experience Lives On

I have homework for you, if you have the energy. And if you don't have the energy now, you'll soon find it after you begin the assignment. Find any collection of the photography of Ansel Adams, anything at all that he did high in the Sierra Nevada Mountains, and when you have digested this magic, I hope you can find a copy of "Mountain Light," by the climber/photographer, Galen Rowell. What Adams' genius revealed in the wonder of the mountains, with the detail of black and white photography, Rowell captured in the glory of the light up there, and in its color.

Meanwhile, I will attempt to recall some of that wonder with a few words. Where I fail, you can insert an Adams image, or a Rowell jewel, and with luck, you will gain a hint of what I'm trying to describe.

Ya see, I'm talking about a place of remarkable, if austere, beauty. Few people have seen it, although if you go there, and you actually see someone else, someone hiking the main trail that traverses north to south, for instance, you might say, "Go away, for you are crowding my space, and I resent you." Because when there, you want it all to yourself, and you do not care if anyone else sees it. Certainly, this is selfish, but a crowd of more than a few detracts from the experience, so you gladly choose to be the hermit, at least during your brief time spent there.

The pass isn't much, just a low spot on the Sierra Crest, but it grants entry to the place. You can see part of the Great Western Divide from there, and as you wander down slope from the pass, the view opens up to include more of it. That spectacular row of 13,000 foot peaks is the western boundary, the awe inspiring Sierra Crest forms the eastern wall, and a less famous row of peaks, the King-Kern Divide closes off the north. You walk down to 11,000 feet or so, and then you can wander wherever you wish, giddy from altitude and awe.

Eleven thousand feet marks the end of the trees, and you pass that line going up or down every day. The trees are foxtail pines, a species that for whatever reason elected to live on the very edge of survival. They are picturesque, weather blasted freaks of trees, and they get even more spectacular after they die, and the wind sculpts them into modern art.

Beautiful lakes dot the sparse landscape, and some hold trout. We caught a bunch one day, under the sparkling high-altitude sun. The photo is of Dan holding his spinning rod in both hands, and the fish are strung along the rod, and my friend has the big grin on his face.

Dan was on the hospice bed, in his living room, and the morphine was doing its job so that he didn't have to know about it, when I brought him the photo. He awoke while we were there, and I showed him the photo, and he remembered, and the grin came one more time. His wife placed the photo in a frame, and it lives there to this day. It's not an Adams or a Rowell, but it captures a piece of a place and a time, and it was special.

April 18, 2010

Inspiration Comes In Many Forms

Inspiration Point, GPS Coordinates: N43. 46', W110. 45', Elevation: 7,200 Feet

This technical description leaves much unexplained, and certainly lends no understanding of the place. What, for instance, is so inspiring about this bit of real estate? Who named it? Do all agree that it is inspiring, or is this simply the opinion of a few?

Don't ask me. It's been too many years and too many miles since I have stood on the spot, and although I remember it as quite the beautiful place, in all honesty it kinda blurs in with a few others. So, why bring it up at all? Well, maybe because we didn't reach it this time.

Let me try to explain… First, you should go to Grand Teton National Park in Wyoming, 'cause none of this makes sense (or maybe it does), unless you experience it. Once there, take the boat across Jenny Lake and hop off onto the dock. The trail climbs a half mile to Hidden Falls, which is worth the hike, but I'm getting ahead of myself, and then head up two hundred more feet of elevation and another half mile of trail, and you will be standing on the Point. Let me know how you like it.

Anyway, Dad first did this hike in 1980, and many times since. If you are heading up Cascade Canyon to do Paintbrush Divide, you will knock off over 20 miles that day, and more if you are climbing behind the Grand bound for Death Canyon, so you can imagine how he might remember the first mile of these treks as the simple part. In those days he left getting to Inspiration Point, as the sole destination of the day, to the more casual hikers.

Now Dad is 88 years old, and he knew we were going back to Grand Teton, and he decided he was going to hike up to

Inspiration Point, 'cause he wanted to wander into Cascade Canyon, the prettiest place in the world, one more time, and that's how you get there. So we all lined up to help him.

My sister Jean led the way up the trail, and I followed closely behind. Dad had his two walking sticks, and he took his time, but all those rocks, roots, steps, and various impediments made it tough on him. Jean pulled him up a few spots, and I pushed from behind when needed, but it was slow arduous duty for Dad. Still, he persevered. He almost fell one time, and I caught him. Reminded me of taking the rock climbing class with him those many years ago.

Bob (r) with his father, Jerry;
Grand Teton National Park, 1980

Dad finally made it to Hidden Falls and back. Inspiration Point was within sight, but not within his reach. But this was no failure. Every time Dad rested and stepped aside to let other hikers pass, he was assailed with, "Atta boy!" and, "Go for it!" and, "You're a hero!" from young and old, all those perfect strangers who passed us on the trail. The most appreciative were florid faced, sweating middle-aged folks who struggled as well. Applause greeted Dad at the base of Hidden Falls. Apparently, inspiration can come from sources other than a point of land.

August 30, 2009

The Morality Of The "Hunt"

As a child, I learned how to fly fish on manmade ponds which were built by a rich guy thirty-five years earlier. I attempted to catch trout with my fly rod, and those few I did manage to hook went home to become dinner for my family. The wooden box at the head of the last pond where the creek flowed in had a wide door on top you swung up out of the way, and inside sat a baby scale to weigh the trout and the record book where you recorded your catch, number and weight, for the homeowners' association. I don't remember how much they charged for a pound of fish, but Mom got the bill at the end of the month. From time to time she suggested that I don't catch so many fish, onnacounta what they charged for a pound of fish.

This wasn't on the Big Horn River in Montana, or some untrammeled creek in Colorado mountains. It was instead in Northern Illinois, not exactly a hotbed of fly-fishing for trout in the 1960s when I was there, or the '20s when the ponds went in. The rich guy built the kind of estate I might consider if I won the lottery. The Roaring Twenties let a few folks get this wealthy, without ever even winning the lottery. Don't know how this guy made his bucks, but he built a mansion with them in the center of 360 acres of hills and forest overlooking the Fox River, and it was a nice place. A series of springs fed a creek that ran through the center of the property, and a sequence of rock dams along the stream left him with thirteen small ponds and the larger one in which I caught those fish. They were still there when the estate became a subdivision and we moved in.

This rich guy built his own hatchery to supply trout for the ponds, and years later as I grew up on that property, I caught hatchery raised fish. And I suppose the money I cost Mom went to the expense of running that hatchery. Without the hatchery and the ponds, there would have been no fly-fishing for trout in my youth in Northern Illinois.

A farm prospered a short distance to the north and west of our family home. Descendants of the first Hallstroms, my father's two uncles and an aunt, worked that farm. Beulah raised the chickens and gathered the eggs. Herb and Cliff farmed the fields, planting feed corn during the times I remember, and fattening a few steers. I recall some sows popping out pigs, too. Somehow I doubt those three ever harbored the notion that dinner magically appeared plastic-wrapped in a refrigerated compartment set strategically to the rear of a chain store.

We miss Clyde (p.92). He was that gray cat who presided over our backyard for those many years. Clyde hammered the gopher population, munching down on those voracious rodents. Our landscaping plants thanked him, for dead gophers don't kill plants by eating all their roots. Without Clyde guarding the farm, the squirrels and gophers ate more from our garden than we did last year.

We want to eat more from our garden, as much as possible. Our own vegetables are not only handy, but they are as fresh as we want them to be. They taste much better, and you certainly can argue that they are better for us than that engineered synthetic rubber in the chain store that is shipped in from who knows where.

We have to compete with the rodents for the fruits of our garden, and I expect to win. That's just life. And death.

Reality involves competition. Clyde ate gophers. We want to eat zucchini and green beans from our garden. So do the rodents. I'll be fencing off and covering the garden this year to keep out as many as I can. And I will kill as many gophers and squirrels as I can. Nothing personal. No blood lust here. It's simply competition.

We eat red meat and the occasional fish. There, I've said it. This can start an argument. There are many arguments I could address. I cannot resolve the rift between big government folks and the individual rights/responsibility folks. I won't solve the abortion debate. I don't step between the Mac people and the PC folks. I'll stop here because of how long this paragraph could get.

This tale is not about the morals or merits of being an omnivore. We eat red meat and the occasional fish. The discussion starts here with this as a given. I'm not going into any of that other.

I wanted to explore here how we wish to go about this. We want to do with our meat as we wish to do with our garden. We want to take the responsibility of obtaining our own meat and fish, and thus improve the quality, freshness, and arguably, the health benefits from this. This is why we may someday feed a steer on our retirement property each year. I'm sure Cliff and Herb would appreciate this. And this is why I hunt and why I will fish when I no longer must work, and thus have the time.

I'm not at all sure how many more years I will be able to hunt for elk. Long our favorite meat, for years I have willingly spent the time and money for the chance to bring home this food. But the mountains are growing taller, and my legs shorter, every year. Someday I will no longer be up to the task. Throwing hay over the fence to our steer frankly would be much easier.

We have considered buying a buffalo calf and feeding it up to eating size instead. We very much enjoy the meat from a bison. But keeping bison behind a fence is much more interesting than an Angus steer. Might not be up to that challenge, either.

Which brings me to my recent bison "hunt"...

Elk hunting is a sacred endeavor to me. Took me years of internal debate before I decided to try this. 'Twas a difficult decision. But from this I have learned the truth of what the native hunters always knew. Without being spiritually ready to pass the test, you don't see any elk. When you have earned them, you do. You can believe this or not, but without hunting elk you cannot know.

A hunt for bison would be much the same, but truly wild bison wander few places in this country. Politics and bad science have put the much needed bison hunt north of Yellowstone Park on hold. A few hunts can be had on reservation land if your checkbook is big enough. Custer State Park in South Dakota holds a small hunt to manage their bison population. And I will be looking into this one.

A lottery is held for the few tags permitting a bison hunt in the Henry Mountains in Utah. This would be a true wild buffalo hunt. But winning this lottery is as likely as winning the one that would set me up on a wooded estate, and it is every bit as physically challenging as an elk hunt.

However, many ranches raise bison instead of beef cattle for the growing market of folks who wish to eat bison meat. I can buy one of these animals, and I can assume the responsibility for the act that turns a living animal into the freezer-wrapped protein we will consume for the next year. So I chose a bison shoot to fill the freezer this winter.

Hatchery produced fish from an artificial pond rather than a wild river. An Angus steer raised on our own land. A bison harvested from a ranch, a fenced-in piece of its native prairie. Not the same perhaps, as bringing home the meat from a wild elk living high on the mountain. But this is not 1830 and I'm not Jeremiah Johnson. It's not the same as that plastic wrapped mystery in the store, either. All things considered, this does in fact, work for me.

January 22, 2012

The Spark That Ignited The Flame

The events described in this piece took place in 1998. What struck me about this essay in particular is the relatively short period of time Bob has been hunting. He has described his hunting adventures as though they've been occurring for a lifetime, and his enthusiasm and detail draw me to pieces like this. (RG)

Published in Bugle [the official publication of the Rocky Mountain Elk Foundation] again! Unseemly bragging here. Please forgive my unabashed enthusiasm.

We broke out of black timber into an Idaho mountain meadow dotted with a few grazing horses. Low-angle sunlight lent color and cast long shadows. White canvas tents lined up in a rough 'L' at the edge of the meadow, with a hitch rail in front of the largest one and a dead tree flag pole to one side, Old Glory hanging limp near the top. I could hear the splash and babble of the creek behind the camp. The tree-clad mountainside rose almost vertically beyond that. And tendrils of smoke wafted up from stovepipes before hanging lazily over the tents, as if reluctant to leave. It was so perfect I had to ask myself if this was actually happening.

The scene was just like the pictures in Grandpa's magazines. This was what an elk camp should look like. I'd waited a long time to see one in the flesh, and it was time to call it home for a few days.

Reaching the hitch rail, my guide Rick easily hopped off his horse. I didn't show quite as much style. I reminded myself that any dismount from a horse you can walk away from is a good landing, so I settled for that and wobbled around to the off side to snatch my rifle from the scabbard. My gear waited in the last tent. I fluffed out my sleeping bag to let it air, then headed for the cook tent where I'd been told there'd be coffee.

The cook tent was a large affair. It had to be to accommodate six hunters, their guides, and the wranglers who led pack trains in and out of camp. Kathy, the camp cook, had two propane stoves upon which to work her magic, rows of pack boxes crammed with food and gear stacked along one wall, and a wood stove blazing away by the door to tame the chill of mountain autumn. Two big black coffee pots lived on the edge of the woodstove, and when Kathy's dinner was prepared, she plopped onto a seat next to the stove with a cup of coffee.

The mice moved into the cook tent in early September, shortly after my outfitter set up camp in their meadow. They lived in the stack of firewood that stood ready to feed the hungry stove, busily scurrying about, time to time poking their heads out of the gaps between the ends of the logs to twitch their whiskers at us.

I sat with two guides and one of the wranglers watching the mice. October was winding down and the next day these men would begin breaking down camp. Everything, save the poles holding up the tents, was packed in on horses and would soon need to be packed out.

I sensed they didn't quite know what to make of me after my inauspicious first day's hunt. Many hunters booked these hunts, and I assumed most knew what they were doing. I wondered if these guys ever had to cope with one who knew as little about this endeavor as I did. Undoubtedly they'd been told I failed to take the shot at a bull Rick put me on earlier that afternoon. Legal elk don't grow on trees. Rick had done his job and I clearly hadn't done mine. But they made small talk with me while we all watched the mice alternately poking their heads out of the holes lined up in that woodpile.

Everyone laughed when I thanked them for providing the mice for my entertainment, the Selway equivalent of Hollywood Squares. That helped to break the ice. When I didn't blame Rick for my screw-up, well, that helped, too. Over a background of stream noise, while a battery-powered radio struggled to deliver some music through the static, and the fire hissed and popped in the stove, we laughed and talked into the night. On this level at least, they welcomed me in.

The term hunter hardly applied to me. I signed up for a wilderness elk hunt having never hunted anything. Heck, for most of my life I hadn't even known anyone who hunted.

I grew up watching Bambi, and from that learned that hunters were vicious slobs. My mother felt that any hunting, subsistence or trophy, was despicable. Mom never was one to hide her feelings, so I heard about this early and often. If she had discovered that I used a friend's pellet rifle to clear pigeons from the roof of the barn down the road, I would have been skinned.

I formed my opinions against hunting with information gleaned from mainstream media and a circle of friends who parroted an anti-gun and anti-hunting mantra. I lived in Berkeley for a decade after college, surrounded by the greatest distortion of reality in this hemisphere. And I trained as a veterinarian, pledging my life to the relief of animal suffering. Hunting and shooting were anathema to me, and I argued long and loudly against both. I was the last person on earth you'd expect to meet in elk camp.

However, people who actually mature, rather than simply age, can learn to look at the complex issues of life from more than one direction. Experience eventually taught me that when I was absolutely, positively certain about some things, I was often wrong.

For most of my adult life I let only one barber cut my hair. If he was busy, I waited. Men gathered in Louie's shop, some for his services and others just to talk. I kept quiet while I sat, because I quickly realized that in this company I rarely held the majority opinion. From these discussions, I learned a little about cars, probably nothing useful about women, and a great deal about other things.

Some of these men spoke of a war I had opposed, a war they had attended and I had not. And they talked about guns and hunting. None of these men appeared to be sociopaths or vicious slobs. I actually listened to their side of the arguments, and they began to make sense. I also read the hunting magazines that littered the place. And I grew curious.

Grandpa had been a fisherman. He subscribed to magazines featuring hunting stories as well as fishing, and as a child I read about western big game hunts. And I soon recalled those stories.

My father had been a marksman before Mom made him sell his rifle. So despite the grief he caught at home, he made sure I had the opportunity to shoot at Boy Scout camp. And sitting in that barbershop I remembered that, well, shooting had been fun.

I set out to learn more, and soon an acquaintance took me to the range. It was still fun. I bought a .22 target pistol and was soon hooked. I spent countless relaxing hours punching holes in paper, and in the process talked with more hunters.

I don't remember when I first considered becoming a hunter, but I know at that point I remained conflicted. I felt I should hunt only if my family was going hungry, but still the idea intrigued me. My internal debate lasted several years before I realized that I could not truly pass judgment except by my own experience. It was time to find out.

Killing pigeons hadn't taught me much. I enjoyed the challenge, but hated the guilt that came when I picked up those limp bodies that I had erased for no good reason. My lesson had to be more meaningful, and so I chose to try an elk hunt. This would not only present a physical, but also an emotional challenge.

I knew elk hunts were difficult. Elk are large animals, but despite their size, they are stealthy creatures that inhabit the most spectacular and inaccessible wild country in North America.

To me, elk also are beautiful, and my brief encounters with them were some of my more treasured memories. In my youth I had driven a thousand miles on more than one occasion to watch a bull bugle against a backdrop of Wyoming mountains, his breath a frozen cloud as he stood silhouetted by the dawn. I admired this animal, but now I needed to meet the side of me that could also hunt him.

I wanted to experience that hunt I read about as a child: of hunters on horseback, and tent camps set in high mountain splendor. Perhaps this was a romantic anachronism, but I made up my mind to try. Life intervened, and it was three years later before I could take the test. I didn't stop thinking about it, but my dreams and fantasies had to suffice.

I was 49 when I went to Idaho in October. I camped near the edge of the wilderness and spent time walking the hills, trying to adjust to the altitude, but also hoping to shift the workings inside my head into a new mode of thinking. I was hiking a forest trail when the bugle of a nearby bull jolted me. My eyes bored into the dark woods to find him, but I failed. Early the next morning, as my camp stove struggled to turn nearly frozen water into coffee, I watched a tree stump in the nearby meadow morph into a moose in the flat light of pre-dawn. She wandered through wisps of ground fog to a nearby pond, where pretending to be a hunter, I stalked her just for fun.

That afternoon I met with my outfitter. I discovered that no one else had booked this last week of the season, and I was to be the only hunter in camp. So much for wondering what I could learn from a group of experienced hunters, and if I might fit in.

The following morning found us at a ridge top trailhead where a string of pack horses patiently waited. They headed down the muddy trail under a leaden sky, while Rick and I hoofed it through the trees. We were going to hunt our way down to camp. That feeling in my gut before a final exam in school was nothing like this.

It's different walking through the woods when you carry a rifle. It's harder still when everything is wet and slippery. Hours of tripping and stumbling passed while I slowly learned the ropes. And yeah, I was supposed to be watching for elk in the process. I was traversing a snot-slick log over a stream when Rick spotted a five-point bull in its bed, only 20 yards ahead. He waved me forward and urged me to shoot. I had zero time to react. I raised the rifle, looking for a shoulder through the scope, but saw nothing but black. I hadn't removed the scope covers. While I fumbled, the bull decided he had had enough and exploded from his bed. Only his scent remained.

I felt like an idiot, my worst fears realized as I let this simple opportunity run away. Rick tried to reassure me, but we both knew I might not get another chance. I had wasted my dream hunt. I finished the descent of the ridge, my mood as dreary as the day.

We struck a trail going up-canyon that paralleled the stream, and not long after found the two horses the wranglers had left tied to a tree. A mile or two in the saddle brought us to that doorway into the meadow, and my first hunt camp. And yeah, that helped, and I did pinch myself.

We were well up a wooded ridge as morning two broke. An hour earlier, I stumbled out to my horse, invisible in the frosty dark, and blindly followed Rick up a trail. I fervently hoped the horse could see better than me. Leaving our mounts tied near the creek, we slogged up the ridge to a point where we could glass into two canyons.

I was supposed to be watching for elk, but it was hard not to be distracted by the spectacular mountain scenery as it played hide and seek through the clouds. At times we were engulfed in a gray blanket, then later we were above the clouds looking down upon white cotton, granite peaks poking up like islands in a surreal sea. Frosted by the mist, trees high above us glittered in the sun.

Later, near a dry pond littered with weathered elk tracks and droppings, a pika chirped his objections from the talus as we passed. That's when my left ankle exploded. I don't know if I slipped on that clump of wet bear grass or if my warranty simply expired, but I heard a pop and felt searing pain as the tendon tore loose. And I was on the ground.

Rick carried my rifle and I leaned on a stout branch for the long hobble back to the horses. The last couple hundred yards was a humiliating slide down a steep slope on my butt. Fatigue, pain, disappointment collided in my head until I turned a corner and finally smelled the horses. For the second time in two days, I thought the hunt was over.

Day three found me sitting alone, back to a tree, facing a forest clearing and hoping an elk would drop into my lap. None did. My ears twitched at every forest sound. An eagle soared past on familiar thermals. I found that I could blend in, compelled by a bum leg to slow down and experience the place.

The hunt camp was quickly disappearing into pack boxes. Rick and I rode up to a spike camp 2,000 feet higher the next day, and we hunted on foot through an area of salt lick and pocket meadows. A light snow fell, and we followed tracks that led to two cows, but they quickly melded into a snow shower and disappeared. Rick was shaking down the country for me, but you cannot find bulls if they are not there.

I could barely walk, had botched my chance for a bull, and yet I felt at peace with this effort. I relaxed as I smelled the air, sensed the breeze and wandered through the dark forest. I walked slowly and saw more.

I'd accepted that I probably wouldn't bring an elk home, so a late start the next morning didn't stress me. The pressure was off. Rick tended to some business and sent me up the trail to the pocket meadows alone. I hobbled the half mile on three inches of fresh snow in the faint light before dawn. The trees were snow blanketed, the air still and the quiet pervasive.

I thought I was paying attention, but I stumbled into a small group of cow elk, quarter-ton animals moving like ghosts through the trees. They crossed a small opening in single file. Five passed. Then a head emerged from behind a tree, this one with antlers.

My carefully concocted plan for this hunt called for a period of soul searching before I pulled the trigger on my first game animal, but I forgot that part as the bull emerged into the opening. I had only seconds before he would disappear. A certain detachment took over, the hours of rifle practice paid off. After the bull fell I tried to unload my rifle, my fumbling fingers dropping cartridges into the snow.

I stood trembling beside a fine bull elk. An old raven flew over and discretely reminded me to give thanks. When Rick caught up, we tackled the arduous task of quartering the bull. I tried to help, but since I knew nothing about field dressing elk, there was little for me to contribute besides hold this or that. This made time for celebration to fade and sadness arrive. I was relieved to discover that I am not a man who kills without conscience.

Now, when I look up at that antlered head on the wall, and the light is dim like it was that morning, the memories return. When we give thanks before we feast on venison I've brought home, I have no regrets.

I learned that hunting is far more than simply killing an elk. Hunting is anticipation and disappointment, exhilaration and sadness, hard work and satisfaction. It is autumn in country so beautiful it truly defies description. It is new friends who become old friends and the gratifying feeling when experienced woodsmen tell you they would hunt with you again.

Subsequent hunts have taught me more. I'm a better man for this knowledge and experience. I don't feel at all like a vicious slob. I'm glad I finally figured that one out.

March 4, 2012

"You're a quick study. Some folks go their whole life and never learn these things. Congratulations, brother."

Harold Jones, DVM
friend and colleague

Kehoe, Revisited

I keep a magic rock in the top drawer of my office desk. Please don't tell anybody, 'cause you know how they get when they hear you have a magic rock. Some don't believe in such things, so they stare at me with that funny look on their faces. And if they know about magic rocks I have to watch them, or they might try to steal mine.

Still, it's worth the risk, for when the day begins to overwhelm me, I can close my eyes, roll the cool smooth stone between my fingers, and immediately I'm transported back to Pt. Reyes National Seashore, to Kehoe beach, where I found it...

I'm strolling the high tide line heading south, and if I choose, I can walk for hours. I might walk to infinity, for I cannot see either end of the beach from here. A fog bank hangs a few miles off the coast, but the sky above is clear, blue, and sunny.

Two ravens swoop and soar on the wind above the sand dunes to my left. On my right, a line of ratty looking pelicans commute to the north, gliding in formation with their wing tips just skimming the waves. They drop into a wave trough, and then reappear above the next crest with just a few wing beats.

Tide's out, so the waves break well down the beach, spreading out into a thin smooth sheet that peters out before reaching my bare feet. This creates a mirror reflecting a foraging gull standing knee deep in the receding water.

With a slight whistling sound, the wind blows into my right ear and out the left. The air smells like no one has used it before.

Nobody is on this beach but me, nobody to interrupt the thoughts crashing around in my mind. I burrow deep into the vault that is my brain, finding memories stacked one upon the other on shelves extending well back into the darkness. It looks like this place hasn't been cleaned for a while.

The View From Here

Brushing old cobwebs out of the way, I stumble across boxes holding the thoughts of a lifetime. Successes and failures, victories and losses, weddings and divorces, it goes on and on. And it is packed nearly to the ceiling. No wonder I cannot think straight.

So I unscrew the top of my head and dump out all this crud into a little pile on the sand.

As I'm picking through it, tossing out the bad and trying to rearrange the good, a half-buried fragment of abalone shell off to the side catches my eye. Turning the shard over, the sand eroded layers inside flash into brilliance in the sunlight, and I marvel at the frozen rainbow that God hides inside each of these shells. I wonder if an abalone, without any eyes, can truly appreciate the beauty of its own home.

I guess none of us do, if we don't look.

Distracted, I get up and wander further down the beach. I watch the shorebirds scurrying about. They poke their beaks into each hole in the sand looking for all the world like street people searching for cans in the trash. Sandpipers hurry off in a group-- a Blue Light Special at the sand flea table was just announced.

I glance out into the surf just in time to spot a harbor seal poking his head out of the foam. Curious fellow, he is watching me. I stop walking to stare back.

My new friend disappears into the next wave, so I go back to my browsing. That's when I find the rock. It's oval, about an inch or two long, and worn smooth by years in the sand. My rock is probably a bit of low-grade jade, with veins of white and brown. It has no real value, except for the magic. I walk along rolling it between my fingers.

Wait a moment... what's that noise?

The beach vanishes and I'm back in the office. I put the rock back in the drawer, next to the one from Death Valley. Time to go back to work... this time, with a smile.

Somehow, I forgot the little pile of brain crud I left behind on the beach for the next tide to wash away.

Guess I didn't need it, after all.

October 2, 2012

Discovering Betty Jane

No doubt Bob counts the experience described in the next two pieces as a highlight of his life. (RG)

I'm going for a ride on Betty Jane this weekend. She may be 70 years old, but she is sleek and she can still dance. Now, don't get all riled up. Yeah, I'm a happily married man, but sometimes a man's just got to do what a man's got to do. And... I have my wife's permission.

Let me 'splain what all led up to this...

They call them the White Mountains, and they named the tallest one White Mountain. Nothing remarkable about this. These mountains are snow capped much of the year. That might be why. I don't recall a Mr. White hiking the place looking for a lost gold mine, so I'll stick with this explanation.

The White Mountains are taller than the Inyos and those cinder cones south of Mono Lake so they hang on to their snow longer, and if you are looking at them from near Mono Lake, and you turn around to look up to the Sierra Nevada summits behind you, the White Mountains won't look like it but they are actually taller.

Most everybody knows about the Sierra Nevada Range, but I venture some fewer know about the Whites. The big highway follows the base of the Sierra Nevada from Reno down to Mojave, but only a couple of lightly traveled roads go near the Whites. No ski resorts up in the Whites. No bed and breakfast places or golf courses. Not much man-made up there at all.

The Bristlecone Pines live up there, and they are worth the visit, but few folks do. Not many people like looking at old trees. Just as well. Those trees like their peace and quiet. But there is a road that runs south to north up the ridge that is that mountain range, and it's even paved for a while. Past the Bristlecones the road thins out a mite. It goes to gravel, and then to bumps, and pretty soon it's not much of a road at all, winding where the mountain lets it, always climbing, up to where the other things thin out, too.

No trees up there. No bushes even. Some flowers that keep their heads down out of the wind. Lichen covered rocks. A few marmots, and they sleep underground. Even the air thins down to a bare minimum, although the wind is a presence.

When you get to the gate, you stop and park just off the road. Down below, which you can't really see from there, you can take breathing for granted. But up here, the gate is at 11,200 feet. Here you sea level folks learn to breathe all over again. And when you begin walking at the gate, and that jeep track you follow continues uphill, sucking in thin air preoccupies your consciousness.

Persevere, and after seven miles, eventually you will reach the summit of White Mountain, which has a little weather station and an old WPA stone building and nothing else. Well, not exactly nothing else. The summit holds some of those intangibles that motivate folks to do silly things like this. A view, for instance. Past your toes it drops off about 8,000 feet to the foot of the mountain. And over there, that entire western horizon is defined by the jagged summits lined up along the Sierra Crest. That part's nice.

To the left along that crest you can see Mts. Whitney at 14,505 feet and Williamson at 14,389. Those are the two tallest in the state. And this is the only place in California where you can say you are standing on the third highest mountain in the state, at 14,252 feet.

Just happened to be standing on White Mountain summit one morning when a sailplane passed by, below me. The valley between the Sierra Crest and the White Mountains generates some wonderful thermals, and the wind hitting the escarpment I was standing on also will bounce a sailplane up. This guy was driving back and forth below me, gaining altitude with each turn. I could look into his cockpit. He didn't wave back.

The first time I looked down upon an aircraft while standing astride a mountain summit, I was on top of Mt. Whitney. That time it was an F-15 I believe. This guy was playing around, passing between mountains and then to our west, slightly below our altitude. I briefly could see inside his cockpit as he turned. He went by in rather a hurry, so he didn't wave, either.

Tagged Telescope Peak at some point in time between these other mountains. It's a pimple at only 11,043 feet, but it does claim one thing. On top there, you can look down to Badwater, the lowest spot in North America, and then turn around to look at Whitney, the highest. This time it was an F-18 that went by, below me.

A couple of years ago, I stood atop Mt. Diablo, our local 3,800 foot "mountain." Drove up to show it to a friend who had not been on the top before, despite living in the area for decades. A good crowd milled about on a Sunday afternoon. We were on the exposed viewing deck of the summit house when I heard a familiar aircraft engine. The plane was approaching, and I spotted it coming in from the north, below us. It went past with an unmuffled roar.

I'd know that engine sound anywhere, although it took a moment for it to register. Wasn't expecting it in that time and place. It came from a restored World War II fighter, a P-51 Mustang. A handful of these birds still live, and I'd heard them fly by before. I knew that sound like an old friend's voice.

I'm a bit obsessed with the story of WWII. I've seen about every movie and television program made concerning that war since I was a child. I have read so many books. Like driving to Wyoming in September just to hear an elk bugle, I've driven hours to an air show simply to hear them start up the old radial engines of a B-17 bomber, and been delighted to see and listen to the other WWII planes at the show, including a couple of P-51's. Gave me that thrill in the pit of my stomach.

Being in the physical presence of such history, and trying to picture the men who rode these planes into danger to halt the evil that drove the other side, lends some harsh yet reassuring reality to my perceptions of the past. They are letting the kids forget this history, so someday they can repeat it. But for us older folks, and our parents who lived that history, these planes help keep it alive. And if it stays alive, maybe the next time won't come as such a surprise.

Now something's come up to put that thrill back into my gut. Once a year the local airport hosts a visit by a B-17, a B-24, and recently, a P-51C fighter. And you can book a ride in any of these aircraft. Which is even better than just listening to the engines start.

If you are standing on top of Mt. Diablo this Sunday morning, listen for the unmuffled roar of a 70 year old Packard built Merlin V-12 engine, and look over, or maybe down. I'll be in that silver P-51 with the red striped tail going by. This is the

Mustang called Betty Jane. You should be able to recognize me by the grin. I expect it will take a crew of five a week to wipe it off my face after I land.

June 5, 2013

Riding Betty Jane

A Plane Ride... Really.

Spock likely would disapprove, but I don't have a logical mind, so I'm not strong in math. But we are talking about solving to an unknown here, and that's math. So I guess I'm not gonna quickly come up with the solution here, and thus I live with an unknown.

I figure I've got X number of mornings left. X more. X is my unknown.

So far, I've seen about twenty three thousand mornings. That's a bunch. There won't be twenty thousand more, in all probability. But if I try to solve for X, if I try to calculate how many mornings are left for me, I don't have a clue. Really, no clue.

What does pass for logic with me is the notion that I should make something of as many mornings as I can of those I have left. Why waste them? So, if this one Sunday morning was to be the first of the rest, I could set a precedent, and maybe try for something truly memorable.

Significant decisions often result from improbable beginnings. I've never had a bad morning in Yosemite. And in the forty years I've been visiting, I've had well over a hundred mornings in that national park, and that meant sleeping in a bunch of different places. But an advertisement in a magazine led me to a different spot, one I had never considered, and it led to two more fine mornings for us.

Two months later, in that same magazine, I fell over another ad (for no better reason than I'd found the last one there so I was poking around), this one for restored World War Two airplanes, and the folks who fly them. And this lit a fire.

The View From Here

The Collings Foundation has been visiting our little city with their restored B-17 and B-24 bombers for a while. One weekend each year. Years ago, I drove to the airport to see them in the flesh, for I have a certain obsession about such things, and I met these aircraft. And that was good.

The Foundation offered rides in the bombers for a fee. But I thought I'd be practical, and I passed on that. But now years later, I did the reconsider, and went to the website to see what a brief tango in a 70 year old bomber might cost these days. And I found instead, their P-51.

We don't have time here for the full story. Someday, if the inspiration and the magic of fingers on keys cooperate, I might be able to explain the full story. Just thinking about this task intimidates me right now. But let's just say I've had a mad passion for the P-51 Mustang for some considerable time.

I'd like to have one. Problem is, I lack the wherewithal. Mega millions might help, but even that might not be enough. So along with a few other preposterous fantasies, I'd put this one on the shelf. I went to the occasional air show, and listened to the sweet sound of a P-51 engine start; and then I melted a little when the craft took off and that sound seared into my soul, and then when one roared past, buzzing the field, I died a little from the sheer lust of the moment. And until now, that has passed for close enough. That's how we get by when we cannot get all that we want.

And then I found the Collings Foundation website, and right there in plain English, was the invite to ride along in their very unique two seat, dual control, P-51C. Betty Jane. And all it would take is a credit card and an hour of my precious time. I gave it some thought. I consulted with folks wiser than me, for emotion should not rule one's decisions, and some logic should be applied.

And then I disregarded logic, and paid heed to my heart, and I made my reservation.

So one of the Sunday mornings that I have left dawned overcast. The marine layer had slipped in under cover of darkness and that meant solid clouds a thousand feet above. That would mean no flying that day, unless it had the decency to clear away. Shucks!

Oh, I'll be fine. It's just a plane ride.

We watched as the clouds backed away from the hills to our east until we could see blue above. Hope began again. We arrived at the airfield early, for that's how I operate. The B-17 and the B-24 sat on the pavement, looking just like those pictures from 70 years ago. The P-51 was nowhere to be seen. Oh, they probably broke it, and just forgot to tell me. No problem. I'll just go home and get on with my life.

No problem.

Nine o'clock and the tables were set up and the souvenirs were set out, folks were showing up with cameras and memories, and the two planes were being prepped by a covey of earnest looking men, the ground crew… and still no P-51. Pretty soon I was going to have to ask where it was.

About then, the electric mule arrived, towing the polished aluminum, red spinner on the prop and red stripes on the tail and elevators, Mustang. Freaking awesome gorgeous in the perfect bright morning sun, my P-51 now sat just beyond the tail of the B-24. That noise was the pulse in my ears.

The Second World War had many parts, and the air war over Europe was a big part of that war. The B-17 and B-24 bombers each carried crews of ten men, and as many as a thousand bombers might head for Germany in a rather large group on any given day trying to win that war. Ten Thousand men at risk.

The Nazis objected to this, and they had many thousands of anti-aircraft guns, the 88s, and also many hundreds of fighter aircraft, the Me-109 and FW-190, and an assortment of others arrayed to stop this. Their job was the destruction of those bombers, and the ten men aboard each. The leading Nazi ace in that war had 200 aerial victories, otherwise known as kills. Most of those victories were bombers which carried ten men to 25,000 feet above Germany, from which they fell to earth. Some survived. Others did not.

The P-51's went along to safeguard the bombers. They were tasked with performing aerial victories against the Nazi fighters. They did well. A battle to the death, and from one point of view, of good against evil. For some then thought the Nazis should be stopped. And contrary to what some teach today, they were right.

This all was a nasty business. I cannot even begin to wrap my brain around the courage those boys carried on each mission, for I've led a sheltered life.

A 737 airliner that we have all flown to 30,000 feet is a small plane to most of us, but they are larger than those WWII bombers, and the P-51 parked next to the B-24 looked like a mosquito next to that green plane. But in the inevitable evolution that war brings, in the survival of the fittest, the P-51 was the best to come out of that war. And on this morning, 70 years later, I'd be allowed to experience a tiny bit of what this airplane meant to history.

The P-51C was an engine, four .50 caliber machine guns, large fuel tanks, and a little space for the pilot to make the whole thing work. And the parts went together very well.

I signed in at the table, and suddenly I was a VIP. I got to go over, beyond the rope, and check out Betty Jane up close. I got to know her intimately. I met Jeff, the pilot. I took pictures, and Joie caught those photos of me next to the Mustang. We all watched the clouds to the north and west, for that's where we were supposed to fly. And we waited on nature. And we waited.

Jeff offered the choice, to fly above the clouds to the northwest, or instead head east over the delta and into the valley where clear sky awaited. The map was marked with no trespassing zones, those places we could not clutter with our presence. The permitted open area past the delta looked fine to me. That was settled. Joie has a photo of Jeff and me, two backs, walking toward the Betty Jane.

You climb up on the port wing by stepping on the landing gear tire, and then on a shackle, and then you get a knee on the wing. The step into the rear seat is a bit of a stretch, but easier than that little move you did on Wall Street, well up on the Exum Route to the summit of the Grand Teton. (This bit is for Dad, who likely will remember.) A ground crew member helps you don the parachute harness, two shoulder straps, a waist strap, two canvas loops between the legs. The seat belt with two more shoulder straps follow.

With a smile, the guy tells you that if you need to "get out" the pilot will pop off the canopy, and you unfasten the seat belts, and pull that 'D' ring once you are "out," and everything will be OK. Comforting.

The airsick bag sits in a recess next to the left elbow. The pilot says to tell him when you get the first queasy moment, but that macho part of you disregards. It's a large zip lock freezer bag. A souvenir, I suggest. The crew member laughs.

Jeff is futzing around in the front seat. I hear a ticking sound. The crew member stands by the port wing tip. I'm checking out the gauges on the panel in front of me. And trying to find a place for my feet so I won't interfere with the rudder pedals. It's very cozy in my seat. I have a control stick between my legs, and a throttle handle at my left. I find the magnetic compass, the gyro compass, the propeller RPM gauge, airspeed indicator, manifold pressure gauge, altimeter, G-force gauge, artificial horizon, temperature gauge, rate of climb or dive gauge, and fuel gauge. This should be easy.

I've never piloted a plane before. I've never even been in a small plane. Those two trips in a sailplane likely don't qualify as practice for this. But these crazy folks are going to let me fly this precious old airplane. Least I can do is do the best I can.

The engine was designed for a racing seaplane back in 1936. Built by Rolls Royce, the Merlin had powered the Hawker Hurricane and the Supermarine Spitfire as Great Britain fought the Nazis to a tie during the Battle of Britain. The original Mustang was powered by an Allison engine, which lagged in high altitude performance, so somebody got the bright idea to put the Merlin in there, and it transformed the Mustang. The engine was manufactured by Packard under license during the war. 1,650 cubic inches, and over 1,400 horsepower, the twelve-cylinder engine also produces that sound that so flutters my heart. No muffler on that thing.

Jeff fires the engine. A whining sound, the propeller turns slowly, and a few cylinders take, but not enough to keep it going. Smoke passes by on both sides of the plexiglass canopy. Wait a few seconds, and try again. A few more cylinders kick in this time, and the engine runs, albeit a bit rough. Finally, all twelve kick in, and the roar settles. The crew member by the wing gives a thumbs up. We are not on fire.

I'd like to go for a ride, but first we must warm the engine at 1,000 RPM. The little line on the temp gauge ever so slowly works through yellow toward green. I wait to die of old age. The cockpit fills with exhaust fumes and the smell of one hundred octane gas. I sit in a tin can with a blast of engine noise and metal rattle. This is a participatory event. I'm loving it.

Finally, after checking with the tower, Jeff taxis off the parking area. All the folks who had been looking at the two bombers turn to watch. The sound we make is sweet. The runway goes west and east, so we must taxi to the other end. The wind dictates this. The P-51 is a tail dragger, so the nose is in the air and you cannot see to the front, so the pilot does slow S-turns the length of the taxiway lest he bump into someone.

I'm excited.

The east end of the runway has a wide spot where you can run up the engine to see if it has any surprises waiting for you. And then after a short discussion with the tower, Jeff rolled us onto the runway headed west. The RPM gauge went to 3,100, and we accelerated down the runway. The tail came up, and the speed came up, and then we came up. We had a hundred feet of elevation as we passed the two bombers, and then further up we went.

We banked left and climbed over the city. Heading southeast and then east, we passed over our house. And then the hills passed below, the two little cities and then the delta, as we gained elevation. At 4,000 feet elevation, Jeff's voice came over the intercom. He was going to do a few maneuvers. He'd warned me that we would see four G's of enthusiasm on this flight. I found a few of those G's right away.

It kinda feels like your guts are going to come out your ass. Jeff leaned the plane over to ninety degrees. This meant that the wings which normally lie parallel with the earth are suddenly aligned vertical to the earth. The plane carves a very sudden turn. And the pilot finds out right away if that barf bag is going to be needed by his passenger. Momentarily, I wasn't sure, until I realized that a gut shift didn't necessarily mean the need for plastic bag. I was fine. I tightened those old belly muscles, and reminded myself to keep breathing, and I was fine. And I was having fun.

And then Jeff turned the plane over to me.

Holy crap!

I learned that the inputs to the control stick need only be subtle. Raise the nose slightly, and then lean the plane to port, and it turns! Easy as that. I know nothing about driving a plane, but this lady is so predictable, that even a rank novice like me can easily make her behave. Turn right, turn left, 360° turn… no problem. I realize how easy it would be to get lost doing this, so I learn to look for the mountain, and when it doesn't change position, I can use it to tell where I'm going. At 250 knots!

Jeff takes over, and we climb up to 6,000 feet, and it's time for some aileron rolls and then finally a loop or two. Weird feeling, looking up through the clear canopy as the ground shows up, up there. This all is very cool. Some quick 'S' turns, and then finally the climb, roll upside down and then dive on the farmhouse below for a strafing attack. Wow, and... Wow!

Then he hands the plane over to me again, and we make our way back toward Concord. I get to try some tighter turns, some 180°s and 360°s. I get nearly vertical in my last turn. I'm flippin' ole Betty Jane around, looking for the Red Baron, and getting a sense for what those guys once did for a living so they could keep on living. I'd lost the need to justify, but clearly this was worth the cost. Priceless is another word for it.

We passed over the airport at 1,500 feet, and then turned round, dropped the landing gear and set the flaps. A touch of throttle, and we touched down gently on the front gear, and then waited for the tail to drop. And then it was just the runoff until Jeff tapped the brakes and we taxied in behind the B-24, turned, and then parked. The engine died. And my flight in a P-51 ended.

A ground crew member helped me with the seat belt and parachute harness, and I clambered out of the cockpit and onto the wing. A quick drop to the pavement, and I was back to earth. A handshake and thank you for Jeff, and a quick look to Joie and her camera.

My brain was a bit cluttered.

I took the moment to wander through the B-17 interior. I waited for the P-51 to take off with the next passenger, and that sound seared my soul again. I wandered about the two bombers a dazed man. And I realized that it might be a while before my feeble brain can process all of this. Not even all that sure what I need to process. But I'm looking forward to whatever I discover next.

Not sure how many more mornings await, but this was a good one.

Worth the price?

Yep.

June 15, 2013

A Bird On The Head Is Worth Two In The Bush

Birds like the top of my head. I'm not sure what the appeal is. It's a nice head, of course. A fair amount of hair still resides up there, at least on the parts I can see. And it is just a little flat on top, which I'm sure the little feathered friends find useful when they land. Lots of people have heads like mine, but they don't seem to have birds using them as often as I have them using mine.

It started when I was a kid, when the family parakeet would seek out my head to perch upon after it tired of flying around the house. All it needed was for me to be standing still, minding my own business, and it would show up.

I would sense, as much as hear, the bird approaching from behind. The hair on the back of my neck would stand on end. Then with a gentle swoosh and flutter, the little budgie would flare into a landing and sink his claws into my scalp.

I could live with the claws, but he always managed to leave a "present" in my hair whenever he landed on my head, so there was always that annoyance to deal with after he left.

Lots of birds have used my head for excretory purposes.

Red Skelton, the comedian, had a TV show when I was a kid, and he used to do a bit about Gertrude and Heathcliff, two seagulls he mimicked on stage. I'll never forget the gag where Gertrude asked Heathcliff, "Have you seen the new sports car?" To which Heathcliff replied, "Yes, I 'spotted one' yesterday." I figured Mr. Skelton had to be thinking about my head when he came up with that joke.

To this day, I always wear a hat when I am at the beach. And the memory of the parakeet swooping in for a landing on my head came back one evening in the Yosemite backcountry. A friend and I were nearing the end a weeklong backpack, and we set up our last night's camp alongside the Tuolumne River, at a place called Glen Aulen. Sunset was fading into dull pink on the western horizon as I stood talking to another hiker. He was looking west, while I stood facing the opposite direction, watching a waterfall slowly blurring into the dusk. Suddenly his eyes widened and I felt that familiar sensation on the back of my neck as a small hawk flew in and tried to land on top of my head.

Apparently I do a fair impression of a tree stump. The hawk only did a quick touch and go; then he flew off when he realized his error. Just as well, for his claws were likely sharper than the budgies I have met.

When the mocking bird is nesting in the bushes behind the clinic, I get to experience the same sensation. I wander out back to walk my dog, and before we get halfway across the parking lot, the dive-bombing starts. That bird always attacks from the back, like the Red Baron, and I can feel him before I hear him. Usually I duck before he delivers his little peck to the top of my noggin.

The largest bird to sneak up on me from behind was a golden eagle. I was about thirteen and a half thousand feet up Mt. Tyndal in the southern Sierra Nevada when I concluded I couldn't reach the summit. I climbed alone, and when the going got too hairy, I decided to retreat and try another day. This mountain was named after the scientist who described why the sky appears blue. I stood on the side of the mountain admiring the deep blue of the high altitude, cloudless sky, and the vista spread at my feet. Rows of jagged peaks stretched to the horizon, and straight down past my toes, I could see the basin dotted with lakes that I walked through on my way to the mountain earlier that morning. I was lost in reverie, in the quiet stupor that high altitude and incomparable beauty inspires. Then I heard the quiet swoosh, hair started twitching on my neck, and the eagle blasted past my left ear, nearly blowing me off my perch. He dove by me, sailing over the valley below, before he caught a thermal and quickly climbed out of sight, leaving me shaking on the rocks. Finally regaining my composure, I climbed carefully back down the mountain.

I was of course, impressed by this magnificent eagle, but I still wonder why birds cannot just approach from the front and introduce themselves like civilized folks.

October 12, 2001

Getting Away From It All

One of many Federal Government "shut downs" occurred from October 1-16, 2013. (RG)

We were the only people in a Kaiser pharmacy designed to handle several hundreds in a day, so we expected to be in and out of there quickly. Seven in the morning didn't figure to be a busy time; the prescription offered nothing of consequence to prepare, but the staff there demonstrated the style of relaxed effort one associates with Post Office drones. They carried on with a lighthearted banter amongst themselves behind the counter, wasting little energy as they pretended to be busy. We sat in our chairs. Time passed. More time. Even more.

Oh, they were so cheerful. One... two... three pills... Working, working, working. See, we're working.

Count the pills. Put the pills in the vial. Let the computer print a label. I've done that. I've done that a few thousand times. Every year. I know what it takes. They must be paid by the hour. It was early in the day in a hospital pharmacy, so no doubt they were tasked with first assembling the morning doses for all those folks in the beds upstairs. They had all night to do that, but likely some doctors were late with their orders. Time pressure on folks only interested in not breaking a sweat. Five pills for room 213 bed A. Three for 309, B. Don't give the anticoagulant anymore to the guy in 145 who has the bleeding ulcer, so take the time to read the directions on the computer screen. Oh, sooooo much to do. Can't stop to fill the prescription for those two sitting out there. Anonymous, insignificant people. Let them wait. That... is real power.

Forty-five freaking minutes waiting for one prescription. Good thing our time meant nothing. Good thing we weren't in a hurry. I watched as the spider wove the web extending from my knee to the chair beside me. Back and forth. Back and forth. The fly was caught and the spider leisurely finished breakfast. Grass sprouted. Steel rusted somewhere. Mountains grew taller. The limited time remaining in my life diminished palpably. We were not cheerful. Cranky bordering on desperate might better describe. Those people were burning our precious vacation time.

We'd hit the pharmacy on the way out of town. We *reallly* wanted to get out of town. It was well past time for a vacation, and we churned that in our core. Too much pathos and tragedy. Too many people sucking the energy out of us. For too long. We needed a break. We *needed* a vacation. We wanted it *now*! We really were not interested in listening to the cheerful banter of the very people who were preventing us from leaving town. They were building the Berlin Wall out of little pills, locking us away from freedom. We did not like those people.

Walking quickly out to the car, we looked up at the mountain trying to inject some calm and beauty into our morning. The first morning of our vacation.

The East County was once a pleasant place, an expanse of farms, pastures, orchards. Now it is a sea of roofs as far as the eye can see. Identical roofs. Every intersection has a Starbucks, a Subway, a hamburger place or two. The shopping center over there is considered a destination resort by the local ants... I mean, residents. Like, wow! It has an In and Out *and* Trader Joe's. Movin' on up to the East Side.

The hospital pharmacy is on one edge of this scourge of suburban sprawl. Our job, should we choose to accept it, was to negotiate our way out the other side. Every intersection sports a set of traffic lights. There are several intersections. On this Saturday morning few vehicles sullied the scene. The road was wide open. We headed east. We should have easily escaped.

The View From Here

First gear, second, third... stop for light. First gear, second, third... stop for light. Repeat as necessary. Thanks, clever traffic engineers. I could sense our freedom out there somewhere, but I could not get there from here. First gear, second, third... stop for light. Every freaking light. A thousand stoplights. My fingers were bleeding as I scrambled up the hill only to slide back down. They've turned this place into hell.

We finally reached the Bypass. Some folks think all this development is a good thing. I'm happy for them. I think the Bypass is a good thing. The Bypass lets me, uh... bypass the East County.

We crossed the bridge, heading north beside the river. "Have you noticed? We haven't stopped for a stoplight for a while."

"There aren't any stoplights up here."

"Yeah! That's it."

Once past Reno heading east, I could feel the cloak of oppression slip from my shoulders. Works this way every time. Behind us... Too many cities. Too many people. Too much civilization wears me down. Love the damn job, but it also wears me down. In front, as we left Reno in the dust, is all that nothing.

I like nothing. Ergo, I like driving across Nevada. There is nothing there. This was so good.

The little German car tripped along on cruise control, just a smidge beyond the speed limit. Nevada. Nothing but open road, mountains and endless long vistas, blue sky with entertaining clouds, the colors of desert in the autumn. The mountains were tipped with snow. The rabbit brush was yellow and all over the place. The aspen groves on the mountainsides were golden. The cottonwoods in the drainages had turned. We saw another vehicle every once in a long while. Hwy 50. The loneliest road in the nation. Perfect.

Ely is only a short nine hour drive from home, but it seemed like the end of the world. The understatement of all time: Ely neither looked, felt, nor acted like... California. It proved we were on vacation. Cheap, old motel. Decent, take-out Chinese food. Early to bed, and early to rise.

We awoke to a cold damp overcast hovering over the small, quiet town. We would be "in between" for the bulk of this day, so I topped off the tank with diesel. Still heading east, the first snowfall began in the first hour of driving. Climbing into the sparse juniper/pinyon pine zone that we love so much, we watched it snow. We were in heaven.

Somewhere in the middle of nowhere, we came to a fork. We chose one, and drove past the entrance to Great Basin National Park. Hadn't been up that road into the hills since 1979 and would have liked to do it that day, but the sign said, "Closed because of Tantrum." Or something like that. Seems somebody elected a president who doesn't deserve a capital P in his title. He didn't get what he wanted, so he took his ball and went home.

The president was feeling peckish. He does that a lot. Barack is an angry man. He has succeeded in life despite having every advantage handed to him. He advanced where others failed because his skin has more color. He has benefited from everything that is good about this country, so of course he hates this country, and its people. Like many others so blessed, he wants to destroy this country. But, some stand in his way. Small wonder he is so edgy.

Sociopaths do that sort of thing. Don't know why Barack does. Closing the national parks hurts the little people, the little people he feels should be kneeling gratefully before the throne. Some, of course, do (kneel, that is). No accounting for taste. But Barack knows that many of those other proles stand in his way. In his vindictive mind, they deserve to be punished. This president thinks a little flogging would turn them to his way of thinking. Likely, he was surprised that they turned on him.

We passed by the park entrance and went on to view those parts of the country not denied us by our president. We found some good stuff. Highways 21 and 130 were simply wonderful, scenic and entertaining. We especially liked the triangular warning signs along the roadside that showed cows on skateboards. Gotta watch those counterculture bovines.

The road from Parowan to Brian Head was simply spectacular. A short spur road east into the national forest presented red sandstone cliffs and height of the season fall foliage. The top of the pass showed 10.2K on my altimeter watch and featured a scenic viewpoint into Cedar Breaks, which the president had also closed. We looked anyway, thumbing our noses at the falling snow, low temperature, and arrogant chief executive.

Continuing to Panguitch, we enjoyed golden aspen groves, pine forest, wondrous views off to the east, and the conspicuous absence of people.

That president tossed us a crumb ("Thank you sir; may I have another?"), for when we reached Bryce Canyon National Park, the gates were open and manned. That bit worked in spite of him, so the notion that billions would soon go down the drain to plug the gaping holes in the president's failed health care experiment slipped out of mind while we could still see some of our country's treasure. And Bryce is such a treasure.

Mommy Nature laid more snow on us, along with the cloud show as we burned up pixels trying to preserve the memories. Beauty beyond any description I might attempt to describe here was on display everywhere.

Cities and crowds, unpaid bills and taxes, biting dogs and bitching clients left far behind, we enjoyed our vacation that day.

November 1, 2013

Grizzly Bears' Place In California Society

The grizzly bear has been missing from California since 1922. The bears were killed off when they conflicted with a growing human population. As far as anyone knows, a rancher killed the last one down near Kings Canyon in the summer of that year.

This paucity of bears doesn't stop us from keeping the grizzly as our state animal. It is on our state flag. Looks good on that flag too, even though these days it might make more sense if we substituted a Chihuahua in its place. Such a timid animal would fit in much better with the direction this state is headed.

California used to host wolves, too. The record is fuzzy, but wolves had also been pretty much wiped out by a burgeoning human population back in the '20s or '30s. So while that backpacker I talked about last week might have expected to see wolves in the Sierra Nevada, that wasn't gonna happen. I'm also reminded of a client I knew years ago who wanted to breed his Malamute female to a wolf, so he turned her loose one night in the woods near Lake Tahoe to mingle with the wolves he thought lived up there. She did end up pregnant, but I suspect that German shepherd with the smile on his face was the likely daddy.

Not surprisingly, considering the diversity of opinion in this state, you can find a few folks who would like to see both wolves and grizzly bears reintroduced to California. I certainly agree with these folks to the degree that I think we have overpopulated and over-urbanized this place. But I do wonder if adding hundreds of large predators to the mess is really going to make this place seem more natural.

I can see it now: "Vote For Prop 1069, The Dangerous Predator Reintroduction Act." It likely would pass if they can just get the media behind it. Supporters of this initiative will certainly point out that there are a few tracts of land remaining in California that actually still have a sparse human population, and they could easily drop a few grizzly bears into these places without having said bears bother anyone these activists know. As long as the bears follow the rules and stay where they belong, those few rural people the bears do eat will hardly be missed. The proponents won't care if those folks vote against bears in their backyards. Rural people are so not progressive thinkers.

Even if this proposition did not pass, we probably will soon have wolves moving into California from the north anyway. They have wandered out of Wyoming into Idaho, and from there into Oregon. I doubt they will respect the black line on the ground between Oregon and us. Those rural people in California, like the ranchers of Idaho and Wyoming, might not be thrilled by this prospect. But I'm sure the proponents of wolf reintroduction who are tucked in each night, deep in the heart of the cities, will be thrilled when the big canines arrive. They can drive out to see wolves, and then head for home refreshed and secure in the knowledge that nobody important was inconvenienced to keep them happy.

November 29, 2009

Franklin Wrong On Eagle Vs. Turkey

I have a bone to pick with Benjamin Franklin. You remember Ben, the inquisitive scientist, clever inventor, and resident wit of the original 13 colonies, back in the late 1700's. He reportedly flew a kite in a thunderstorm, invented the Franklin stove (is that how he got his name?), and actively participated in the birthing of this nation. Why, he was even in on the selection process to designate our national bird. Early on in that selection process, anyway.

Seems that when the committee actually made their decision to nominate the bald eagle for national bird in 1782, Ben was in France and wasn't consulted. This slight may have annoyed him, but the selection of the eagle annoyed him more. For Ben was no fan of the bald eagle. Somebody actually saved the letter he wrote to his daughter in which he expressed his discontent. Can you imagine somebody saving such a missive these days, especially if you simply texted your kid off at college, and it showed up over two hundred years later?

Anyway, Ben had some harsh words for the bald eagle. He suggested that eagles have bad moral character, because they were known to steal fish from the grasp of ospreys. And he called them cowards for those times when these large birds were seen flying away with much smaller birds in hot pursuit. As such, he didn't think they represented the finer characteristics one might prefer in a national symbol.

Ben's choice apparently, would have been the turkey, a bird he thought quite noble. The turkey is also a large bird, intelligent, and interesting in its own right, but I gotta draw the line here, for in my experience, they don't hold a candle to a bald eagle on my scale of one to ten. I'm sorry Ben, but you got it wrong this time.

Ben was referring to what would be today's wild turkey, and not that large-breasted blonde bimbo that graces our Thanksgiving table. Our domestic turkey cannot fly or reproduce itself, and it is dumb as a rock. But I still think he was mistaken about the wild birds. I've seen a skirmish line of wild turkeys wandering through a suburban neighborhood aerating the lawns and leaving little presents for the lawnmowers to fling around. Sorry, but not national symbol material. And that time we saw a lone tom trying to cross busy Kirker Pass Road, darting awkwardly amongst the traffic, looking all the world like a drag queen in top gear... well, I don't think even Ben would have voted for him that day.

Once you have floated the quiet river, and watched the bald eagle leave its perch high in the tree and sail down to snatch the fish from that smooth spot in the water, and then you listen to the cries of the juvenile eagle as its parent approaches the huge nest atop a jagged snag, fish held firmly by yellow talons, you will vote for the eagle. Once those yellow eyes lock on yours, unblinking and unflinching, you will vote for the eagle.

And once you hear the turkey gobble... you will vote for the eagle.

August 23, 2009

A Picture Worth A Thousand Words

The great escarpment of the Grand Tetons stretches across the horizon, with the wide forested valley of Jackson Hole arrayed at its base. New snow dusts the tallest of the granite peaks.

A curve of the Snake River enters on the right from behind a bluff, passes below through a gorge cut into the alluvium, then turns left to disappear around the next bend. The rapids seem smaller when viewed from up here, smaller than I remember from floating this stretch of the river.

Weathered trees fill the foreground. My eyes, however, are drawn to the clouds. A storm is breaking up over the summits, and the billowing cumuli and remnants of thunderheads fill much of this photograph.

Ansel Adams was a genius at capturing and accentuating the myriad of details that clouds present, the shadings of white and gray, and the way the light dances on and around them. And he did this all, somehow, with black and white film.

I've stood on the very spot where he composed this photograph, with the same mountains and trees and river, and a reasonable assortment of clouds to work with, and tried to make the magic with my own camera. So far I haven't come close.

I mostly take pictures. A fair number are pretty pictures, and I sometimes have the camera shop enlarge these, and my friend builds frames for them, and I hang them on my walls. But, only every once in a long while do I take a photograph.

A photograph is different from a picture. A picture is simply a moment frozen in time, valued for its own sake. A picture helps preserve a memory, perhaps of a place or an event, or more importantly, of a person. The vast majority of film expended each year goes to make pictures.

The View From Here

There is nothing wrong with a picture. It's just that a photograph evokes far more. A photograph somehow captures and preserves a more magnificent or compelling image.

Some photographs result from serendipity, when someone accidentally trips the shutter at just the right instant to catch that look in a lover's eyes, or the tragedy in a clown's face, or a sailor kissing a young woman at the end of a war.

Other photographs are planned and executed with precision and forethought, and then the light and chemicals are massaged in the darkroom to produce an image on paper that simply overwhelms the viewer.

A picture is a picture; a photograph is art. A photograph compels the viewer to say, "Wow."

Ansel Adams created many photographs that make me say, "Wow," but that image of a storm clearing over the Tetons is my favorite. I had the chance to purchase an original print once, and I passed. It was hanging in the gallery in Yosemite, in a dark metal frame about four feet square, the first thing I saw as I entered the building. I'd seen copies, reprints in books and on posters, but the real thing simply took my breath away. I couldn't even see anything else in the room.

I should have bought it. I had room on my credit card and I could have managed, somehow, to bend the budget to accommodate it, but I thought I should be practical, so I left this photograph on someone else's wall.

I have regretted that decision for nearly thirty years.

I suppose you might make the argument that no one can truly own a piece of art. Perhaps they should not, for art must be shared with anyone who knows what, "Wow," means. But I don't blame someone who wants to grab and hold onto that feeling, if only for a little while.

I had never even heard of Grand Teton National Park when my folks loaded all three kids into the old Rambler and we made ul from Illinois to Wyoming. We camped next to ior a week, hiked some of the trails that pierce the country, gawked at the moose and elk, and breathed the air.

When the time came for us to leave, a part of my heart stayed behind.

I try to get back to the Tetons every year, but I can't always make it. When I do return, the little piece I left there fits right back into the empty space in my heart... just like finally finishing a jigsaw puzzle.

Eventually I'll get kicked out of this place, and I've asked them to scatter my ashes into the Snake River, so I can take one more float through Jackson Hole. I can't think of a better place.

The Tetons live in my memory, and I've got my own pictures to remind me of them, but none of my pictures give me a, "Wow." When I desperately need to be back in the Tetons, and I can't go, I sure wish I hadn't been quite so responsible that day in a gallery in Yosemite. During those moments, I'd really like to have Mr. Adam's photograph hanging on my wall.

October 4, 2001

Seeking A Photograph, Redux

Years later, Joie and I found ourselves in southern Utah, each day seemingly more beautiful than the previous. 'Twas hard to imagine that the state could keep it up and harbor any beauty that could trump the previous day, but that piece of the Beehive State scheduled next would. I kinda knew this, because I had passed through once before, some twenty years earlier. I couldn't remember all the details, so there were moments that were as much a surprise to me as they were to Joie. So I made sure my camera was handy, and Joie saw that her phone was fully charged, for that is her camera of choice. Two steps out of the motel room door presented a striking mountain range catching dawn light to the north, and yet another red sandstone cliff to the south. Here we go again.

We motored past pleasant small farms, with the green of well-irrigated pastures and trees in autumn color. Streambeds glimmered with willow and cottonwood. The mountains around were tipped in snow. And here and there the exposed rocks of red, gray, and various purples poked their heads out to watch us speed past.

Where we had looked down into Bryce Canyon and its kaleidoscope of colors and shapes, on this day we looked up instead at the gather of garishly painted cliffs and towers in Kodachrome Basin. Several pixels bit the dust there.

We entered a sparse forest, leaving the colored rocks behind. My memory blurred, and I stated that all we'd have for the next two hours would be a pleasant cruise in the trees. My memory erred.

Shortly, large eroded cliffs and a curved canyon resplendent in riverbed and golden leaves led to the huge reef near the town of Escalante. Then we crested a ridge, and the viewpoint parking area beckoned. Pulling off the road, we noted that the view indeed opened. It spread before us in a 180°, toe-tip-to-horizon explosion of beauty. While the engine ticked quietly behind us, we stood looking, silent, mouths gaping, forgetting to breathe.

Intense blue sky and fairy clouds. Hundred mile views. Colored rock in cliff and dome, patterns in the rock, rock carved by canyons, speckled with sparse green trees, the Grand Staircase lay naked in the sun. She was beyond gorgeous. And I remembered none of this from my last visit.

Our road pierced this wonder, narrow and sinuous, with the occasional guardrail when there was room, and otherwise not at all forgiving of the careless. The view was on both sides as we dropped into the place. Each turn brought awe, ooos and ahs, giggles. We each pointed out wonders at the same time, on opposite sides of the vehicle. We laughed. We may have cried at times. We lost our breath. Utterly spent, we followed the road as it climbed out of this wonderland, and then crawled the spine of a ridge with merely wonderful views that almost disappointed after that which we just left behind.

Neither of us had taken even one picture. The camera and the phone sat unused. We openly admitted that they were not up to the task. The place as a whole was simply too massive, too beautiful, too overwhelming. If we had a year, and could pick the best pieces, a million photographs lay hidden in the Golden Staircase for us to discover. But they would all be pieces rather than the whole of the place.

So we'll just have to go back and do it correctly... soon.

November 7, 2013

Backyard Offers An Escape, Even As An Adult

When we were kids, the best tent we built in the backyard came about when we took Dad's old canvas painting tarp and dragged it over the metal frame of our swing set. It even looked like a tent, a cavalry tent from those black and white movies we once watched. Our tent smelled a bit musty, with a hint of oil paint and yep, old canvas. But we kept it erected for weeks, over Dad's protestations, 'cause it was a really neat thing to have when you were a kid. We didn't sleep out in our tent. We just played in it during the summer afternoons.

A couple of times every summer, we talked the parents into letting us camp out overnight in the backyard. They first made sure it wasn't going to rain, and that the other kids had permission from their folks to stay over with us, and then they turned us loose.

We dragged the sleeping bags out onto the lawn, and settled in as it got dark. We didn't want a tent, because we wanted to watch the sky. That's where the shooting stars lived.

The house lights blinked out around the neighborhood, and it grew quiet as darkness fell and the stars popped out. Few cars passed by on the highway behind the house, so all we could hear was the breeze in the leaves, and perhaps an owl or two. The stars didn't make any noise at all.

So, flat on our backs we looked for the Big Dipper and the North Star, even though we knew where north was. We always marveled that one star could always stay in that place, up in the north, while all the others moved around the sky.

The rule was you couldn't fall asleep until you saw a shooting star. Most nights we made it, but with all that staring at the sky, sometimes sleep caught up with us first. If anyone had been listening, they would have heard us arguing over who saw the first shooting star. And then later, they would have heard nothing at all.

Sometimes I woke in the middle of the dark night. Took some getting used to, that not being in my own bed realization, but then the marvel of the splatter of stars across the black sky and the quiet and the smells of the night reminded me why I did silly things like sleep on the lawn in my own backyard.

The Big Dipper would have moved since I last saw it, since it circles around the North Star when most aren't watching. I couldn't tell time by it yet, 'cause that takes more than one night to learn, but it was worth watching, anyway. By then, cool air would be making its way past my neck and into the sleeping bag, so I tucked in a little tighter, and was soon lost in sleep, again.

The birds woke me before the sun each time. The air was cool and damp and it smelled wonderful.

A short half-century has passed since those times, but when the world intrudes a little too much, I still like to escape, to sleep out in my backyard. We use the trailer now, which I suppose is cheating a bit, but my back isn't what it once was. There is more traffic noise than I remember from my youth. And I cannot see the stars without stepping outside. But, if we leave the windows open, the cool air with its smells still slips in, and the birds are still there in the morning.

I've slept out below sea level in Death Valley, and above 13,000 feet in the White Mountains. I've slept in a swamp in Florida, and in the snow under a full moon. At times the elk were bugling, or a moose walked by. Deer have sniffed me in my sleeping bag, and once that bear walking under my hammock set me swinging. And I've listened to coyotes and things that go bump in the night in places where it would take days to walk back to civilization.

Each and every one of these places was worth waking up in. But none of that takes away from the simple pleasure of sleeping out in my own backyard.

August 6, 2006

Intermission

Cooperisms

Bob's enthusiasm for firearms, the Second Amendment, and the personal freedoms that come with these items is simply unmistakable. Jeff Cooper (5/10/20-9/25/06), the creator of modern handgun handling technique, left a legacy among all responsible gun owners, and Bob made it a point to collect some of his written wisdom. (RG)

Selections from the ramblings of a wise and well-traveled man:

"Life is hopelessly complex for people who have no principles."

"Pick up a rifle and you change instantly from a subject to a citizen."

"Personal weapons are what raised mankind out of the mud, and the rifle is the queen of personal weapons."

"The rifle itself has no moral stature, since it has no will of its own. Naturally, it may be used by evil men for evil purposes, but there are more good men than evil, and while the latter cannot be persuaded to the path of righteousness by propaganda, they can certainly be corrected by good men with rifles."

"The rifle is a weapon. Let there be no mistake about that. It is a tool of power, and thus dependent completely upon the moral stature of its user. It is equally useful in securing meat for the table, destroying group enemies on the battlefield, and resisting tyranny. In fact, it is the only means of resisting tyranny, since a citizenry armed with rifles simply cannot be tyrannized."

"Remember the first rule of gunfighting… 'have a gun.'"

"Safety is nice, but it's not first. Life is first and life is not safe."

"Do you care about freedom? Dreams may have inspired it, and wishes prompted it, but only war and weapons have made it yours."

"The media insist that crime is the major concern of the American public today. In this connection they generally push the point that a disarmed society would be a crime-free society. They will not accept the truth that if you take all the guns off the street you still will have a crime problem, whereas if you take the criminals off the street you cannot have a gun problem."

"The will to survive is not as important as the will to prevail - the answer to criminal aggression is retaliation."

"One bleeding-heart type asked me in a recent interview if I did not agree that violence begets violence. I told him that it is my earnest endeavor to see that it does. I would like very much to ensure - and in some cases I have - that any man who offers violence to his fellow citizens begets a whole lot more in return than he can enjoy."

"We continue to be exasperated by the view apparently gaining momentum in certain circles, that armed robbery is OK as long as nobody gets hurt! The proper solution to armed robbery is a dead robber, on the scene."

"The police cannot protect the citizen at this stage of our development, and they cannot even protect themselves in many cases. It is up to the private citizen to protect himself and his family, and this is not only acceptable, but mandatory."

"The 1911 pistol remains the service pistol of choice in the eyes of those who understand the problem. Back when we audited the FBI academy in 1947, I was told that I ought not to use my pistol in their training program because it was not fair.

Maybe the first thing one should demand of his sidearm is that it be unfair."

"A free man must not be told how to think, either by the government or by social activists. He may certainly be shown the right way, but he must not accept being forced into it."

"The conclusions seem inescapable that in certain circles a tendency has arisen to fear people who fear government. Government, as the Father of Our Country put it so well, is a dangerous servant and a fearful master. People who understand history, especially the history of government, do well to fear it. For a people to express openly their fear of those of us who are afraid of tyranny is alarming. Fear of the state is in no sense subversive. It is, to the contrary, the healthiest political philosophy for a free people."

"One difference between a liberal and a pickpocket is that if you demand your money back from a pickpocket, he will not question your motives."

Part Four:
My Invisible Friend

Just Why Must We Debate Death?

> *Bob's invisible friend was a recurring character in his weekly column over the years. The civility with which he maintained their "conversations," and the duration of their "friendship" ought to be an example to us all in this era of hyperpolarization and political correctness. (RG)*

I have an invisible friend with whom I argue. She and I rarely see eye to eye. She is well intentioned and moral, as I try to be, but we inevitably end up debating the issues that trouble thinking people. Some of our arguments become heated, and I must be careful to restrain my responses when we are out in public, for if I begin to shout and gesticulate when she provokes me, people tend to stare, because only I can see her. Still, I love these arguments. My invisible friend forces me to question and grow.

Recently, as we browsed through a craft fair, she tried holding me to task because I have not renounced eating meat. Realizing that we were headed for another nasty confrontation, I desperately tried to change the subject. However, when she charged me with the crime of insensitivity, of not caring about the lives that ended so that I might eat, I had to respond, for I am intimately acquainted with death. I know that death changes things… and it is forever.

I discovered many years ago that nothing is the same in death as it is in life. My invisible friend was shopping for a dried flower arrangement, dead flowers, to decorate her home. So I asked her if those dried flowers, as pretty as they were, could compare to a natural garden of live flowers tousled by the breeze in a sunny mountain meadow. Of course, they could not.

Near where we stood, a display of photographs hung on the wall. One depicted a rare beauty, the late Marilyn Monroe. I have seen her movies; they captured some of her essence, even the sound of her voice. But I can only imagine how this might compare to time spent with her, the soft whisper of her breath in my ear, the smell of her hair, or even the brush of her skirt on my arm as she passed by my chair.

My friend doesn't know it, but I have a trophy mount of a bull elk hanging on my wall. I like to think it serves as a fitting memorial to the fine beast that has been feeding my family for a year. A taxidermist did a marvelous job with the bull, he looks very life-like, but I am fully aware that his presence on a wall overlooking the pool table is not the same as the living bull elk I heard bugling in the mountains of Wyoming last autumn.

I concede that death is inevitable. Every seed that sprouts, every egg that hatches, every bawling newborn calf is going to die. Sometimes a life is wonderful and its death a tragedy; often the opposite occurs, a miserable existence but a merciful death. Nobody gets to choose, but nobody escapes, either.

Sometimes I try to deny death, for the images of death disturb me. I turn the page when the newspaper presents photos of a thousand bloated corpses filling a mass grave in some country most couldn't find on a map. I don't look at the tiny calico kitten struck on the road, never to snuggle next to a little girl again. And as a child I ran away from my strangely plastic looking Grandma, lying in a purple box at the front of a room that smelled funny, a room filled by evil sounding organ music and crying aunts that I never saw anywhere else.

But I am concerned with the *how* of death, for as a society we have no consistency in the way we deal with this. We are horrified by the grisly murder of a child, but would stand in line to torture her killer to death. Some people carry signs to protest a man hunting for elk, then go home to watch endless TV hours of cheetahs that feed their young by chasing down and killing impalas.

A part of a veterinarian's job is to offer relief to animals that are suffering an intolerable existence, a humane death we call it. In effect the doctor conveys a gift of death. This is considered a good thing. But if he were to offer the same relief to his ailing father he would be thrown in jail.

My invisible friend recoils at the thought that I eat meat, that an animal died to feed me, while she is comfortable eating fruit, the unborn babies of a tree. I wonder how anyone decides if any of this is right or wrong?

I'm not proposing we should "kill 'em all and let God sort it out" as some might suggest. But since we all have to live with that person in the mirror, shouldn't we have some latitude to judge ourselves in these matters?

I often ponder how to reconcile the causing of death. I know men who have killed their fellow humans in war with no apparent residual embarrassment, but were paralyzed with grief for accidentally killing their own dog. This year alone, I killed ten thousand ants in my kitchen for no more reason than they bothered me, yet I felt no remorse. And I killed one animal with a rifle, a resoundingly difficult task for me, to put food in the freezer for my family.

Years of introspection preceded, and no doubt will follow, the decision to hunt my own food. To the charge of insensitivity, I plead not guilty. I don't know all the answers, or even if there are answers, but it is not for lack of consideration.

And the next time I see my invisible friend, maybe I will ask her this question: If it is wrong to hunt for food and be a taker of life, how can it be right to end suffering and be a giver of death?

March 30, 2000

Don't Take Rights Away
From Wrong People

My invisible friend showed up the other day waving a newspaper clipping which reported the first slight increase in violent crime numbers in nearly a decade. It's probably just me (you know how I get), but she seemed almost delighted over the prospect. Needless to say, we had another one of our arguments.

We'd both like to see less crime in this country. We still need to look over our shoulders for muggers when we walk the neighborhood and neither of us enjoys locking our car doors just to drive downtown. But let's face it, there are some bad people out there who spend their lives hurting others and it's best to avoid them.

My biggest gripe however, is that whenever my invisible friend is reminded about crime, she argues that I need to surrender more of my freedom in the faint hope that somehow she could feel safer. My friend watches the news so she is convinced that drugs and guns cause most of the crime and death in America. She argues that both the War on Drugs and complete gun control are solutions. So I wanted to play a little game with her, a game of crime, violence and death in the hope that I might lend a little perspective to the next round of our argument.

For my game we need a big football stadium with 100,000 people in the stands. We'll call this America. Now send 5,000 of these people down to the field. That's how many get caught breaking the rules and spend some time in jail during their lifetime. We'll let about two-thirds of them back into the stands eventually, because they didn't do anything real scary and they straightened out after they learned their lesson. Leave the rest on the field however, for they do the nasty crimes, and many of them do them over and over.

Now put 700 folding chairs out on the grass and fill them with the assorted folks standing on the field. This represents the two million criminals we actually have in jail in this country right now. They don't stay there for long, of course, because we let them play musical chairs with the rest of the criminals down there. Those left standing on the grass when the music stops get to run around committing mayhem on the rest of us.

Out of our little population in this stadium about 700 people die every year. Most die from "natural causes." Illegal drugs kill only one. In contrast, our popular legal drugs, alcohol and cigarettes, kill over 200.

Seven people in our family of 100,000 are murdered. That is a lot compared to a soccer stadium in England or Europe, where only one or two die that way each year, but it still looks good compared with similar stadiums in Mexico, where the number is 17, or South Africa where it is 75.

A lot depends on where you put the stadium. In most American cities, the number is less than one; in others, it is almost 80. It seems that most of our murders take place in a handful of urban stadiums, and the rest of the land isn't a whole lot less civilized than the countries my friend compares us to. By the way, people who get out of their folding chairs before they are scheduled commit almost a third of these murders.

Not surprisingly, nearly 80% of the murderers and 50% of the murdered are those folks already down on the field.

Five of the seven murders in our little stadium are committed with guns. This number provokes my friend to demand that all 30,000 people in the stadium who own firearms must give them up. Meanwhile 16 people in this stadium die in automobile crashes and 33 more from medical mistakes every year.

This game could go on much longer, but every time we get this far my friend changes the subject.

I get tired of this same old fight with my invisible friend, but I haven't figured out what to do with nearly 2,000 folks down in the field. I don't know why there are so many career criminals in our little stadium, but I do know they are perpetrating most of the violent crime. Logic would suggest that we do something to reduce their number, or at least try to constrain them from further criminal acts before we start restricting the 98,000 decent folk up in the stands who rarely hurt anyone.

If there were fewer people standing around on the field there would be less crime. If they were in school or working they wouldn't be standing around. If they were sitting on those folding chairs they wouldn't be standing around, either. Sadly, since the War on Drugs began we've seen far more people out on that field.

I really don't know what causes a person to become a criminal. I do know that some of our population will commit crime after violent crime as long as we let them, and they only stop when they are confined to those folding chairs. And we don't have near enough folding chairs.

February 22, 2001

Havana & Berkeley Sister Cities?

My invisible friend dropped by the other day, fresh from her poetry group in Berkeley. I'm not sure why she doesn't just move over there because she does something in that city nearly every day. On Mondays, she is on campus to protest the war. On Tuesdays, she marches in front of the Marine recruiting office. On Wednesdays, she pickets the largest employer in town because it is the largest employer in town, so it must be corrupt, polluting, and unfair to its workers. And on Fridays, she works the phones in some storefront raising funds for obscure left-wing political wannabes who promise a brave new world.

Her poetry group meets in a coffee shop, where over the course of many hours, they suck down dark brew and complain about the current president.

It doesn't matter which president it is. It does matter which coffee they drink, for they take that very seriously. They choose their coffee shop and rarely visit another, although the topic of conversation is pretty much the same in each place. They all complain about the current president.

The countdown is on. They know exactly how many days George W. Bush has left in office. It's up there on the blackboard, along with the muffin of the day. The patrons sit in their same chairs all day, every day, drink their coffee and complain, and plan their celebration for inauguration day. The worst president in history will soon be history. They cannot wait.

These folks hate Bush because of his Patriot Act and those pesky wiretaps.

This tyranny has taken away all of their freedom. They worry about the concentration camps soon to be filled with hundreds of thousands of Americans, and the sense of big brother always watching them. So except for the newspapers, the radio and TV reporters and commentators, the protests in the streets, the many books and movies produced by the president's opposition, and the coffee shops overflowing with criticism of him, all dissent has been crushed. Until next January, they will be oppressed.

I couldn't help but notice that another world leader is leaving office.

Fidel Castro announced his retirement. It's easy to draw contrast between Castro and Bush. Castro has had good approval ratings, especially in Berkeley. Castro's polls always show slightly above 100 percent approval, and no one in Cuba criticizes him in public. Of course, it helps that his pollsters carry automatic weapons. And Castro has been re-elected many times over the decades with virtually no opposition. Now he will pass on the reins of power to his brother, who certainly will maintain the decades-old tradition of prosperity and freedom the Cuban people have enjoyed.

Hopefully, Raúl will maintain the fence Fidel built around his island, so the U.S. population will not shrink further from the mass exodus of Americans escaping to freedom in Cuba.

Meanwhile, my invisible friend hopes our next president will do something about the danger emerging in the East County, where it seems that every school has been given a patriotic name. Don't people realize the harm that will befall our children if we don't stop this attack upon their moral and social development? My invisible friend is trying her best, but she could use some help.

March 2, 2008

Don't Take Care Of Stray Cats

My invisible friend's husband was doing the vegetable garden thing in his yard the other day, toiling away in the soft soil he had roto-tilled the previous weekend. Down on his hands and knees, he carefully planted a row of tomato plants, digging with the brand new trowel he just received from the catalog folks. Soft sunshine warmed the back of his neck while he crawled around his little plot. All was right with the world.

That's when he discovered the little "souvenir" one of the neighborhood cats left for him, buried in that same soft soil. Now my friend is not averse to using "natural fertilizer" in his garden. In fact he expounds at length at dinner parties, to anyone who will listen, about the advantage of cow origin verses horse origin by-product. My invisible friend just loves that part.

Anyway, her husband hates cats and everything they do, including what they do in his garden, so it was all she could manage to keep him from running for the shotgun. It was a perfect set-up, with this guy running around the yard screaming about those dang cats, and his neighbor over the back fence screaming back, for she feeds any stray cat that shows up. And they all show up.

Of course I got caught in the middle.

Talk about your no-win situation. I've sat in on discussions about religion and politics, and gun control and abortion, but nothing will set previously rational neighbors at each other's throats faster than a straying cat.

Folks who love cats *know* they can do no wrong. Cats are God's chosen creatures, beautiful and graceful and infinitely wise. Even when a cat creates chaos by knocking a precious knick-knack off the shelf, all you will hear from a cat person is, "Isn't that cute?"

People who hate cats mostly hate them because they are so perfect... and they know it. Some despise cats because of their arrogance. My friend's husband knows that darn cat figured he created that garden bed just for the cat's private potty, and that drives him nuts. He wouldn't be caught dead doing something nice for a cat.

My invisible friend would love to diffuse this situation peacefully, so she wrote a letter to her county supervisor wondering why the government hadn't started a licensing program for cats like they have for dogs. She knows in her heart that licenses can solve all of society's problems, so surely once we have cat licenses, both her husband and her neighbor will be happy.

I wasn't sure how to break it to my invisible friend, but I figure licensing cats is a lot like licensing the wind. It might look good on paper and make a few bureaucrats happy, but it wasn't going to change anything in her backyard.

Dogs, like people, are semi-domesticated. Society can lay out a set of rules and sometimes, you-know-sort-of-maybe-occasionally, those rules get followed. I'm afraid you won't see anywhere near this kind of compliance with cats, or cat lovers.

The lady feeding all those cats behind my friend's house won't ever license them. She can't even afford to feed them, much less take proper care of them, so she will never pay a license fee. Besides, she doesn't claim ownership of those cats. She is just "saving" them.

Like most folks who feed stray cats, this woman thinks she is helping. She does it because it makes her feel better. This neighbor does love cats and her motives are as pure as snow, but she is doing irrevocable harm to the cats whenever she feeds them, and thus encourages them to crowd together. And she is making enemies all over the neighborhood.

Because she crowds them together, she is spreading viruses among the cats, stressing them, increasing their injury rates from fights, and generally creating more harm than good. And I have it on good authority that her yard was written up in a coyote tour guide as a five star dining establishment. So although she sleeps better thinking she is helping the cats, my friend's neighbor really is inadvertently helping my friend's husband by killing them off.

May 10, 2001

Part Five:
Veterinarian Behaving Badly

Homemade Baby Food

Bob was one of the early contributors to Veterinarians Behaving Badly, self-described as "a sarcastic veterinary blog dedicated to all of the money grubbing vets out there who are fed up with the insanity of the American public." It was (and still remains) controversial both outside as well as within the veterinary community. It's heyday was an 18-month period overlapping 2012 & 2013. As of this printing, two of the most-read posts and many columns that generated the most worthwhile comments came from Bob's 'puter. While there have been a variety of entertaining contributors to VBB over the years, Bob represents the genuine writing talent of the bunch.

As the above history relates to this particular column, references to VBB Hospital appear in many posts on the blog. The truth is, there are Veterinarian Behaving Badly Hospitals all over the country, and we liked to refer to them as one collective unit. (RG)

Mandy makes baby food for our use in VBB hospital. She buys the cheap turkeys just before Thanksgiving, putting a couple in the freezer when they are on sale. One client brings in a turkey every year just for this purpose, because his puppy began eating as it finally recovered from Parvo, and what it ate was Mandy's homemade turkey baby food. He's been doing this for years.

We have a stove in the break room, and Mandy boils a whole turkey on that stove, all day, day after day, until it is mostly mush. The entire hospital smells of turkey when this happens. Like Thanksgiving Day at Mom's. Then into the blender goes the remnants, and from there into ice cube trays, and then the freezer. Ice cube trays provide individual servings of Mandy's homemade baby food, which thaw quickly in the microwave, or with hot water. We call this food magic, because puppies and kittens, old lady cats and ninety pound pit bulls will eat this before they will eat anything else in the world, and sometimes this saves their lives.

Ya see, thirty-five years ago, Mandy had a baby. The baby came a bit early, and it weighed all of 4.5 pounds, and he took a little work to get him started. Eventually he got to where he'd eat baby food, and since money was just a mite tight back then, Mandy made her own. This set a precedent.

Mandy will tell you that the homemade turkey baby food is magic, but she won't tell you the entire truth. Sure, the baby food smells great, and it tastes great, and it slides down easy when eating is too much work, but what Mandy won't tell you is that there is more than mushed turkey and water in those ice cube trays. Nope. That's not all that goes into that baby food.

What Mandy won't tell you is that she also infuses a generous serving of love into that food. And the other thing that Mandy won't tell you is that there isn't enough room in that baby food for all the love she has to give, so she serves up some more love on the side, every time she feeds her baby food to puppies or kittens or old lady cats, or ninety pound pit bulls. And thus we have magic.

Mandy works for me and thus I'm always giving her things to do around here. Most times she does them. But every once in a while I'll go looking for Mandy onnacounta something not getting done right away, and I'll find her in the back, sitting next to an open kennel door. The kennel floor will be covered with one of those warm, colorful, padded kennel floor covers that Mandy sews. The water dish will be clean and full. The cat box, if needed, is clean and over there. And the puppy or kitten or old lady cator ninety pound pit bull is curled up in the bed that Mandy makes for them.

Mandy talks quietly with these patients of ours, so she disturbs no one. She'll generally have a little plastic bowl of warm homemade turkey baby food with her, maybe a spoon or small syringe, or maybe just that second finger on her right hand that delivers fingertips of baby food gently to the nose of a puppy or kitten who just might lick it off, and thus jumpstart a recovery.

Mandy will have already been sitting there for two hours, talking with her patient, petting or combing or cleaning softly, fussing with and touching and passing on the love she serves up with the magic of her baby food. Mandy learned that you can pass love through your fingers and your voice, and your fussing... pass it on to a tiny premature baby or a puppy or kitten or old lady cat or ninety pound pit bull... and that is what she does. That, and the homemade baby food.

I have tests and drugs and a scalpel, and I do what I can. Mandy follows with the homemade turkey baby food and her love, and she brings the miracles I don't have in my box.

This morning we arrived at the hospital early. We wanted to see how Icarus was doing. This cat had come into our hospital yesterday, and he looked like shit. Sorry. He did. Mostly, he looked like flea dirt, which is flea shit, and he felt like a handful of sand when you picked him up. He had so much flea dirt all over him that the wet parts had turned red.

Icarus lay there on my exam table, limp. His right eye bulged nearly out of its socket. According to the owner, "He ain't eatin', and he don't move much." That much I had figured before Mrs. Einstein opened her mouth.

Of course she didn't have any money. Heck, she still owed me a hundred bucks from February. Couldn't come up with a hundred bucks in three months, although it looked as if her tattoo artist got paid. So no tests or anything useful this day. I got permission to drain the abscess, correct some of the dehydration, start the antibiotics. We'd have to hope for a miracle to do the rest.

So I turned Icarus over to Mandy. She fussed over him for three hours. When she was done, he was clean, about a hundred fleas lay dead on the battlefield, he'd been talked to, petted, touched, fussed over. His drugs were in him, his fluids delivered, and now his bed was warm. And a finger with a bit of homemade turkey baby food was touching ever so gently on his nose. He licked it off. And he rolled over to have his belly rubbed.

When we left for home Icarus could stand, and he had eaten some considerable amount of baby food, and even a bit of canned cat food. And he purred. Maybe, just maybe…

Icarus was dead in his bed this morning. He looked better dead than when he arrived, for he was clean and he died in a relaxed position. But yeah, he didn't make it. That crying and cursing? Well, that's what Mandy does sometimes. Especially when she is standing over one of the dead ones who shouldn't be that way.

She hasn't done this work as long as I have, and while I walk away muttering something about god damn f****ing stupid ass people, Mandy still screams and cries. And then later she said to me, "You're right, you know. You can't love them more than their own people. You can't, or this will kill you."

"Yeah, and good luck with that."

She'll be there for the next one. You watch.

May 11, 2013

This Shouldn't Be Necessary, But Here...

Bob wrote a number of columns foundational to my philosophy of the day-to-day economics of veterinary medicine. None more than this. (RG)

From 1948 until the late 1970s our little city had one veterinary hospital. A guy built this hospital, sold it to another, who sold it to my boss, who eventually retired and sold it to me in 1981. The city was and is kinda the ugly sister in this area. The residents who worked, worked factory jobs, had Bob or Stan stenciled over the pocket of their shirts, inhaled asbestos, got dirty hands. At best our city was lower middle class, except for those bad neighborhoods that lay claim to the worse economic titles critics lay on the unemployed, the old and lonely, or that bunch they simply dismissed.

We kinda had the corner on crime, ignorance, and irresponsibility, and our clients reflected this. For decades, nobody else wanted to try to run a veterinary practice here. And then some doctors I knew announced that they were going to open a veterinary hospital in our city, and this made it into the local newspaper. I found out about it when one of our more annoying clients, Clair, threw it in my face. She was not a sweet lady. She was a bit profane, a touch more than a little crude, monumentally ignorant, and lacking in the social graces. She sneered into my face, and with that same tone that a nasty sixth grade girl uses when she really wants to hurt your feelings, she told me about the new hospital, and then to really rub it in, she injected that now that we would have some competition, we would have to lower our fees.

You know, those fees that were always too high for her comfort, the ones that were making us rich at her expense. We cost her more for her cat than her own medical care. She'd tell you that without having to ask.

Now, I knew the doctors who were gonna be across town, and they liked to practice the highest quality medicine possible in those days, and they charged appropriately for their work. So they were going to have much higher fees than this woman had ever seen, particularly at our practice. So I quietly mentioned to this woman that if we used her logic, flawed as it was, we would actually be able to raise our fees. She was dumbfounded. She had no clue then, and probably still does not.

Today I did a little research. Very little, very quickly. Pardon if some of these numbers are a tad inaccurate, but even if they're a bit off, this makes what I checked out far more accurate than the information many use to draw certain conclusions. For they are working from little or no information, whatsoever.

According to the *Wall Street Journal*, there are 954,000± physicians in this country. According to the Bureau of Labor Statistics, a government agency, we have 691,000 people working as physicians in this country. Which either means we have a heckuva number of unemployed physicians around here, or some folks aren't real good with numbers. Who do I believe? Eh, I don't much care.

I just needed some numbers to make a point. And since these are simply numbers, albeit big numbers, and figures don't lie, but liars sure can figure, I will toss out some of these for your perusal. Hopefully, what I have to say, using actual numbers for illustration, will carry a bit more weight than the spouting of those folks who have no bleeping idea what they are talking about. Or about which they are talking, if the niceties mean that much to you.

According to the Bureau of Labor Statistics 2,737,000 registered nurses work here. And although I think this number a bit low, the Bureau says we have 61,400 veterinarians. From this I hope you will agree that we are a small profession. We don't have a lot of clout. Up until recently we were more like a friendly club than an industry. We operate in this tiny niche, and try to get by without making a lot of waves. And we deal with our clients as individuals, and not from the perspective of massive industry.

Calling upon the BLS again, I noticed that the median income for physicians is about $166,000 per year. Median is not the same as "average." It translates into half the physicians make less than this figure, and half more. The median income for veterinarians is $82,000. And in case you were wondering, the registered nurses' median income is $65,000. For comparison, truck drivers have a "mean" salary of about $40,000. "Mean" is a bit different from median. This one does mean average, and the BLS uses the average earnings for most jobs and apparently reserves median for those overpriced professionals. So I guess they are "mean" to those plain ole workin' folks.

In case you are wondering, I'm here to defend my fellow veterinarians against the charge that we are money grubbing liars and thieves. I'm not here to attack the earnings of physicians or nurses. And I'm certainly not going to disparage truck drivers. Truth be known, I've always wanted to drive a truck, long haul, cross country. Might even try it after I retire from this nonsense.

I like truck drivers, and admire them. Any driver that borrows $100K for his own rig, deals with the cost of diesel, the retard four wheelers, the inconsistency of insurance companies and the irrational insanity of government regulation earns his/her money. And every time they get on the binders in time to keep from squishing that mini-van full of women and children they should be paid brain surgeon money. But let's be real here. You can get a CDL after days of schooling and with some proper mentoring, you can do that job just fine.

Registered nurses are angels, and I've trusted my life to them on occasion and I admire what they do. I absolutely fold when I have to deal with sick people. Nurses are worth every penny and more. Many have advanced training and advanced degrees, but you can become a nurse with an AA.

Physicians put in those eight years of college, plus internships and residencies. That truck driver has been working for ten to fifteen years before the physicians draw their first serious paycheck.

Well, veterinarians put in those same eight years of college, and many have the internships and residencies. We also bring a little something to the table. For this we do twice as well as the "mean" truck driver, a bit more than the median RN, and less than half what a median physician nets.

So why did Clair think we cost her more to care for her cat than she paid for her own medical care? Well, mostly because Clair was *wrong*! And she had no clue.

Ya see, Clair had a good job that paid benefits. One of those benefits was a medical plan that gave her access to doctors and hospitals whenever she wished, and it cost her a $5.00 co-pay to see her doctor and another five for her prescriptions. Small wonder my charges were higher. Her doctor visits were worth about $75.00 in those days, and the prescriptions many dollars more. Her hysterectomy cost somebody over $30,000, but she paid five bucks. When I spayed her cat, I charged far less than 0.5% of that $30K. But yeah, I cost *her* more than her own medical care.

That medical benefit cost her employer more than $1,000.00 a *month* for Clair's family. But Clair never saw that. She just expected it. I cost her more than she *wanted* to pay. She *wanted* to spend her money on fun stuff. I ruined that. My fees infuriated her, for she thought I took everything away from her and took it home. So I was getting rich off of her.

Don't matter at all to Clair what I was actually making. After expenses, at that time I was taking home about 14% of what I charged, before taxes. Clair never figured that out. I was not outperforming her physicians, or their nurses.

But to Clair, I was simply a money grubbing liar and thief. And that, was that.

April 22, 2012

I'm Tired

This is the first one of Bob's columns I remember reading. As the previous piece was foundational for Ryan, so this one was for me. It helped me see what could, what couldn't, and what needed to change in veterinary medicine. (EM)

Decades in this profession teach many lessons. For instance, I've learned that there are two kinds of tired in this business. One version comes from being so busy during your hours in the hospital that you blindly stumble out to the car at the end of a day, pick up a bake-at-home pizza as you try to remember where you live, cook it up while gulping down one neat bourbon, and then fall asleep in the chair in front of the usual reruns before you finish the third piece. More on this later.

The other kind of tired happens when nothing of consequence happens for days at a time in the hospital, and you wear out the solitaire game on the computer, and thus at the end of the day when you peek at tomorrow's bank deposit, it laughs at you. And when you sneak up on the bill file and peer inside, it laughs even louder. On these nights you hit every red light, stalled truck, radar trap, and road repair on the way home. When you finally make it to the house, the good bourbon bottle is nearly empty, but the cheap shit will do, and you have one or six, and the usual reruns are on the tube, but nothing in the house will matter. You ain't gonna sleep that night at all.

When the economy sucks like this one, those in our profession get to know both versions. There is no rhyme or reason to what comes through the front door, and you simply go with the flow, busy or slow, for the boat has no oars, just like those oarsmen in government who would tell you they can fix this mess. We are utterly at the mercy of what comes through the front door, as are those folks who come in through the front door.

Today was one of those crazy busy, exhausting days.

I fired up the computer when I walked into the hospital at 7:15. The day's appointments popped up. Two procedures booked for the 10:00-12:00 morning slot. A teeth cleaning on a dog belonging to a friend, and a double enucleation, surgical removal of both eyes, on a cranky old Shih Tzu with glaucoma in both eyes, and likely chronic pain. He has been blind for a while, and now I will make him comfortable for the rest of his days.

The rest of the morning was completely booked, seven appointments from 8:15 to 10:00. I ran through the usual things I must do to prepare for the day. My receptionist arrived in her usual flurry of noise and chaos, setting my stress level alarm off before I even start the day, just before 8:00. I could hear her talking with someone in the parking lot. That couldn't be good.

I knew the guy. He has two Dobermans, one an absolute doll, and the other so afraid of her own shadow that she thinks anyone petting her will kill her, so she kills him first. She is a joy to work with in the hospital. Of course he brings in the psycho one. She had been vomiting since one AM, and the puke looked and smelled like poop. Bad sign. Oh, and she had been eating those parts of the kong toy that the other dog chewed off.

The xrays were classic obstruction of the small bowel. Time to forget everything else and go to surgery. My receptionist went about calling clients and moving their morning appointments to free up the time I would need. We were in surgery shortly after nine.

The last of the morning's surgery was done by 12:30. I hit the bank, and the Chinese takeout, and I was back writing up the surgery records by 1:00.

The afternoon began at 1:30. Sixteen appointments awaited. I was approaching tired already, and when the "I paid for part of this clinic and I deserve special attention so forget my tomorrow appointment cause I'm here today" walk-in showed up at 2:00, we tried to find a way to see her, too. I hope she enjoyed the wait, for the courteous folks somehow got seen before this one.

I did finally see the mouth, and her cat wasn't all that bad off, and as she was leaving somebody noticed the weird people standing in front of the clinic so I went out to see if any unreasonable crimes were being committed. Introduce the filthy pet owner holding the puppy in a towel in her arms. The guy translating for her, for her English was missing a few pieces, told me her puppy wasn't eating, was throwing up, and the diarrhea was bloody. Oh, and no, the puppy had not been vaccinated.

I can describe tired pretty well, but I'm not sure I can describe the sinking feeling this revelation rewarded me. I've watched hundreds of puppies die from Parvo during the thirty plus years this disease has existed. Every one died because somebody didn't vaccinate a puppy. Every freaking one. And they all died horrid deaths.

Personally, I haven't been hiding the fact that you can vaccinate against this disease. I have no reason to. I thought it was common knowledge. And I've tried to get the word out. But some folks are well-isolated from common knowledge.

I had clients waiting patiently to see me. Some were the very folks who moved their appointments that morning so I could save a life. These were clients who try their very best to be good pet owners. I suppose I could screw them over to see this despicable person holding a sick puppy. That's what the puppy owner would prefer. And she will pay me later... she promises.

Thirty years of treating Parvo in puppies belonging to irresponsible people. I've heard this promise before. It's not worth the paper it is printed upon. When I turn and walk back into the clinic to take care of the nice people, the memory of all those lies, all those thieves, all those lying cheating irresponsible people whose reprehensible behavior killed all those innocent puppies burns in my memory and my gut.

The woman hung around for a while. She walked into the waiting room with the puppy so we had to lock the room and disinfect it... yet again. When she finally left, she swore at us, the evil in her voice, the hatred. But I was serving the people who pay my bills so I can stay open as a veterinary hospital in these difficult times.

I'm sorry puppy. I'm sorry I can't fix the mess that horrible person inflicted upon you. But I cannot afford to carry the weight of every irresponsible asshole. There are far too many irresponsible assholes. I'm barely surviving here at all, and those nice people and their animals need me.

I left for home at 6:30 in the evening. Everybody else left when we closed at 5:30. Eleven hours. And I was tired.

October 10, 2012

Judge Not Lest Ye Be Judged

This is one of the absolute truths of veterinary medicine: you can't tell who has money or who'll spend it. And the two are surely not the same. (EM)

I think if you count down the list, I've had at least one of each. Each kind of person, that is. And no, clean up your dirty mind. I've had one of each kind of person as a client. Where do you get these thoughts?

Been doing this veterinarian thing for a long time, and at the end of every leash, and carrying every cat, there's been a person or two. People. Male and female. Young, middle and old. About every race and culture available, rich and poor and undecided. Misers and philanthropists. Educated and... uh, less so. And though not the same as educated or not, I've seen smart, or the other. Dedicated and indifferent. Professional athletes and folks in chairs with wheels. Saints and sinners. Cops and criminals. Politicians and professors. The very honest, and the bare faced liars.

I haven't learned everything, but I have learned some things. You cannot judge the book by its cover, and some people will fool you, too. Let me tell you about two.

She was not an impressive looking woman. We get that a lot. This is not a wealthy area, so few women wear designer clothing, carry designer handbags, or for that matter own designer dogs. And they don't fritter away hours at spas or visit the polite gentlemen who style movie star hair. She looked a bit tawdry.

Her puppy was pure mutt, the product of a shameless hussy and a traveling salesman. Somebody had played 52 Pickup with the gene pool with this little guy. But, he had a busted leg and needed help.

This was back in the day when a hundred bucks was a good deposit. Because yeah, even then folks would lie about paying their bills. And she didn't look the type to have much cash just laying around. But she promised to come back with the money.

She did.

Five times she came in that afternoon, with $20 each time.

I didn't ask, but we all wondered if she wasn't hunting up a few traveling salesmen or whatever. But she kept her promise and I fixed up her dog.

He was a minister of a local church. Several of my clients knew him. They said he was a neat guy, kinda hip for a minister. Young and handsome. With a wink they also mentioned that he was a bit of a ladies man.

He dressed well, and yeah, he seemed kinda hip for a minister. The dog had some small problem with which we quickly dealt. Then my receptionist presented his bill for service. He was outraged.

It seems he was accustomed to certain favors from local businesses, for he was, after all, a man of God. He flat told my receptionist that he expected a discount at the very least, and free would be nice. She looked at him with the quiet determination of a good receptionist who was accustomed to folks trying to con her. And she got her money, but boy was he never coming back.

And he stomped out to his Porsche and drove away.

Next time, dude... don't drive the Porsche.

I'm not saying that I've never been ripped off by a hooker, and watch that dirty mind of yours again, or that all of my minister clients have been arrogant reprobates. Not saying that at all.

Just saying that ya can't tell by appearance, and it really is content of character that tells in the end.

May 2, 2013

Murder, By Internet

One of our veterinary colleagues, Shirley Koshi, died by suicide on February 16, 2014. She was the victim of relentless bullying, both online and in person at the hands of what can kindly be described as the mentally ill wackos among us. After her tragic death, the bullies proceeded to celebrate the outcome in the most cruel of manners on their blogs and message boards. It truly illustrated the depravity of mankind, as well as a portion of the animal-owning public.

We in the veterinary community were simultaneously saddened and outraged. Some of our colleagues called out the bullies for a time on their own turf, but that was simply in the gutter, and struggling in the gutter is exhausting, fruitless work. Bob, on the other hand, had his say in his own unique way, and in the opinion of this editor, his way was the most artistic of all. (RG)

I apologize in advance for the length of this, but the story is a bit involved, and I believe illustrative.

Blood ran down my arm, across the back of my hand, and dripped onto the exam table. I stood there quietly taking the verbal abuse from an outraged pet owner, my hands resting on the metal surfaced table. It's better to let them rave themselves breathless rather than trying to interrupt. Ya learn this after a while. Once they've spewed their piece, they eventually stop to take a breath. Then they are not talking. No one can listen when they are talking. It's an A/B switch kinda thing.

I'm pretty thin skinned. Don't mean by this that I'm overly-sensitive. Far from it. Nah, I'm just old. Skin gets thinner when you get old, so when the dog rakes you with those front toenails little furrows appear, followed shortly by that red stuff. And when you follow the physician's advice and take those little aspirin daily, this inhibits platelet aggregation. Oh sorry. Big words, This means you bleed with enthusiasm from little furrows.

I learn from such encounters, even after all these decades of playing this game. I listened intently to the young man, occasionally glancing over at his embarrassed wife. I wanted to learn what he thought I'd done incorrectly. She was dumbfounded by his tirade. I was a mite taken aback myself, but I, too, stood there taking it in.

By the time he finished, it was completely obvious that I need not try to respond. Why waste the oxygen? This guy had it all figured out, and reality had nothing to do with our little predicament. The first words out of his mouth when he had entered the exam room with his dog, "We didn't like the last vet," would be the first words out of his mouth at the next veterinary practice. Nothing I had to say was going to change that.

I shook my head and turned away, ignoring that little bit of his spittle hanging off his lower lip. I left him puffing in the exam room. Time to bandage the arm again.

"We should have listened to your internet reviews."

Yeah, you should have. Thought it but didn't say it. I don't read my reviews. No point in that. But someone (the mayor of our little city) had mentioned those reviews just the week before. Apparently next to all the good ones were two rather nasty ones. I figured I knew what those were about, and when I replied the mayor simply nodded.

One was a young woman who was incensed when I excused her dog before my exam could even begin. It had something to do with not being able to touch her vicious little dog. Her boyfriend had screamed into my face that I get paid to get bit, and I took some small exception to that bit of misinformation.

The second bad review concerned another client who announced as she entered the exam room (yep, another who didn't like her last vet) that she was dissatisfied with the dose of the pain killing drug the last doctor had prescribed for her cat, so she had raised the dose without asking if this was appropriate.

The second sentence out of her mouth was to demand from me more of the drug, long before I had the opportunity to become familiar with the animal's condition, the history and the physical exam. I didn't jump at this opportunity for a fast sale, inasmuch as this was a controlled substance, and prudence suggests we not simply supply these to the public.

Numerous other demands poured from this woman's mouth with each new statement she made. And then the complaints as I began my exam. I was to do it the way she required, and how dare I do it my way? I smiled and continued my exam. She continued to rail against every single thing I did. I smiled again.

Goodbye.

The mayor has been a client of mine for roughly thirty years, so I don't know why he consulted those online reviews, but I'll get back to this thought later.

Anyway, the young couple and their dog entered my exam room. It was a busy Saturday morning and we were completely booked. We'd set aside the usual 15 minute slot for what should have been a routine visit. The chart hinted at an ear problem, and they needed a Rabies vaccination. I greeted them in my usual ingratiating fashion. I'm a heck of a nice person after all. The dog was about 45 pounds of one and a half year old mixed-breed.

Warning #1: "We didn't like the last vet," they say.

Warning #2: Dog is wearing a harness rather than a collar. This is where self-preservation kicks in. It's kinda like how you feel when the guy walks into the convenience store wearing a ski mask. Maybe he just has bad acne, but ya still watch 'em closely.

Warning #3: I get down into my squat that I use to greet every dog that comes into my exam room. This is diplomacy in the dog world. It invites the dog to come over and make friends. It often begins the process that defuses doggie anxiety in the veterinarian's office. It makes the job easier. The friendly dogs just love it. The clients love it. And I really enjoy the dogs. This dog approaches to a four foot distance, stares at me, raises it's lip about a half inch, and then runs behind the man.

Warning #4: "The last vet took a foxtail out of his ear," they say.

"When was this?" I ask.

"Last July."

OK, that's foxtail season. Seems reasonable.

"But it didn't get better," they add. (Seemed he intimated that the other vet faked taking a foxtail out of the ear. Heard that nonsense before, too.)

"OK, how long has he had this ear infection?" I inquire.

"I don't know."

"Well, how old was he when you first noticed it?"

"He was about seven months old."

So, about last February.

"And it's been infected ever since?" I prod.

"Yes. It didn't get better after the last vet treated it."

Small wonder. Ears infected for a year, treated once, didn't get better. We gonna need more than fifteen minutes for this.

Dog had erect ears, so from across the room I could see a bit of the inside of the ears. They were pigmented black. Bad sign. Usually takes years of neglect before the ears turn black. Turning black is scaring from chronic inflammation, and it portends other damage that is not only permanent but often requires what we call salvage surgery to keep the dog from suffering needlessly. Poor dog's owners clearly lacked the clue.

The young woman showed me the crinkled flattened tube of ear infection medicine. Way back it contained plenty to treat the ears for the usual ten to fourteen day treatment. "We've been using this ever since, and he didn't get better."

Sigh.

Without understanding the reasons for chronic or recurring ear infections in dogs, the poor owners who are treating these ears are unlikely to get it right. No knock on owners (this time), but when not handled correctly such infections often turn into disasters, and even when handled correctly they are often not cured, but merely managed. The sun comes up in the east, and some dog ear infections are extremely challenging to treat. That's just how it is.

Educating pet owners is the single most important thing veterinarians do. This is how we best help the animals. It is critical. It prevents a lot of the preventable disasters. It is also the most challenging aspect of the job. (There he goes, picking on pet owners again.) So I spent a half hour explaining the basics to this young couple. My receptionist stopped by to wag two fingers in my face. The next two clients were already waiting. But I was getting somewhere with these two and I didn't want to stop. They seemed to be learning.

Now you might wonder why I still hadn't examined this dog. Normally, this would precede the education part, but I like to give the fearful dogs time to become accustomed to the room and me, and it gives me time to defuse some of the anxiety or hostility residing in the owners, for they set these dogs off by how they react. So I laid on the whole lesson, going back over each concept in different ways when they didn't understand. I'm good at this. Done it for decades. Most clients thank me once they figure things out. I made my other clients wait while investing important time with this couple. It began to feel as if we might make this work.

The time arrived when I would try to examine the dog. Prospects for this hadn't improved much. The dog still would not come over to sniff me. It had sniffed the entire room, wandered out of the room when the owner didn't pull him back by the leash, but never once approached me. You don't simply reach for a dog behaving like this.

I got into my squat again, and it approached to that same four feet, and then headed for the other side of the room. The man holding the leash stood right beside me. His dog was over there, giving me the eye. Silly veterinarians often wonder why the owners don't simply use the leash to pull the dog to them so we can actually do our job. Rarely happens. So after a bit, I reached up and took the leash from his hand, and gently pulled the dog toward me. He stopped at that magic four-foot distance. A bit more tug on the leash as I entreated the dog to come. Harness goes up and over head, landing limply on the floor. Dog hurries over to stand beside the woman, over there.

I held up the useless harness and turned to the man. "This is why you don't use a harness. They give you no control over your dog."

Woman stands next to dog. Doesn't grab his collar. Doesn't try to bring the dog over to me. Man does nothing. Woman speaks, "Maybe I should leave the room. He gets real protective of me."

Ah... **Warning #5**. I shouldn't need to explain this one.

I turn to look at the man standing next to me. "Why don't you go over there, take the dog by the collar, and bring him over here?" A novel concept he had apparently not considered.

He squats next to me, dog cradled between his legs, biting part facing out. Perfectly wrong set up for dealing with an untrained fearful dog.

I take collar and pull dog in front of me. He lunges left, he lunges right, he lunges left again. I hold collar. He stops lunging and I turn him to face away and induce him to sit. Soft calming voice, praising him for a sit, petting and scratching his back. He settles a bit. I touch an ear.

Dog lunges left, dog lunges right. For expediency I will not repeat this part over and again. The dog did. Take my word for it. After some considerable time, I give up on examining ears. I turn to look at the man who is still squatting right next to me. No attempt whatsoever to control his own dog.

"Your dog really needs a good obedience training course. Not only will it teach him to behave, but it will impart him with some badly needed confidence so he won't misbehave like this." Nothing.

OK, enough wasted time. I give the dog his rabies vaccine, and go to stand up. Dog launches one more time, spinning in a circle, which locks my hand in the collar. Not a good thing if he begins to nibble on my arm. Manage to untangle my hand without injury, but dog rears on his hind legs and rakes my arm with his claws. I know that feeling. I'm done with dog and turn him loose.

I'm washing the blood off my arm when the man launches on me. He doesn't like how I held his dog by the collar. Really? How else does one hold a dog by the collar? Silly me. Took me a bit before I realized that he didn't want the dog held at all. That thing where I always say that the use of a harness is the owner's concession that he has no desire to control the dog at all. That's this guy.

So I stood beside my exam table, bleeding, while he assailed me. And then I walked out of the room, bandaged my arm, and then put on my smile for the next client. Excuse me for trying to help. The day went on, as they have for all these decades.

Will this guy put up a bad review online? Don't know. Don't care. I don't read reviews. I don't defend myself when a bad one shows up. Don't care. My practice has been growing for decades because satisfied clients send their friends to me, and people who don't like how I try to help their animals are welcome to find someone who does it differently. Lot's of ways to skin a cat. (Sorry, cat lovers.)

Does it hurt my feelings after all these years of dedicating my life to helping people and their pets to have someone scream at me like that? Yeah... a little. I got into this profession to help, and I've sacrificed a lot to continue doing this for a lifetime. Mostly it is rewarding. Sometimes it breaks my heart.

So why the long story? Well, last week a few people killed a veterinarian I know.

Oh, they didn't poke her with a knife or shoot her with a gun. But they killed her.

Shirley was in practice for over thirty years, and although a bit unconventional at times, she was always compassionate, up to date, hard working. She finally got the chance to start her own little practice. On a shoestring budget, she opened a small place in the city of New York. As with all start-ups, it was a struggle. The economy still sucked. The weather sucked. The likely illegal collusion between landlord, banker, contractor and maybe even organized crime nearly bankrupted her. But it took crazy cat ladies to kill her.

A feeder of feral cat colonies in the city adopted a cat from a shelter and then turned it loose in a city park, in the snow and the 2014 winter, to struggle on its own. This lady thinks this is good for cats. Some friends of hers brought the sick cat to Shirley for a medical problem, but of course declined most everything necessary due to cost. So as she had done in the past, Shirley asked them to surrender their cat so she could care for it and then try to find it a nice home. Because they could not provide properly for the cat, they agreed. Later, the woman who had turned the cat loose in the park showed up to claim the cat, and Shirley refused. She didn't want to see the cat abandoned again. And she didn't at that point even know who owned the cat. For she had been duped into believing the first two people had owned it.

That's when it started. Vicious evil people have the same voice on the internet as the rest. An organized assault on Shirley began on the net. An online blog that specializes in character assassination zeroed in on her. Protesters with signs lined the street in front of her hospital, and had to be removed from her clinic by the police. People who had no idea of the facts hopped on board with the mob because the evil rich veterinarian deserved it. They were vicious, conscienceless, and evil. But they got their wish.

Shirley killed herself the other night.

And the vermin on the blog celebrated, cheering her death in their posts.

Ask any veterinarian out here. This hurts us. So I guess they win.

February 23, 2014

A Soft Spot

"Open confession is good for the soul."
                              Old Scottish proverb

Have you ever made a mistake?

"I thought I had made a mistake once, but I was wrong."

A comedian said that once. So have a few sociopaths. I must confess to having made mistakes. There, my soul feels better now.

Actually, during the middle of the night, that time when I cannot hide from elements that wander about my brain, I sometimes discover the list of mistakes I've made in a lifetime. Something reminds me of an error I'd thought I'd put away, and then the others line up obediently for my leisurely perusal. Nights are long, so there is plenty of time.

A colleague has a friend, a physician, a pediatric surgeon. Once a year, every year, on the same day, this doctor receives a letter reminding him of a child who died while under his care. This has been a regular thing for 25 years. Best as we can tell, this doctor did nothing wrong, but a patient died while under his care. And somebody has not forgotten. From the look of things, somebody is not likely ever to forget. And they wish to assure that the doctor never forgets.

I can assure you that the doctor will never forget, and the letters have nothing to do with this. But the sender gets a wish granted, for the letters cause pain.

Years ago we used a brand name drug as part of our anesthetic combination for cats. The drug was manufactured in two strengths, one for horses and the other for ten pound cats. Since we don't see horses, we always used the cat version. One day the drug sales rep mentioned that a generic version of the drug had become available, so we ordered it from that supplier. Used it for a short while, and frankly didn't much like the new version. This occasionally happens with generics. Then a cat nearly died.

The horse version of the drug had ten times the concentration as the small animal version. Guess what kind the supply company shipped to us? I didn't catch it. I ordered one drug, received another, and used it. And a cat nearly died.

I suppose I might argue the point, but it was clearly my responsibility to catch this error. I was the one who had to tell the cat's owner. I was the one who paid for the emergency care the cat received. I was the one who had to respond to the board complaint she filed. I am the one who relives this periodically, late in the night.

The owner tried to get my license revoked, and she swore that she would never come back, and I didn't blame her. Two years later, when she called to schedule an appointment to euthanize another of her cats, because our fee for this was less than the practice she now utilized, I refused to see her. We like to think we keep the fees for euthanasia low as a kindness for our clients. We are not attempting to attract...

Several months later, we ordered that same drug from that same company. We specifically mandated the small animal concentration. And we told them why.

They sent the wrong one, again. We caught the error this time.

I'd be ripe fodder for the hate obsessed lady with her hate veterinarians website. I confess... I've made mistakes.

Twenty years ago my own dog died while under my care. The details are not relevant. Suffice it to say that Jake was another casualty of my career, another sacrifice I made in the life-long obsession to try to help the animals and their people. So yeah, I know what it feels like to hate the doctor that you think killed your pet. And no, I likely will never forgive, ah… me.

People tell me I should "let it go," but ya know how that goes. So yeah, I do sympathize with the woman who started an internet website who so hates veterinarians. Her cat died while under the care of a veterinarian, so she blames that doctor for that death.

Sure, the cat was twenty years old and it died like most every other twenty year old cat that dies, of kidney failure. Back when this happened we didn't have dialysis for cats. Truth is we had so few things that could be done to delay the death. No doctor on earth could have kept that kitty going indefinitely. Fifteen years later this woman still hates veterinarians virulently and with enthusiasm and persistence, and she uses the internet to prosecute her vengeance.

When Dr. Koshi died, a cat that she had tried to save from a lifetime of neglect in a park was instead given to the self-styled "cat rescuer" who reportedly has said she will release it back into the colony of feral cats living in that park. Despite all the evidence that feeding feral cat colonies is not only bad for the cats, but also bad for wild birds and animals, and a risk to public health… a gaggle of "cat rescuers" joined in celebration of the return of the cat to this woman. And another woman with a hate-website chimed in with her own version of hate. She of course, directed her hate at the doctor.

Don't know if you caught any of this. But if you did… did you notice this part? Did you notice that other than the vicious veterinarian hater on the web, everyone else, those people in the street aligned against Dr. Koshi pretty much said the same thing? How wonderful that the cat was given to this person. Not a thing about any benefit or harm to the cat if it was to return to the park. Not a word of how well it had fared under Dr. Koshi's care. Nope. How wonderful for the "cat rescuer" was the theme.

This was never about the cat at all.

Ask any veterinarian, "What do you do?" They will tell you, "I practice veterinary medicine."

Ask any veterinarian, "*Who* are you?" They will tell you, "A veterinarian."

After a while in this profession, that *is* who we become, it *is* who we are. And pardon the self-promotion here, but we take intense pride in caring about and for the animals and their people. That is who we are.

The haters try to take that away from us, and yeah… that's where they go because any bully knows you go for the sensitive place first, the soft spot. They attack who we are. They went after the part of Dr. Koshi that was the caring, helping, sacrificing essence of who she was. Those people who attacked Dr. Koshi took *her* away, from her.

What was she left with?

February 27, 2014

Bums And Bullies

VBB Small Animal Hospital occupies the street end of the property, with the hedges, bushes, and trees arrayed to one side across the parking area and scattered about the back half of our land. We have plenty of room to air our dogs in the back half (away from the street), and the time spent patiently waiting whilst the dogs finish their sniffing and their other tasks can be spent listening to the birds. One bunch of bushes sports red flowers, and the hummingbirds nest in there. We've had killdeer nesting in the weeds, and there generally are some mockingbirds and jays lending their noise. I invite the dogs to go "out" often, for back there is a haven of sorts away from the crazy and the stress that packs the inside of the hospital.

It's not a national park back there. But then I don't need to pack the travel trailer and tug it for hours to get there. I'm generally better adjusted when I return to the grind. I love the place for doing that for me.

So perhaps you can understand our outrage when each spring some folks find our back property the perfect place to dump pickup-loads of garbage, mattresses, old furniture, and tree prunings. We so look forward to spring cleaning time.

Oh, and the relative solitude and peace is a draw for the homeless people who make their nests back in our bushes (p.88). Most times they move in after dark, and move out in the mornings, unseen except for their trash left behind and the sure knowledge that as the local McDonald's has put locks on the bathroom doors, so they only buzz in their customers, the homeless are now left with only our bushes and the back walls of the hospital when they need to go "out."

For years we were nice guys, and we didn't hassle them unless their behavior demanded it. Too many needles back there, too many broken bottles in the parking area, too many visits from the local police because of too many outstanding warrants, and we'd tell them to leave. We wouldn't kick them out if it was raining. We'd give them some time to find a new nest. But we'd eventually ask them to leave. They earned that.

I won't suggest that we felt sorry for them, for they clearly had earned their lot in life. But we tried not to punish them for their lives. We simply didn't wish to sacrifice too much of our lives to their bad judgment and behaviors.

These are not traditional people. Most have addictions. Many are mentally ill, with most all the varieties that make up that lot. And some are vindictive, dangerous folks. So sometimes we've paid for our audacity in asking them to leave.

Our cars have been broken into in broad daylight a dozen times over the years. Broken as in broken windows, that of course we paid to fix so that we could still afford auto insurance. Shortly after we told one guy to leave, he confronted me in the parking area. It was a week after Easter.

"Damn rich doctors, living in your house on top of the hill. You don't give a damn about the little people."

Sounded like some of my clients, but that's another story.

"I'll bet you'd kick Jesus Christ off of your property."

I looked him right in the eye.

"You aren't Jesus Christ."

The woman had lived in her tent in the back of the property all winter. We knew she was there, but she made no mess, didn't walk through the parking lot when clients were around, and you couldn't see her tent. She even had someplace else to, uh... go "out"... for she left none of that mess either. Then a guy moved in with her, bringing his drinking buddies.

When they began breaking bottles in the parking area at one in the afternoon, we tossed them out. The woman apologized. And I told her she was not the reason she had to leave.

A week later, the glass exit door at the front of the hospital was smeared with human feces: locks, handles, glass. It was a thorough, dedicated effort. We figure we know who did it, and he wasn't Jesus Christ.

A couple of months ago, we found a new nest way in the back. They'd rigged a camo tarp over the gap in the trees, so we'd not seen them for some time. They'd built a two room house from tarp and cardboard. One of my canine officers stopped by with a problem with his dog, and he was kind enough to invite them to leave. They left behind several truck loads of trash for us to clean.

A week later, my wife left the passenger window of her car open two inches. The car was parked behind the hospital. Someone urinated into the car. Pretty sure that wasn't Jesus Christ either.

So yeah, we know these folks are not right. And they can respond to normal situations with a variety of abnormal, often harmful and even dangerous behaviors. Like monkeys in the zoo that throw their shit at the people outside their bars, they make do with the most powerful weapons upon which they can lay their hands. And even, or especially when we try to help them, they eventually turn on us. And they hurt us as best they can.

No, they don't know any better. They likely think they are in the right. They likely think they are entitled. They are making do with the most powerful weapons upon which they can lay their hands to harm those they feel harm them. Us.

Kinda like those folks that show up on the net with their virulent, irrational hatred of veterinarians. They are condemned to their own reality. And when we try to help them, and their reality collides with the actual reality, they simply cannot recognize their role, their blame, for the harm that they feel was deliberately laid upon them. Instead, they turn loose their hate. And we are handy target for their irrational response.

I suppose we should feel sorry for them, but we won't. Still, we won't punish them for how they fruitlessly try to cope with their own lives. But we will look both ways if we think they are around. For folks like that make the world a more unpleasant and dangerous place for the rest of us.

March 13, 2014

Penny And Ed

Penny was six weeks old when she first visited back in 1996. Sounds like a century ago, and yeah, it's been a while. A little red dachshund, Penny showed personality already, which meant she fit in with the gentleman who brought her by. She looked around my office as if deciding whether it met her expectations. Yes, you may pet me, but no… I'd rather you not look into my mouth nor touch my feet. Assertiveness training would not be needed to complete her package.

Her person was a man older than I but how old was a bit difficult to divine. Neither tall nor overweight, I guess you'd call him wiry. Whoever chiseled his face out of that rock had cleverly lined it with the wrinkles of both wisdom and laughter. His dress was as casual as the old pickup truck in which he arrived. The truck sported a stained formerly white camper shell that looked like it was actually used for camping, and I had no problem visualizing a spot under a large pine, lake over there and white granite boulders here, an old fire ring and a comfortable chair, with books to read and sunsets to ponder. And at one time a glass of something to help with the memories, the ones you really don't need to remember. Did get the impression that the man was comfortable alone.

I don't believe he worked. I hope he wrote, but I never asked. Always seemed he had something to say worth listening to, but you would have to start before he joined in. Below the cuff of his left pant leg lived the wooden leg. It was exquisitely stained a deep reddish brown and then lacquered to a mirror finish, with a black round rubber "foot." A peg leg. Ed could have passed for a pirate direct from central casting had he so wished.

Penny stopped by for her puppy vaccines right on schedule, endured the hysterectomy at six months, and then periodically over the last 17 years, we'd cut her toenails. Nobody else could. She wouldn't allow this. Not an uncommon trait in the wiener beast. We always managed to get the job done with only the minimal amount of persuasion. She didn't like it, but it wasn't a deal breaker for her. And it gave me a chance to get to know Ed better. He always saw that Penny got whatever she needed.

Eventually, we got around to that wooden leg.

War is not healthy for people and other living things. I knew all about that, I thought, except for that where I actually learned first hand. I skipped that part. Ed didn't.

His war was Korea. If it were not for the M*A*S*H TV series, no one around here would remember Korea. It was the first war we fought to a draw on purpose. And like soccer, that made little sense to Americans. Likely that accounts in large part for our amnesia. We've grown accustomed to this now, since apparently that's the new proper way of doing war. But unless you talk to one of that war's veterans, you probably missed it. Ed remembered.

I kinda walked Ed into this discussion with both feet in my mouth. I probably mentioned his leg, and then I pried a little too far. He got the faraway look in his eyes, the eyes that suddenly lost their sparkle. Real quiet filled the room. Even Penny stood still, eyes on her person. I felt it in the pit of my stomach. I went to change the subject, but he stopped me. I guess he felt like talking that day.

Much of that war involved fighting over hilltops with numbers. No features, just numbers. You generally want to be fighting downhill in war, so this made some sense. Ed's unit was entrenched upon such a hill, and when the other side showed up in the middle of the night they did it with thousands more men. The usual mess ensued; the position was overrun and then retaken later in the day. Just another hill with a number.

When things settled down, they made a pile of the Chinese bodies over there, and the American bodies over here. Somebody was having a smoke when he saw a finger twitch on one of the American bodies deep in that pile. That was Ed's finger.

Anyway, that's how Ed got the wooden leg, and presumably this exerted some influence over the next 45 years of his life before I met him. He was a neat guy, but I wouldn't have traded places with him.

Ed was married, sorta. His wife Vivian was also an interesting person. I believe he said they met over a bottle, or maybe at one of those meetings on the rebound after the love affair with a bottle ended. After Ed passed she brought Penny in, mostly for toe nail trims. Got to know her well, too, and liked her. But then she also grew sickly, and so an adult son began bringing Penny in.

He got the house and dog when she left. Dan wasn't near as interesting as his mother or Ed, but he got by. And for years more I saw Penny infrequently, took care of the things Dan would let me do, and cut her nails. There were other things that could have been done for Penny, should have been done, but as these things sometimes go, we didn't get the chance.

Dan met me outside the clinic when I unlocked the doors after lunch on Monday. He looked like heck. I'd seen the appointment on the schedule, five o'clock, euthanasia, Penny, age 17. He didn't have any money, but would I still put Penny to sleep that afternoon? He'd pay me later.

Sometimes you break the rules, the rules you force yourself to follow because of how easy you can make it for people to steal from you if you don't. But for Penny the rules don't apply, so yeah, I'll do it.

Penny looked pretty bad. She was fat as usual, and those various large growths were still poking out of her like they had for the last few years. Her mouth was horrid, thanks to Dan postponing all those suggestions to deal with that. But she was still in there, and her personality still filled the room. So why are we putting Penny to sleep this afternoon?

Well, Dan finally lost the house, and he has nowhere to live. Nowhere. He has no place for Penny anymore.

Life puts you into situations sometimes. It put Ed on that hill once, and Penny on my table many times, and now it put her fate into my hands. And the best thing I could do for Penny, and for Ed's memory, and for Vivian's sweetness, was to let Penny go. I didn't do it for Dan, for although I'd known him for years, I felt no connection there. He followed his own path, because of or despite whatever Vivian and Ed had done for him. I owed him nothing.

But if there is one simple sentence that sums up why we humanely end some lives, it would be this: If it genuinely feels like you are doing a beloved pet a favor by letting them go, you are.

And so, I did.

March 21, 2013

Petting Puppies

I've had occasions to share Bob's columns with many friends, colleagues, employees and associates, and I'm not sure there's a piece that induces tears quite to the degree that this piece does. See what you think. And don't be terribly surprised at the ending. (RG)

Once upon a time, in a land far away... I approached the Canadian border on a deserted two lane highway. I'd traveled for days up the coast from California, turned inland at the end of Washington, ferried across the water, and then forgoing the interstate highway, found a small road that headed north. I hadn't considered this to be anything suspicious. It simply seemed more fun to be riding the motorcycle on a winding back road than on a boring crowded interstate.

The border crossing was not crowded. In fact, I had the place to myself. The officer in the kiosk was efficient if not exactly effervescent. I figured he was simply doing his job. But I was a bit surprised when he invited me into the little building over there for a few questions. The gent in there was efficient, but not polite.

Where was I from? Where was I going? No surprises here. Straight answers from me. Just hoping to see some Canada, I said.

What do you do for a living? Oh, I'm a veterinarian.

Ah... so you can get drugs, right?

Excuse me? Dawned upon me right about then, the *why* for why I was sitting in a chair across a table from a law enforcement agent in the always welcoming nation of Canada. This guy thought I was smuggling drugs. Apparently, that's what veterinarians do.

And all this time I'd thought that veterinarians just petted puppies and kittens, and cashed the checks so we could get rich. I had no idea I was supposed to be smuggling drugs, too. All these years I've wasted by not scoring drugs for sale. Probably could have retired by now.

Petting puppies is a major plus in the "Why do I do this job?" column. Puppies are nice. They mostly arrive on my exam table simply really glad to see me. Too young to know any better, a puppy trusts everyone, loves everyone. They march right up, eyes locked on you and mouth spread in perpetual grin, they match their tails with their enthusiasm. Puppy breath. Puppy kisses.

All of the negatives in this deal, all the disappointments, all the tragedy, all the frustration and pain this job nets us… melts away with just one puppy lovin' on you. A good day in this business is puppies, all day long. The more puppies, the better.

Today… The four o'clock… three puppies. Saw this show up on the appointment schedule, and my heart sank. I wanted to cry.

We get to see the puppies often for the simple reality that the best way to keep the devil away, that virus we call Parvo, is to vaccinate the puppies early and often. I won't bore you with the details, but when we have the opportunity to vaccinate every three weeks or so, most of our puppies won't catch that disease, and they will live to be the companions we so value in our dogs. And they won't die lying weak and helpless in the puddle of vomit and bloody diarrhea that this particular disease inflicts upon them.

Something went wrong with this litter. The dam was vaccinated, according to the owner, so her immunity should have protected the puppies for weeks more than it did. The puppies had started their vaccine series so they should have been in a pretty safe state. We don't much see eight week old puppies catch Parvo anymore. Eight week old puppies have never had much of a chance when Parvo showed up. That's what we saw back in the day, when we watched so many die in agony.

These days, usually they wait until they are older and they have a semblance of a chance of surviving even if they do catch it. If mom's immunity transferred to the pups works like it should, only the older pups will get sick, and our opportunity with proper care, of saving the pups who do catch this disease, hangs in the pretty-good-chance percentages. Of course, when we cannot apply what we can, that damn disease will still kill off most of those precious babies, just like it has for the last thirty years.

Seven pups were born into this litter. The first puppy had been sold, and within a day it was diagnosed with Parvo at another hospital. Not quite eight weeks old. A day later, the first of the rest showed up at our hospital. It tested positive, but wasn't too badly off, so a few simple things which might help if the gods approved were tried, and we sent it home. Two days later, we got to kill the first two.

Ya see, the plan was to sell the pups for many hundreds of tax free dollars. No money was set aside for the puppies' care if anything went wrong. These folks had no money to spare at all. Proper care of a Parvo sick puppy costs many hundreds of dollars at a good hospital, and even at our little place it ain't cheap. And the puppies' owners weren't going there. So rather than watch the puppies die puking and shitting blood, and crying and twitching in agony, somebody gets to "put them out of their misery."

It's the humane thing to do. And guess who gets to do it.

The puppy at the other hospital had already died. The one I'd seen two days earlier died at their home. These two had the zombie look that Parvo gives us, but they still tried to wag their tails and smile at us as we killed them. My poor tech was crying, and pleading, "I'm sorry baby, I'm sorry, I'm sorry..." I kept it together, because somebody had to hit a tiny vein in a tiny leg so these pups could die in peace, and tears get in the way of that.

So today we got the last three. They weren't eating and they could not play. They were vomiting and barely moved. The drool seeped from their mouths and horrid stuff leaked from the other end. The first two died quietly, just like it's supposed to be when I do my job right. My tech was more stoic this time, as the job here had killed a little bit more of her.

The last puppy sensed something. Perhaps he wasn't ready to die at only eight weeks of age. Nobody should be ready to die at eight weeks of age. This puppy railed and cried, and struggled, and then I killed him, too. My tech left to go scream in the bathroom.

The owner turned to face me, after all this. He asked me for a discount on the bill, for this had involved so many pups, and the cost was more than he had hoped.

June 23, 2013

Pot Calling Kettle, Uh... Names

ABC aired a 20/20 episode entitled "Is Your Veterinarian Being Honest with You?" in November of 2013 It was a usual media hit-piece, but this time it included a formerly licensed veterinarian claiming to be sharing insider secrets. In reality, he was promoting his own product. There was some outcry from the veterinary community, and while I can look back now and say there has not been any lasting damage to the profession, it was a public relations fiasco at the time. (RG)

The one building is taller, lit by floodlights, signed with massive gaudy multicolored flashing moving lights that glow to the horizon. It cost tens of millions of dollars to build and equip and it is staffed with a large number of cleaning and maintenance workers, many more others whose duty is to ensure the comfort of the people who arrive seeking to win, and a core of well-trained experts who determine in large degree whether these people win, or lose. The building was built with one goal in mind. And it generally succeeds in satisfying this goal.

The second building is not as tall and lacks the floodlights. It is signed with modest informational lighted and arrowed directions that facilitate finding the right doors in the dark. It does not light up the sky. It too cost tens of millions of dollars to build and equip and it is staffed with a large number of cleaning and maintenance workers, many more others whose duty is to ensure the comfort of the people who arrive seeking to win, and a well-trained core of experts who determine in large degree whether these people win, or lose. The building was built with one goal in mind. And it generally succeeds in satisfying this goal.

Many people seek out these two buildings, all with the goal of winning, and the risk of losing, occupying their minds. Each of these people knows there is a degree of chance, a degree of randomness but also some predictability, to whether they will win or lose inside each building. Many hope for luck as they arrive. Others pray for divine intervention. Some think they are preordained to win. Others sense they might lose, but they try not to dwell upon this. But they show in great numbers, because the chance to win, however nearly certain or only a prayer, is a powerful drive.

From these brief descriptions you might conclude that there is considerable similarity between these two buildings, and perhaps even more similarity between the people who built them and manage them. Surely these folks have the same goals if the buildings seem so much the same. Obviously, someone spent the money to build, equip and staff these two buildings. They presumably expect some reward for doing this. I think we can conclude that these would not be reasonable investments if some profit did not flow from the people visiting the two buildings into the hands of the people who work in those two buildings and also into the hands of those who paid to build, equip and staff them.

There is one significant difference between the people who built and manage these two buildings. The first of these groups of people is admired and even celebrated and the people flock to their building wearing smiles, and they mostly leave the building at the end of their stay with a similar smile. They spent some considerable amount of money in that building and thus the building served its purpose for the people who built and manage it. Some leave having won, and most do not. Most lose.

The second group of people is sometimes admired and even celebrated, but is often not. This second group is instead very often a subject of distrust and even scorn. The people who visit the building don't generally arrive wearing smiles, and only some leave with one. The people who visited spent some considerable money in that building, and thus this building also served its purpose to those who invested to build and staff it. Some visiting people leave the building having won, and others have lost.

So again it might seem that these are two nearly identical situations. And to many it might seem that this is so. But one very significant difference does exist. For you see, the first group of people who built and staffed their building fervently hope that the people who visit their building will lose. They structure every single aspect of that building to encourage people to lose as much and as often as possible. This first group of people cares nothing more than for how they can create an environment in which people will lose. And they lie, cheat, and steal to insure that this happens.

The second group of people is subtly different, for they instead do everything in their power to see that the people who visit will win. And they spend very little time plotting how to scam more money from their visitors.

So why does the public in general generally like the first group of people more than the second, and they instead often accuse the second group of the nefarious behaviors?

Well... in case you haven't guessed, the first group of people built and manage a casino, and the second group of people built and manage a hospital. And the people who like a casino and accuse a hospital of lying, cheating, and stealing... well, they are a bit unclear on the concept.

I'm going to make a leap of faith here and assume that at least some of you reading this see the truth. And then I'm going to ask you to extend some understanding toward your local veterinary hospital. And when I suggest that I want you to consider the recent 20/20 program in which a known self-serving quack spent considerable effort to discredit the people who built and staff veterinary hospitals, I hope you will realize that we manage them the way we do because we fervently hope that the people who arrive with misgivings will leave after having a win. The ravings of a quack notwithstanding, that is what generally happens in a veterinary hospital.

November 24, 2013

Wasting Time

I learn something every once in a while. Usually from folks wiser or more experienced than me. I've been at this work for a while and I've picked up some tricks along the way, but my knowledge base always has room for expansion and enrichment.

So anyway, this friend of mine, a veterinarian of some renown, was once talking about the frustrations of scheduling appointments with clients who just could not manage to show up. Not show up on time, or not even show up late. Nope... Not show up at all. No call. No excuse. Sure as hell no apology. Just don't show up. Somebody else, another client, might have filled that slot if the doc only knew, but there it goes, forever empty.

Now, if you work for the government, or if you simply work for some other boss you don't like, an empty appointment slot means you don't have to work for a bit, and you still get paid, and that's a fine cup of coffee you enjoyed while you didn't work. But suppose you own a veterinary practice, and your day is meticulously scheduled to convenience your clients and yourself, and you can maximize the work and the benefit you provide for those clients if there is some semblance of order to the schedule. Since you work for, and thus are paid by those folks who come through the front door, when someone books a piece of your time and they don't show, you have still invested that time, but that time will be wasted.

So at the end of the finite day, when your employees are home and enjoying their families, you sit there in your office with the light on, with the medical records and bank balances and that never shrinking stack of bills, and that serious need to pay all those people who work for you for the time they have spent... and there is that piece of time wasted. No choice. You struggle to stretch the smaller piece of money as far as you can. You've done it before. You have to.

We are not just about the money in this job, but without enough of it, we go away. It costs a tremendous quantity of money to run a veterinary hospital, generally thousands of dollars a day, every penny of which comes from the people we serve, and all of which must be paid before the owner of the practice sees one red cent. This is the simple reality the owner of every small business faces even before her need for oxygen.

But beyond reality is that nebulous thing we call life. And our life is marked by time, not money. And as my friend taught me, we might make up the money, but we can never make up the time. For the clock only runs in one direction, and it is most unforgiving.

The draft horse, Boxer, in George Orwell's <u>Animal Farm</u> had a simple solution for when not enough was coming in to support the farm. He simply vowed to work harder. And that sufficed for a while to keep things going in the story. But when the draft horse finally died on the job, there was no one to take his place. Bad times fell upon the farm. And of course, he also was dead.

I'm reminded of this as I choose to work ever longer hours to keep things going during these difficult economic conditions. If I keep this up long enough, I'm eventually gonna be dead. I'm burning time that will never come back, and time is finite.

Suppose someone approached you in your youth with this offer…

I've two jobs for you to consider. You must choose between the two. One you will generally conduct with a passion and with a sense of satisfaction, but it will cost you much of seven days a week. Welcome to the ownership of a veterinary practice. The other job will pay you as well, or often much better, and likely will offer that same satisfaction, or more. You will invest only a normal workweek, and you will go outside to play in the evenings after work, on the weekends, and during those vacations. Which would you take?

Oh, just for jollies… What if you take that first job, and out of sheer self-indulgence you steal one weekend away from your practice every few months to go play with your family, and the people you pledged to serve bitch and whine because you failed them by not being there for them on that one weekend?

Which job would you take?

Did ya notice the lesson here? You can make back the money, sometimes… but you can never get back the time. And Jack may eventually become a dull boy, despite doing the work he loves.

Now let's throw in one more, ah… variable.

Suppose you took that first job, and just for jollies we'll say you own a veterinary hospital, and you are a good citizen so you registered to vote. And then the letter arrives because of this registering to vote thing suggesting you show up for one day of jury duty rather than go to jail for not. So you bite your lip because some time will go away forever while you are at jury duty and take away with it that day's earnings intended to pay the bills. Your clients will complain because you are not there to serve them on that day. But what a good citizen you are! And the judge thanks you for your service, and makes you a fine offer…

"How'd ya like to spend, oh say, the month of November playing juror?"

Well, heck, yeah. I'd love to. I'm a good citizen and I'd be a good juror, much better than a few of those seedy looking folks lounging around the jury assembly room down at the courthouse who look like they really should instead be sitting up there next to the public defender.

Of course, they won't let me know if I'll be serving that whole month until the very last minute, so the notion that I could find a relief doctor to keep my practice open at least part of the month becomes a little, uh, unlikely. But suppose I do luck out and hire a good doctor. I will pay that doctor more than I would make myself doing that same job, and that doc will generate less for my practice than I do. Then I'd have the bills and the payroll mostly covered. But I'll pass the whole month with no paycheck for my family.

Well, tough titty, said the kitty. The judge proclaims this does not constitute a hardship, so don't bother asking him to change his mind and let me go serve my first master instead of his catch and release fishery.

And don't forget the property taxes due in early December. Make that two months with no paycheck. Merry Christmas.

But it gets better if I cannot find a relief doctor. Then I get to eat the whole thing. Tens of thousands to pay the bills and pay my loyal employees, out of my personal savings that don't really constitute tens of thousands, because my practice will generate no revenue during that time. This is how it will feel when I finally have that heart attack and cannot work for, oh a month. Real sorry about that, goes the judge, but thanks for your service.

Sure, I could call this a vacation from my practice, and just forget any silly notion of taking an actual vacation for some considerable time. Felony trials are hecka fun. Hells bells, I sure never have even considered taking a month long vacation in my adult life, even though I wouldn't call a real vacation completely lost time. We'll call the jury trial a government mandated vacation. First time they ever did that for a boss.

But I might have saved up for an actual vacation, having enough sense not to bankrupt myself just to run off and have some time for my family and myself. After all, you can plan for a vacation.

Oh yeah... and on top of this, my clients will still complain because I'm not there.

October 11, 2012

Bourbon And Bandages

Today I ran out of Band-Aids. Actually, they were some off brand from the chain of drug stores. But I ran out of them, anyway. The last two days have not been a celebration of intact integument. Sorry. For those of you without medical training, integument means skin. Don't mean to be huffy and disrespectful of those without a medical education. Far from it. You all know the joy of skin poked through with sharp objects, and torn asunder with similar implements. Of this is what I speak. So please pardon the big words. My skin has been rent full of holes, so I used up all the Band-Aids in the place.

Yesterday, the penetrators were the usual six month old cat, immersed deeply in the brat stage of cat development, and a joy filled young pit bull who just wanted to love me to death. The little kitty simply drove a few claws into my arm during a moment of indecision. And the joyous pit bull was merely overcome by the moment, because she thought I might pet her. The dog claws tore off a much larger piece of my skin, or integument, than the cat could manage. She didn't mean to. But this put a dent in the Band-Aid box.

Today's animals weren't so well intentioned. When I first met the German shepherd, she was only eleven weeks old, and she should have been delighted to meet some strange bearded man who approached her across the exam room table. But no, she wasn't all that well adjusted, and she was pure freaky scared and dangerous at eleven weeks of age that I could not even pet her. I remember thinking that by the time she was a year old, I wouldn't be able to enter the room with her.

And the little one, the Chihuahua mix... well she nearly screamed when I tried to touch her when she was only eight weeks old. I remember wondering just what it takes to completely ruin a darling little puppy at this tender age. What horrors can you expose it to that will take an animal that wants nothing more than to love total strangers, and turn it into a cowering, snarling, vicious, totally harmed puppy monster. So now that she is five months old and a huge nine pounds, she is actually a dangerous dog that should be killed for its own good, for the terror it lives every day is intolerable torture. But you cannot say a word, for we must respect the culture that destroyed her, because that's the politically correct thing these days.

So tonight I sport five Band-Aids on my arms and fingers. I was wrong about the German shepherd, for she did let me touch her, but when I touched her chest with my stethoscope, she launched into the air, wild-eyed with terror and rage, and the left hand of mine on her collar held her tight. She raked my arms with her claws, and thus my blood tumbled to the floor as I auscultated her heart prior to admitting her for the anesthetic and surgery. The mop cleaned the floor, and the bandages stemmed the flow of blood, and we spayed her so, thank the Lord, she will never have puppies condemned by genetics and a mother's teaching to a life of terror and violence.

The Chihuahua cross showed up scheduled for a vaccine, but once here the man who translated the other language into English for my benefit told me that the puppy had been vomiting and now would not eat. So I thought some version of a physical examination was in order for this puppy. She now was five months old, and she trembled on the exam table. She squirmed when I touched her. Her tummy seemed OK, and so I thought a peek at her eyes and mouth in order. Well, that was not to be. My blood flowed again as the puppy's claws tore into my wrist, and when I wrenched my arm free, I carelessly left my finger available for the sinking of those tiny teeth we call needle teeth. I might have mentioned to the owner that such behavior was a tad inappropriate in a puppy that should run unabated to any stranger for hugs and pets. But such was a waste of breath and effort. I did mention that I hoped the disease present was the self-limiting version, for if the puppy needed more care, it was going to die, for no one could help the nasty little, ah, creature.

So tonight I wear the five Band-Aids, and I wonder why.

Last week was one of those times you hate when you are the veterinarian. I spent the week telling wonderful owners of wonderful pets that we were dealing with incurable, painful diseases, and the only thing of value I could offer was the quiet and humane ending of miserable life. We had too many such last week, and we thought we could not possibly cry any more.

So tonight, after stopping by the drug store for more Band-Aids and some more bourbon, I wondered aloud… just what is worse, the killing of wonderful pets for wonderful people when that was all we had to offer, or the dealing with the dregs of humanity who have destroyed their animals with neglect and cruelty, whose animals leave me bleeding and hurt, and they could not care less. And I had no answer to my own question.

So I opened and then destroyed the bourbon, and tried to type this. And I have no clue right now why I do this silly thing with my life.

March 8, 2013

Real Doctor

Who among us veterinarians hasn't experienced the following? (RG)

I watch the faces, I think. The "I think" part is because I'm not really sure what I do all the time, or even some of the time. I watch the faces in the exam room because so much of what happens in the exam room has nothing to do with what the people think they know, or what they want me to know. I'm looking for the truth, and for those bits of useful stuff that I learn from folks when they don't know they are telling me these things. This is all a part of that thing somebody once said about veterinarians, that thing about how the animals can't talk, so the vet just has to know. Well, we don't just know, but we can often find out.

To do my job I need to know what my patient has been doing. I'm hoping the people have seen what the animals are doing. I ask questions of the people, and they generally answer. Sometimes they tell me what the animal is doing, and sometimes they tell me why they think the animal is doing it. The difference between these two answers is that sometimes they tell me what the animal is doing and I get a useful answer, and sometimes they tell me what they think is the *why* the animal is doing what it is doing, and that is often wrong. If they fool me, and I accept as fact their *why* instead of their *what*, I may make serious mistakes in my diagnosis and treatment. And these mistakes can have grave consequences.

The best example of this dilemma would be an old friend of mine, a retired physician. He has brought his pets to me for the best part of 40 years. I believe he was once a skilled physician. He certainly thought he was a pretty special doctor, but he was only trained on that one species of animal, and not all of his knowledge transfers over to the species I work with.

When I watch his face in the exam room, he puts on his "I'm the real doctor here, so shut up and listen to me and I'll tell you how to take care of things" face, and I guess I'm supposed to be impressed, and compliant. As a client bringing his pets to me, he was, and is, a trial. Mostly, he is a trial because he will not, or cannot, tell me what his animals are doing, without injecting the *why* that his doctor brain has already concluded. Now, all this would be fine, except that he generally is wrong. And that makes my job much harder.

I walked out of surgery the other day after amputating this physician's dog's tail. All because of that cancer on the tail that he had been treating on his own with the antibiotics because he thought for a while it was just an infection. We had talked about the thing and how it could be a cancer, and he was convinced that the old dog could not survive a surgery to remove said tail, so he simply discarded that notion and did what he thought best, which was wrong. And finally he decided to do what I told him to do, which was to amputate the tail, and I let it be his idea and I did the surgery. And the dog is fine now.

And then later that day I went into the exam room with another man and his young, innocent child and their puppy. He was a nice man, and the boy was bright and asked good questions, and the puppy was a doll. And when I did my examination, and I listened to the puppy's heart with the stethoscope, and it was OK, and I handed the stethoscope to the boy and he listened to a puppy's heart for the very first time, I watched his face. His face was quizzical at first, and his eyes moved back and forth, and then he heard the lub-dub... lub-dub of a living heart, and his eyes froze for a second, and the astonishment came, and then the smile, and I saw it in his face, and my heart sang with his. And in that instant I knew that he had learned a precious thing that I could not have taught him any other way.

I will never know what becomes of this child, but I will always know that he knows that a heart beats inside a puppy, and that may change him just a little as he moves on into this harsh world.

The day before, I bent over a friend's kitty that had had the misfortune of beating up a car, and there was a hole in this kitty's diaphragm that let his guts slide into his chest, where they certainly didn't belong, and they made sure he couldn't breathe right. And I was needed to close that hole.

On paper such a surgery is a simple thing. You anesthetize the kitty, and open the abdomen, and pull those things out of the chest and put them back where they belong, and then you find the torn parts of the diaphragm and suture them together, and all will be well with the world. In reality, such a task is a bit more exciting, and when you contemplate such a task, it feels a bit like Bullwinkle the moose, and, "Hey, Rocky, watch me pull a rabbit out of my hat."

You don't want to know how often, "That trick never works."

I have this machine that sits in surgery, and its job is to beep every time my patient's heart beats, and show me numbers that mean the lungs are taking in oxygen and putting it into the blood. It is a useful machine...

But when you are doing the surgery, and you can actually look into the kitty's chest through that hole in the diaphragm, and you can see the heart beating, and it bumps into your finger as you putz around in there, and the lungs are blowing up and emptying out, it just means so much more to you than a machine can convey. If at that point you could look into my face, you might see the quizzical look, and then my eyes might freeze for a second, and the astonishment might come, even after all those decades of playing this game. You might not be able to see into my future, but you would know that I know that a heart beats inside this kitty... and that is a precious thing.

August 28, 2011

Peddling Your Ass About Town

> NatGeo's #1 grossing program in the early and mid 20teens was The Incredible Dr. Pol, depicting a veterinarian in his 70s practicing the type of veterinary medicine that led to a number of disciplinary actions from the Michigan Veterinary Medical Licensing Board.
>
> For veterinarians like Bob, who made a career out of providing services that his clients could afford while continuing to uphold standards of veterinary medical care, this television program was a slap in the face. (RG)

Why prostitution is not the world's oldest profession, after all... and what does this have to do with Dr. Pol?

I've been sitting here, sipping some Bulleit, and trying to remember all that nonsense they tried to pound into my head back then.

First off... why the word "nonsense?" *They* thought it very important, not nonsense at all, and that is why they pounded it into our heads.

First year in Veterinary College. Note capital letters and spelled correctly. The first week of class. Orientation. *They* were gonna spin our heads until we got it right.

I don't even remember how many of us sat in that classroom. 75? 76? I was 19 years old. The old guy in our class we called Gramps, was 40. The men at the front of the class were much older. They were, each and every one of them, veterinarians. We wanted to become veterinarians, and to a man, and five women, we wondered about this nonsense they were laying on us. Where was the important stuff, the how to make animals better stuff? Who cares about this?

I remember *they* were a bit stern. No foolin' around at all. They took this seriously. OK, I was not there to get kicked out. Much as I wished to object, I listened. My momma didn't raise no fools.

VETERINARIAN.

Now spell that... V E T E R I N A R I A N.

We were not leaving that room without knowing how to spell VETERINARIAN. As they carefully, and sternly explained, some people didn't get this one right. We were not spending four years at the taxpayers' expense to learn how to be a vetinary, or a horse doc, or a vet. We were about to join a profession, and we were going to become VETERINARIANS. If they caught us talking about becoming a "vet" they'd shout us down.

Forty-seven years later, and I still cringe when my colleagues refer to themselves as "vets."

They very carefully explained to us the definition of a *profession*. This is the part I don't rightly remember, but it had much to do with learning an entire bunch of stuff, and then spending the rest of our productive lives learning more stuff. Special stuff, or what they called specialized knowledge. Specialized knowledge was part of what defined a profession.

They talked about a code of conduct that sounded much like the Boy Scout oath. We were to be held to a higher standard, so we were going to merit that by behaving to that standard. We were gonna be cheerful, loyal, thrifty, brave, clean and reverent. Or words to that effect.

We were going to be honest with our clients and with our colleagues. We would police ourselves because no one else could do as good a job as we. We would have a code of behavior that was far higher than what one expected from someone who was not a professional.

We would respect our fellow professionals, never denigrating them to profit ourselves, yet always holding them to the same standard to which they held us.

We were to pledge to always advance our profession, our knowledge, our tools, for that was to the advantage of our patients and our clients. This was our obligation.

How could we argue with any of this? We realized that this was not, in fact, nonsense after all.

Those men at the front of the class... They'd been there when this was less than a profession. They'd seen "horse doctors" and various frauds pretending to do what we were training to do. They'd seen the neon signs over "pet hospitals" with the wagging tail and the "today's special" signs. They'd seen the fish hooks on the xray cassettes and filthy surgeries. And they had fought to rid our calling of this fraud and nonsense. They'd seen a profession emerge from the muck, and we damn well weren't going to ruin that. And so, they were stern.

My class and I inherited the most respected profession in this land.

The entire point of this orientation course was to introduce us to the notion of a profession. A profession is different when compared to a trade or a job.

There are many honorable trades in this world. Folks learn a complicated skill, practice it until they get it right and then they can call themselves a tradesman/person.

There are many jobs in which one can earn respect by showing up and doing prescribed duties. Lord knows we need folks to do this.

A profession, on the other hand, has special requirements, special knowledge that must be acquired and then augmented over time, and rules of behavior far more constraining that one finds on a job. Professionals are held to a higher standard than tradespersons or folks with a job.

Thus, there are fewer professions than there are jobs or trades, and those within a profession *earn* a degree of respect. Which might be why prostitution isn't really a profession.

Sure, there is that one whore with a heart of gold, and certainly some of these pros can claim to offer special knowledge. Somehow, when it all shakes out, it ain't the same.

When push comes to shove, a prostitute will do, not what is right, but what is paid for. And thus, a prostitute does not join a profession when she spreads her legs. She merely gets paid for what she is willing to do, and what she is asked to do. Right or wrong.

Which brings us to Dr. Pol...

April 4, 2015

Did I Do OK?

I hope you kind readers will bear with an old man as I try to come to grips with that world out there. Things are changing, things I don't quite understand.

I am a veterinarian. I'm proud to say this. I have poured my heart and soul into this profession, this helping and caring endeavor. I've been a veterinarian for a while. I'm now seeing the pets of the grandchildren of the folks I started with. Over decades, I've made friends, and met many and varied personalities. Some have been a trial, as anyone who works with the public understands. Some have left me muttering obscenities in the sanctuary of the back ward. Others left me laughing. They've mostly made this work fun, but not always. And the animals... bless them. They are the reason, the chore, and the salvation for all the effort.

I have saved lives and lost some, exalted and cried with thousands of people over the years. It's been hard work and it's been mostly worth it. This is not a wealthy area and economics have always defined what I could or could not do for the animals and their folks. But I have mirrors in my house and I can look into them with a clear conscience. I always tried my best, figured and connived and invented around the limits set for me, and put the animals welfare first and foremost.

I've made a living at this profession, and will retire with enough to get by. Never got into this line of work to get rich, and I was right about that. I've helped thousands of animals live healthy lives, and then quietly assisted them when 'twas time for them to leave. I've advocated for the animals, and sympathized with their people. I've done my job as I saw it, and I think did my best.

I figure I've shown up to work in my clinic, to help animals and their people, almost 13,000 mornings over my career. That sounds like a lot, but when you do them one at a time it only takes forty some years. Doesn't make me an expert, but I'll put my opinion up against some of those loud people who haven't yet done this even once. They claim their right to a voice, and I'll claim mine.

Don't know if it is introspection or retrospection. It's the process an old man endures when wrapping up a life's work. I find myself spending too much time with old clients in the exam room, talking. Remembering. Telling stories. Coming to some peace with my life. Takes some thought and time.

I awake in the middle of the night.

The guy behind me honks when the light turns green.

Don't quite understand the process, but it's about this.

Did I do OK?

Should be obvious... right? Client after client, old friends and new, when we tell them we are putting the practice up for sale because it is time to retire, voice the opinion that I cannot leave, that they won't know where to turn when I'm gone. Of course they are trying to be kind, to thank me for those times I tried, and this is the best way they can say this without going maudlin. They tell me I did right by them when they say this. And that's OK.

This should be enough. But they weren't there on those many nights over those many years when I woke in the dark wondering if I'd done enough. And I now have far too much time in which to wonder... did I do enough?

And now, new voices chime in, and they are the motivation for this essay.

Consider this notion. Suppose... just suppose, that the next reality TV show featured someone whose behavior set back, oh say that stuff we call high tech. Suppose he so influenced people through some misguided notions, that they should discard all that useful stuff, like computers and smartphones, and just go back to the days of party line phones hanging on the wall, and those clunky mechanical adding machines. Would that make any sense to you?

Suppose the next TV show featured a confused guy who argued that we should lose modern jet airliners, highly trained pilots, radar controlled air traffic, modern weather forecasting, and instead resurrect the venerable Ford Trimotor in which you could head out into the dark, not knowing if Omaha was socked in with fog or not. Would that make much sense to you?

Would you watch a TV show where the celebrity chef dropped the steak on a filthy bathroom floor, wiped it off with a paper towel, and then proceeded to prepare dinner for the panel of judges, using curdled milk, cheese with hair, and green bread all kneaded together with his bare hands, with that one finger dripping pus from the rat bite?

Would you watch any of these shows, and then cheer them on, and rabidly defend the star from criticism by shouting down high tech, modern air travel, and a safe food supply, solely because the way the stars of these shows does things is cheaper than doing things correctly?

Well, apparently some of you would.

And that is part of why I now wonder if I really did OK.

His name is Dr. Marcus Free. Dr. Free is a physician who practices in Michigan. Dr. Free is vocal in his opposition to those veterinarians who have asked the *National Geographic* people to cancel *The Amazing Dr. Pol*.

In case you just woke from a 50 year nap and you know not who Dr. Pol might be...

Dr. Pol is like many veterinarians in that he sometimes wades into boot deep mud and manure to administer to a downer cow. On his show he gets kicked by the occasional horse and gets rained on, snowed on and sunburned in the course of any given day. And he sees dogs and cats when not out on the road in his truck. So far, so good. Sounds like a regular James Herriot. Kind and caring, dedicated, and most importantly... he works cheap.

OK for myths. The reality... James Herriot worked in rural, pre-war England some 80 years ago. Veterinary medicine has advanced some since the 1930s, as has communications, air travel, and food safety. In his day, James Herriot was on the cutting edge of his profession, and over the years constantly improved the quality of medical care he delivered to his patients and for his clients. The man is dead now, but I would venture that he would be appalled at the malpractice portrayed frequently on the reality TV show that celebrates the incredible Dr. Pol. For James Herriot in the mid 1930s practiced more advanced, and effective medicine than Dr. Pol now does. And for the record, James Herriot was never cheap. And he heard about this constantly from the clients who were cheap, and he endured this just like the good veterinarians of today.

Getting back to Dr. Marcus Free...

Like all professions, veterinary medicine tries to police itself, to protect those animals and their people from bad veterinarians. So when our family of veterinarians witnessed the horror that is Dr. Pol's show, we petitioned *National Geographic* TV, and the various regulatory agencies that oversee our behavior, to put an end to a TV show that pretends to amuse folks with a charismatic (cheap) veterinarian, all while showcasing unadulterated malpractice and subsequent abuse of animals. The show is popular, and makes *National Geographic* a ton of money. So screw the animals, Dr. Pol stays on the air.

On a Facebook page dedicated to ending this travesty, Dr. Pol supporters appeared. Some were amusing, some quite sad, and a few overtly threatening. And then Dr. Free spoke up, "If it is true that the standards of care were broken by Dr. Pol, then the standards have grown out of control. Let's keep in mind that we are discussing non-human animals here. If they die it is unfortunate, but certainly no tragedy. We have enough skyrocketing expense on our side of the fence."

By this I'm sure Dr. Free means to say that the use of sterile technique and inhalant anesthetic is the reason why the costs in human medicine have climbed so in the last two centuries. Because these things are right up there in our discussion of Dr. Pol's oversights. He could fix these things for a few dollars per procedure but apparently he thinks it unnecessary. But according to Dr. Free, if a few animals die because of this callous indifference, both to the animals and their people, that's just tough shit. Because Dr. Free apparently doesn't care about animals, and ya gotta wonder about Dr. Pol.

Dr. Free is a surgeon, and his comments beg the question: do ya really think it would improve human medicine to go back to the Civil War when a bottle of whiskey passed for anesthesia, and four guys held down the victim, I mean patient, while he chewed on a stick as the surgeon lopped off his leg with a hand saw and then seared the stump with a red hot iron?

Presumably, the good doctor would say that wasn't what he meant, but heck, it would be cheaper.

So far, every person I've heard, and there have been many, who defend Dr. Pol's malpractice state one, and only one thing in his favor.

He is cheap.

Oh, they also say he's compassionate, but they say he shows his compassion by... being cheap.

As long as it doesn't cost folks money, the horse doctor can drop the steak on the floor, crash the ancient plane into a mountain, and listen in on the party line call.

And those veterinarians who try to do the best they can... well, they just be a bunch a crooks.

Amongst all the things I reminisce about, about did I do all I could, did I do my best, did I help, this reality surfaces. A whole bunch of people don't care squat about their animals or the care their animals receive from veterinarians. And if I have any advice to pass on to the young ones who dream of becoming a veterinarian, it would be to only do this if you really care, for the folks who have these animals often do not, and if you don't really care, and if you are not prepared to die inside daily for a 13,000 day career because you do care more about their animals than their owners do, don't go there. For this profession will then kill you if you cannot convince yourself every freaking day that you are doing the right thing.

April 9, 2015

Bob provided care to many K-9s through the years.

Why Bother?

This one is gonna jump around a bit, from here to there and then back again. Hopefully by the end I will have made some version of a point. If you don't get there at the end, and don't get it, please try not to blame me. Ya see, I'm trying to make some sense of this myself and I'm not sure I can. So if I cannot 'splain this cogently to you, imagine the fun I am having churning it into sense for me.

I was introduced to a sick, demented, and fortunately tiny subset of humanity when a veterinarian I knew through the interweb was driven to suicide a short while ago. Dr. Koshi tried to rescue a cat from the demented efforts of a cat rescuer. Saving a cat from folks who think they are saviors. This is what ya call a no win situation. Dr. Koshi put the cat's welfare first, while the cat rescuers put their own selfish needs foremost. The crazies won when Dr. Koshi killed herself, and they celebrated long and hard in their lonely homes and on the web.

One of the loudest haters on the web was a woman who had watched as her 20 year old cat died of kidney failure 20 years earlier. This woman never forgave the doctor who had tried to prolong the life of the doomed cat, and failed. Rational people, and those of us who know a few things, realize that the only 20 year old cats that don't die from kidney failure will be the 21 year old cats who die from kidney failure. The sun comes up in the east; always has, and likely always will.

This poor woman, bless her heart, thought more could have been done for her cat, and to this day, twenty years later, she has waged a one woman war against the profession of veterinary medicine for the slight visited upon her when her beloved cat died. This is her right, and the internet is her weapon, and the world goes on without even bothering to mock her futility. But as each day grows old, this woman seeks out any opportunity to rage against veterinarians who she thinks don't do enough to help animals. She is rather obsessed with this crusade. Death to veterinarians who don't do enough to help animals. She celebrated on her bit of the web when Dr. Koshi died. And daily she does all she can do to harm veterinarians that she decides have not done enough to help animals.

Please, remember this part.

Some time ago, a young man talked the *National Geographic* TV people into a reality show featuring his father, a quirky, aged, and arguably self-dedicated veterinarian who operates a mixed animal practice in Michigan. Folks love veterinarians, or at least they used to. The show has been entertaining at times, and the TV folks have made a fortune off it. This alone makes them happy. This is a win-win for everyone, right? The ratings are huge. Dr. Pol is the next James Herriot. We should all celebrate.

Well, not quite.

Ya see... on film, the incredible Dr. Pol has committed egregious malpractice, time and again, and some of us, the veterinarians dedicated to doing things right for the animals and their people, have objected to this. We've seen animals suffer at the hands of this man. We've seen him cut corners for no reason other than the fact that he doesn't care to do things correctly. We've seen his arrogance when charged with the abuse of his oath to reduce animal suffering. We've watched him cash the checks from his victimized clients and the TV folks, and walk away smiling.

So we have tried to stop this television program. We are proud of our profession. We are proud of the progress we have made over decades of time in the quality and effectiveness of the care we can provide your animals. We strive over our entire careers to improve this care. And we do this for the animals, and for you folks, and sometimes in spite of you folks. Thus, we want to stop that one doctor, because he mocks the progress we have made, and he attempts to elevate himself by denigrating the good that we as a profession have done for the animals and their people.

What? What do you mean, in spite of "you folks."

Yeah, sadly... in spite of you folks.

We stirred up a hornets nest when we asked *National Geographic* to stop popularizing a fraud posing as a Doctor of Veterinary Medicine. We did this because we are proud of our profession and the care we provide, and because this one TV program is harming animals by undoing decades of progress in the care of animals.

"It ain't what you don't know that gets you into trouble. It's what you know for sure that just ain't so," said Mark Twain

When some dedicated veterinarians asked the National Geographic people to discontinue this show, because this TV show harms animals in the long run, of course nothing happened. The money is far more important to the TV people than any harm they might cause.

So some veterinarians filed complaints with the regulatory folks in Michigan, suggesting that they should enforce their own regulations against malpractice in the practice of Veterinary Medicine. Dr. Pol clearly demonstrated a need for sanctions on numerous occasions while he was being filmed. God only knows what he did when not watched.

The regulatory people have acted twice now, finding clear evidence of substandard practice, malpractice on the part of the TV star doctor. The man has been shown to be a hazard to the animals put in his care, and a fraud as he sells his services to a gullible public.

Some celebration might be in order here, but instead, a throng of Dr. Pol supporters have surfaced to oppose any constraints on this show and this practice. Anyone interested in the welfare of the animals, and also aware of reality, would want the Dr. Pol show to go away. But, this is when it's what you know that just ain't so gets in the way of this.

With the throng of rabid Dr. Pol supporters speaking out, a variety of opinions have surfaced. All these folks think they know for sure, and sadly don't. Allow me to compress them into an easily digested few.

"Dr. Pol cares."

"Dr. Pol doesn't use all those fancy tests."

"Dr. Pol is cheap."

Let me translate, for convenience.

"Dr. Pol cares."

This means that Dr. Pol is cheap. Those doctors who want to do things correctly cost more money. Dr. Pol doesn't care about doing things right, and he cuts valuable corners to the detriment of the animals. Dr. Pol is cheap.

"Dr. Pol doesn't use all those fancy tests."

This means that Dr. Pol refuses to use the best methods to help peoples' animals, but instead does something far less. Dr. Pol is cheap.

"Dr. Pol is cheap."

Well, never mind.

Just for jollies. That woman who has pilloried veterinarians for the last 20 years because one veterinarian didn't do enough for her cat in her demented mind. Didn't do enough… Death to those who don't do enough to help an animal. The woman who celebrated when a veterinarian killed herself.

This woman has come out in defense of the substandard care offered by Dr. Pol. Because he is cheap.

Now, try to work with me here for a moment. I want you to wrack you brains, think long and hard, and then answer these questions.

Can you think of any time when you see someone doing a job, performing a trade, or practicing at a profession where people consistently and persistently beg, argue, demand, cajole, and whine… in order to get that person to do a poor job rather than a good job?

Do you, as a functioning human, beg the chef of a restaurant to do a horrid abortion of a medium rare steak? Do you ask the mechanic who wrenches on your Harley to please to a terrible job? Do you ask the surgeon who will attempt to save your baby daughter to please cut a few corners because you don't really want the surgery done right? How about the guys who will paint your house, your plumber, the airline pilot taking you to O'Hare, your kids' teachers, those politicians in Washington (oh never mind that one, forget Dr. Pol here), the dude at Starbucks making up your morning coffee, a damn cab driver.

Please do a shitty job, but please do it cheap.

I don't know for sure, but I'm pretty sure I'm right here.

The only time all those people are gonna demand, "You do a shitty job, but please do it cheap," are the folks we veterinarians are pledged to help.

And you wonder why I write such things in the dark of night, trying to figure why I bother to go to work every day. In spite of you people.

April 16, 2015

Almost Perfect

In this piece, Bob showed us the rewards that come from staying in the practice for the long run. Sometimes you find out, years later at times, not only did you do alright, but you did better than alright... you did almost perfect. (EM)

Some good comes from putting a few decades behind ya, but sometimes it seems as if the negatives outnumber the pluses. This is a closely held secret, but after passing the magic 45-50 year old barrier, and the letters from the AARP folks start showing up uninvited in your mailbox, your eyes go off warranty. And your arms get shorter. Those who didn't wear glasses... begin to wear glasses, and if you can't find your reading glasses when you need them, look first to your forehead before you trash the entire house. And if you do wear glasses, get used to the lower part of the lenses going weird on you.

I won't go into the adjustments this requires in surgery, or in tying a fly to your tippet while standing thigh deep in a Montana trout stream. But I will tell you that this new development plays havoc with your target shooting. You can still see the target, standing still waiting for you way out there, but the sights on your pistol or rifle take on a whole new dimension, or dimensions if the truth be told. Shooting by braille has some entertainment value, but what might once have represented precision soon takes on more of a comedic turn.

Which is why I've been adding telescopic sights to some of the old rifles, for I still enjoy playing with them, and I'd still like to do it well. Scoped rifles don't care if your eyes are old.

The ancestors of this particular rifle go back to the military over fifty years ago, and thus it had no provisions for attaching telescopic sights. Took a little ingenuity and time spent on the net to assemble the parts, but said parts were attached to the rifle last weekend, and I got to shoot it today. But first I needed to "sight it in."

I won't bore you with the details, but certain adjustments to a newly mounted scope sight need to be made so it points you in the right direction. Long story short, you fire the rifle at the rather large target placed not all that far away, and then adjust the scoped sight so that you put the bullets you send down range into that little part of the center of the target. You look at the holes you just made in the paper, and then you adjust the sights until the holes show up in the correct place.

If I had not forgotten my spotting scope, the device capable of significant magnification so I could actually see those small holes in the paper target, this would have been a simple task. Fortunately, the guy shooting from the bench next to mine offered to spot for me, using the higher magnification of his rifle's telescopic sight. With his help, within minutes I'd made the appropriate adjustments, and my holes were where they belonged. Such friendly cooperation is the norm at rifle ranges, and I thanked him for his assist.

During the next ceasefire, I moved my target farther out, to the 100 yard line, and then I had a moment to talk with my neighbor. He remembered me from some years ago.

His dog was named Sargent. She broke with Parvo back in the first days of the disease, in the early eighties. We saw way too much Parvo back then, and watched so many die. Sargent was a corgi/beagle mix, and I had conned him into treating the puppy with the notion that beagles could survive anything. She did eventually recover, but she had a long and difficult time. I asked if this was the pup I'd assigned a nickname. And he said, "Yes."

I called her Sarg, during those times when I went back to the isolation ward to talk with her and pet her and hopefully cheer her on with something besides drugs and fluids. And for all the years later, she was Sarg to me. And he remembered that.

This man talked of how in the beginning, he had tried to talk his wife into just dumping the little pup at the pound rather than treating her. He talked of how he had grown up on a ranch where the dogs were tools and if one ran under the truck tire, you simply got a new dog. He had seen no need to invest effort or money into medical care for a pup they had just acquired. And he remembered how I had talked him into treating her.

And then he talked of how surprised he was that Sarg was always thrilled to come see us, and she got excited as the car drove near, and then ran into my clinic. And he talked of how he grew to like her, and she slept in his lap and next to him in the bed, and he had wondered how he had once lived without such love and devotion.

And then he said that after 20 years the time came when Sarg was so old and so sick that the only choice remaining was a quiet release into the other side. And he stood there at a rifle range, and he said to me that he must have been the worst, the most pathetic sobbing mess I'd ever seen as his dog left this earth with my help. And yet he seemed so grateful, as we stood there, and I could read it in his eyes, and then he offered me his hand to shake. For the unspoken… that I'd given his pup the chance to love him for twenty years, and him the chance to love her back.

The range master released us, and I went to my bench and loaded my rifle and sent one round downrange, and then I stopped and unloaded the rifle. Only one round sent downrange. I sat there for the ten minutes, and then during the next ceasefire, I walked out to my target.

The hole in the target was within millimeters of a perfect center hit. It was as close to perfection as I am likely to ever see.

And as I contemplated the time spent with this man, and remembered his wonderful little dog and saw how he had loved her, and I looked back on four decades of this practice of veterinary medicine, all I could conclude was… it was as close to perfection as I am ever likely to see.

July 8, 2013

Acknowledgments

The book you now hold in your hands is the direct result of a combined effort on a number of fronts. Every one involved played a vital role.

Bob has displayed his writing talents for decades in one form or another, and his interests and professional talents gave him ample subject matter. His willingness to be open and blunt about his thoughts, feelings, and experiences have enriched the veterinary profession. Clearly, Bob is the foundation of this project, and he deserves all of the praise coming his way.

That we were able to keep this project a secret from Bob is mostly a testament to Joie's ability to keep quiet, for she is the one person involved in this endeavor who saw and spoke with Bob on a daily basis. It must have been a challenge! Joie's excitement for the project was palpable during our first phone call early on in 2015. She sent me many photos and *all* of Bob's columns. Fewer than 20% of his columns are contained between these covers, and perhaps one day they will all make it into book form in subsequent editions.

Eden Myers' coordinating abilities and encouragement along the way were, and continue to be, priceless. Only one spent more time on this book's publication than she, and it wouldn't be a fraction of it's present form without her wisdom, insight and contributions.

While I'd like to thank this next person by name, she requested anonymity, so let's just say I am indebted to the nice lady at the *Contra Costa Times* who sent me the dates upon which *Dr. Bob's Sunday Columns* were originally published.

Richard McAroy wouldn't have thought he'd be acknowledged here, but it isn't a stretch to say that the events of his exit from the Veterinary Information Network were vital to this project even getting off the ground. Without his unceremonious dismissal, I never would have crossed paths with Bob, and Eden and I wouldn't have learned of his writing.

Hillary Israeli deserves her fair share of credit for bringing Bob's writing to a greater audience.

The Ducks of the Cuyahoga Falls Veterinary Clinic, Inc., were wonderful focus group participants for many of the included columns.

My father, Doug Gates, instilled in me an appreciation for real world veterinarians. I'm convinced that this foundation contributed to the recognition of just how good of a veterinarian Bob has been.

My wife, Jenn, was not only patient with me as I devoted a significant amount of time to this project, but she also willingly listened as I read many of these columns (and others yet unpublished) aloud. We had a blast moving through them.

There are no doubt many influences in Bob's life who he'd name at this point if he had knowledge of this book prior to the first edition. As I mentioned above, there remains a mountain of observations, wisdom, and insight in written form on his 'puter that could fill four or five follow-up compilations, and he can write a list of acknowledgements as long as he sees fit when those make it into print.

The ship sank some time ago. The ocean, it stretches to the horizon, and then hundreds of miles in every direction. Too deep for my feet to touch the bottom, by a thousand feet or so. Haven't seen any sharks yet, but they can't be far away. The water isn't cold, but it is cold enough to suck the life out of you. Waves break over my head from time to time. More now than before. I cling to a timber. I'm tired and getting more tired. I could quit at any time. No reason to continue. I could quit at any time.

Then the life raft floats near. It isn't easy getting to it, and then climbing aboard, but somehow I manage. It changes everything. Now I can float above the water and the waves, and the sharks don't matter. I'm not out of this yet, but boy does this raft help.

Took another Sunday drive, 300+ miles, of white water river canyon and mountains and trees, smooth pavement and curves and more curves. Sun and not a goddamn thing to worry about. The dream catcher is working again. It's just a damn car, but it changes everything.

Bob Hallstrom
The Vet's Corner, August 24, 2015

ABOUT THE AUTHOR

Robert Hallstrom was born in Illinois in 1949. His twisted sense of humor began while working on a bull farm during his college years. (His Curtis Breeding Service ball cap graced his head for decades afterwards. It was a great conversation starter until it was lost in the Snake River in Wyoming in an unfortunate kayaking accident.)

After graduating from the University of Illinois College of Veterinary Medicine in 1972, he moved to northern California to begin his career as a small animal veterinarian. This was also the liberal hippie period of his life, where he grew a spectacular mane and beard reminiscent of "Grizzly Adams." (If you don't remember this show, please Google it!)

This is also when I came into his life, spending my childhood, quite literally, following in his footsteps, growing up in his clinic, and discussing lovely topics over dinner such as maggots and pyometras.

Like Grandpa, Dad loves the outdoors, and I loved following him everywhere – hiking through forests, past lakes, and up mountains (because they were there!). Whenever we got tired, he would say, "It's just over the next ridge."

Dad taught me sarcasm, how to belch, and how to string curse words together like poetry. But he also gave me an appreciation of life and nature, and he encouraged independent thought and strength of character. He taught me to find my way, both in the wilderness and in life, and has always been my example of how to be a great and compassionate veterinarian. He is considerably more conservative now, but the beard remains.

Bob, now retired, still lives in northern California and is ready to see what is over the next ridge.

With love,
Jody Hallstrom, DVM

Made in the USA
San Bernardino, CA
05 April 2017